THE ART OF FRESCO PAINTING

in the Middle Ages and the Renaissance

MRS. MARY P. MERRIFIELD

DOVER PUBLICATIONS, INC.
Mineola, New York

Copyright

Bibliographical Note

This Dover edition, first published in 2007, is an unabridged and slightly corrected republication of the work originally published by Clarendon Press, Oxford, in 1984 as Volume 11 of the International Series of Monographs on Chemistry. An errata list has been added to the present edition on page xii.

Library of Congress Cataloging-in-Publication Data

Wilson, S. (Stephen), 1950–
Electron correlation in molecules / S. Wilson. — Dover ed.
p. cm.
Originally published: Oxford : Clarendon Press, 1984, in series: International series of monographs on chemistry ; v. 11.
Includes index.
ISBN-13: 978-0-486-45879-3 (pbk.)
ISBN-10: 0-486-45879-2 (pbk.)
1. Molecular theory. 2. Electron configuration. I. Title.

QD461.W6 2007
541'.22—dc22

2006102935

www.doverpublications.com

CONTENTS.

THE ART OF FRESCO PAINTING.

PART I.

PART II.

CORRIGENDA.

Page xl, line 6, for "*useful*" read "*used.*"
,, xli, line 25, for "*Civita Vecchia*" read "*Orvieto.*"
,, xliii, paging, for "*xlii*" read "*xliii.*"
,, liii, line 4 from the bottom, after the word "*imitation*" add "*The use of black as a local colour, especially in draperies, is of course excepted.*"
,, 61, line 11, for "*os*" read "*yo*"
,, 61, last line, for "*Pemtres*" read "*Peintres*"
,, 63, last line of text, for "*remainded*" read "*remained*"
,, 68, last line but one of notes, for "*Il*" read "*El*"
,, 69, line 1, for "1563" read "1663"

INTRODUCTION.

THE revival of the art of *Fresco Painting* in the nineteenth century, will be an epoch in the fine arts, and, will probably, be the means of forming a great school of painting in this country, and lead to the improvement of the sister arts of sculpture and architecture. The moment it was determined to decorate the new Houses of Parliament with fresco paintings, it became important to ascertain the mode adopted by the great masters of the Italian and Spanish schools. To accomplish this desirable object, it became necessary to recur to the old treatises on the subject, especially those written in the Italian and Spanish languages. This inquiry was fortunately undertaken by a gentleman fully competent to the task. The result was presented to the public in the valuable reports of the commissioners on the fine arts. The path of inquiry was well traced out in these reports, and the subject coinciding with my own pursuits and inclinations, I was induced to pursue the inquiry, from the persuasion, that the introduction of the art into this country, would be the means of founding a great English school of painting.

Independent of other considerations, there appear to me to be certain analogies between Italy, during the period the fine arts flourished in that country, and England at the present time, which strengthens this persuasion. The same wealth and splendour of our nobles and merchants, the same commercial prosperity, and, above all, the same spirit of inquiry, which characterised Italy at the period I have mentioned, is applicable to England at the present moment. The advantage is on the side of England.

Almost all the writers of eminence, mention fresco painting, as the highest branch of the art. The most competent judges have expressed opinions, that in comprehensiveness of subject, boldness of design, facility of execution, and in durability, it exceeds all other kinds of painting, especially for the decoration of temples, palaces, and great public buildings. It has been practised by men of the highest order of genius. It is only necessary to mention the names of the Carracci, Michael Angelo, Raphael, and Correggio, to shew how highly this branch of the art was formerly appreciated, even if the value set on the cartoons, the rough drafts of paintings in fresco, were not sufficient to establish its superiority. These considerations, added to the favorable reception of my translation of Cennino Cennini, on painting, encouraged me to follow the path of inquiry, traced out in the Reports of the Commissioners.

By long discontinuance, the art had become almost entirely lost. The practice of painting on walls, in the manner described by Vitruvius, that is, partly in *fresco,* and partly in *secco,* appears to have been continued throughout the dark ages, by the Greeks, who instructed the Italians. According to Zanetti, the Greek style was taught by a Greek artist of Constantinople, who, about the year 1200, kept a school for painting, at Venice, to which many foreigners resorted for instruction, and from the same author we learn, that the Greek style was practised until the middle of the fourteenth century.

The earliest modern writer, whose work has been preserved, is Theophilus, a monk, who is supposed to have lived between the ninth and thirteenth centuries, but the exact period is unknown. He professes to teach "all the knowledge of the Greeks respecting colours." A manuscript, which I examined in the Bibliothèque Royale, at Paris, dated in 1431, contains a version in old French, of some parts of the work of Theophilus, which shews that his treatise had then become known.

The following series comprise the principal authors, who have treated practically on fresco painting:—

Theophilus MS. between the years..	1000-1300.
MS. in the Bibliothèque Royale	1431.
Cennino Cennini MS. (published in 1821.) ..	1437.
Leon Batista Alberti	1485.
Vasari	1547.
Guevara	1550-1557.
Borghini	1584.
Armenini	1587.
Cespedes	1608.
Pacheco	1641.
Pozzo	1693-1702.
Palomino	1715-1724.
Mengs	1779.

Commencing therefore with Theophilus, the series of writers on fresco painting, embrace the periods of its commencement, progress, and decline. I believe there is no important practical point, which has not been explained by some one or other of the above series of authors, most of whom were also artists. The reader will be able to judge, by the extracts in this work, how perfectly the practical part of the art had been preserved and transmitted, by a succession of authors, treating expressly or incidentally on the subject.

Between the period when Cennino wrote his treatise, and the publication of the work of Vasari, the art had advanced rapidly. Leonardo da Vinci, Michael Angelo, Raphael, and Correggio had lived and died. The Sistine Chapel, the Vatican, and the Duomo of Parma, had been painted. The practice of fresco painting was changed in some important points; Cartoons were prepared with the greatest care, the figures being drawn either from the life, or from models in clay, from which, when placed on the wall, the picture was traced, and correctness of outline secured. The old custom of painting much of the drapery in secco was discountenanced, and the perfection of fresco painting, as far as concerned the mechanical part of the art, was considered by the best writers on the subject, to consist in completing the picture at once in fresco, without retouching it in secco. The practice however of retouching in secco, was at no period wholly discontinued, except by a few very expert artists, formed chiefly in the school of the Carracci.

In a work which contains translations from so many authors, repetitions will unavoidably occur; and, as every author has his own mode of expressing his ideas, variations will be found. There is however a concurrence, generally, among all the authors, which leads to the conclusion, that the practice, by contemporary artists, was nearly uniform.

We must expect that the introduction of the art, will be opposed and condemned by many of those who love the arts, and to whom we are much indebted for their advancement, but who have grown grey in other practice. It were too much to expect otherwise. But the young artist may be assured that fresco painting will succeed, and be most extensively practised in this country. The commencement has been most auspicious. The patronage of government has been offered. The assistance of parliament has been obtained; and with such encouragement and patronage, ability and genius will not be wanting. No opposition can now prevent its success. The die is cast; the path will be trodden. The art has been already revived, and practised with success, on the continent, especially in Germany. It has commenced in this country, and it may be safely predicted, that it will hereafter form the principal part of the decorations of our public edifices. The great, the wise, and the good, with the actions and works, for which they were most celebrated, will be appropriately represented in our public buildings and palaces, if not in our temples. The illustrious dead will be represented as instructive examples to the living, and the art, which it is the object of this treatise to promote, will, by these means, become subservient to the best interests of the country. These are my anticipations. I firmly believe they will be fully realized; and that fresco painting will be extensively and successfully practised in this country, by our own native artists, and will ultimately attain to a perfection, equal to that for which the Italian schools were so justly celebrated.

With respect to the translations in this volume, I may be permitted to notice, that the greater part was made by my sons, *Charles* and *Frederick;* those from the Italian by the former, and those from the Spanish by the latter; and like most translations by very young persons, are almost as literal as the genius of the respective languages will allow. I have carefully collated and corrected them with the original works, without however altering their literal character, deeming it preferable that the ideas of each author should be presented, as nearly as possible in his own words.

Besides the translations already mentioned, I have collected and added such notices and extracts, from various other authors, as I considered might be useful, relative to the preparation of the walls and roofs, proper for the reception of fresco paintings, the preparation and use of the pigments, and the mode adopted, for the reparation and amendment of the walls and paintings, when injured by time or accident.

The importance of ascertaining the pigments or colours, used by the old masters in fresco painting, induced me to inquire into the nature of these colours. In pursuing this inquiry, it became necessary to consult the old lexicons, and old and modern works on chemistry and mineralogy, in order to ascertain by what modern names the minerals, earths, and pigments formerly used, are now known. This inquiry was not unattended with labour and difficulty. The result is prefixed to the practical part of the present volume.

In my researches, both in this country and on the continent, I have been greatly assisted by *Lord Francis Egerton* and *Sir Robert Peel*, and it is with feelings of pleasure, and a lively sense of gratitude, I acknowledge, that without the assistance and facilities afforded me by these distinguished patrons of the fine arts, I should have been unable to pursue my inquiries in those foreign libraries and public institutions, from whence I have derived the most useful part of the present publication.

The *notes* to which the letters *Ed.* are affixed, and all those to which no reference is appended, were added by the author of this treatise.

M. P. M.

Brighton, 20th December, 1845.

AN INQUIRY

INTO THE

NATURE OF THE COLOURS

USED IN

FRESCO PAINTING,

BY THE

ITALIAN AND SPANISH MASTERS.

PRELIMINARY OBSERVATIONS.

THE selection of proper colours [a] for painting in fresco is among the most important parts of the art. All the best authorities on this subject are unanimous in the opinion, that natural colours only, are proper to be used in fresco painting. Armenino observes, "artificial colours never do well in fresco, nor can any art make them last long without changing, and particularly in the open air ; the wall will not take any other than the natural colours which are found in the ground, and which consist of earths of different colours ; and you may leave to foolish painters those secrets of theirs which no one envies them, of using vermilion and fine lake, because, although they make grounds for these colours with various tints of white, it is nevertheless well known, that in the long run their pictures become ugly daubs."

[a] The authors quoted, almost uniformly use the term "colour," and therefore both that and the term "pigment" have been used throughout the work as if convertable terms : otherwise, "pigment" would in most cases have been preferred.

Vasari uses nearly the same terms. Pacheco observes, "the colours must be natural colours," and Palomino says, "they must be all mineral," by which he means natural and not artificial colours. These and numerous other extracts to the same effect will be found in the subsequent part of this work.

The natural colours are neither numerous nor brilliant, but the frescoes of Raphael, Michael Angelo, and others, irresistibly prove, that the colours used by them, were amply sufficient for all the purposes of fresco painting. Some of these colours have for a long time fallen into disuse, and the knowledge of their value, application, and use, is in a great measure lost. Artificial colours and pigments have been improperly substituted, and failed of their object. The consequence has been, that the highest branch of the art of painting, and from which the greatest masters have derived most of their celebrity, has declined and fallen into disuse. The object of the following treatise is, to restore this knowledge, and with this view I have endeavoured, by a diligent examination and perusal of old authors, who have treated on these subjects, to investigate and ascertain the colours formerly employed in painting in fresco. The subject has extended to greater length than I had anticipated, for my object being to re-discover the old and valued colours used at the period when fresco painting was in its greatest perfection, it was necessary to adduce satisfactory evidence as to what colours or pigments were actually used by the great masters of the Italian and Spanish schools. The importance of employing proper pigments, on which the beauty and durability of the painting so much depends, will, I trust, be considered a sufficient reason for having extended my observations and enquiries to a length, which, otherwise, might have been considered unnecessary.

The following passage in the truly valuable Report of the Commissioners on the Fine Arts, namely, that "the problems yet to be solved are, the speedier preparation of a lime, adapted for fresco painting, and the preparation of durable colours of the more *florid kind*, such as lake and crimson," (III. Rep. 53.) prompted me to the following investigation, and induced me to consider the subject, with a view to ascertain the nature of the pigments used in the Italian and Spanish schools, to produce these florid colours. I shall first endeavour to ascertain the colours formerly used, to produce the lake and crimson colours in the old fresco paintings.

RED COLOURS.—AMATITO.

DIFFERENT NAMES GIVEN TO AMATITO BY AUTHORS ON PAINTING. —It appears quite clear, that the old masters used a natural colour, which, when opposed to the other colours, appeared like lake, and that this colour is mentioned in terms of praise by many writers on art, who however call it by different names. It also appears that this colour was much used by the school of Giotto, but had almost entirely ceased to be used in Italy previous to 1584, and in France long before the time of De Piles, who was born in 1635 and died in 1709; but it was preserved in Spain at least until the publication of Palomino's work on painting in 1715-24.

The earliest Italian writer who mentions this colour is Cennino Cennini. In his Treatise on Painting, ch. 42, he says, "there is a red colour called amatito. This is a natural colour, and is prepared from a very hard and firm stone. It is so hard and firm, that tools are made of it to burnish gold on pictures. These become of a dark colour, and are as perfect and good as a diamond. The pure stone is of a purple or morella colour, and has striæ (or fibres) like Cinnabar. Break this stone first in a bronze mortar, because if you were to break it on a porphyry slab, you might split it. And when you have broken it, put what quantity of it you wish to grind on the stone, and grind it with clear water; and the more you grind it the better, and more perfect will be the colour. This colour is good for painting on walls in fresco, and it makes a colour such as cardinals wear, or a purple or lake colour. It cannot be used in any other way or distemper." And in chapter 136, he says, "choose a piece of *lapis amatista*, firm and without veins, with its striæ or fibres running longitudinally. Grind it on a grindstone, and make it very smooth and polished, of about the width of two fingers, if you can. Then take some of the dust of emeralds, and rub the stone, until no inequalities remain. Round off all the corners and put it into a handle of wood, with a ferule of brass or copper, and let the handle be round and polished, so that the palm of the hand may rest well upon it. Then give it a lustre in the following manner. Put some charcoal powder on a smooth porphyry slab, and rub the stone on it exactly as if you were burnishing with it, and your stone will become firm, dark, and shining, as a diamond. You must be very careful not to break it or to let it touch iron; and when you would burnish gold or silver with it, put it first into your bosom, to get rid of any dampness, which would soil the gold."

The next author who mentions the pigment is Borghini (Riposo 168-169.) His words are, "Another red colour is made of *Lapis Amatito,* (by some called mineral Cinnabar); it is a very hard natural stone, which the sword cutlers, and those who gild leather, use to burnish gold; and because it is very difficult to grind, it is thought a good plan first to calcine it, that is, to make it red hot in the fire, and then quench it with strong red vinegar, and grind it a little at a time on a porphyry slab. This, tempered with clear water, makes a beautiful red for painting in fresco; but, as this stone is not very common, and as it is very difficult to reduce to powder, it is not much used by painters; but there is none of it but what makes a beautiful colour like lake, for painting in fresco, and it is very durable.

The next author I shall quote is Baldinucci. (Voc. Dis. Tit. *Amatita, Lapis Amatita, Matita).* The following are extracts:—

"*Amatita,* a soft stone like gesso, with which drawings are made; there is some black and some red. See Lapis Amatita and Matita." "*Lapis Amatita, Matita,* otherwise called Mineral Cinnabar, a very hard natural stone, used by painters to make designs on leaf gold, where it leaves its colour, which is red. This being ground, although with great difficulty on account of its hardness, makes a beautiful colour, like lake, which serves for painting in fresco, and which is very durable. The sword cutlers use it for burnishing gold." Again, "*Matita,* a kind of soft stone used by our artists in drawing. It is derived from the Greek word *hæmatite,* because it has the colour of blood, which they call *hæma.*" Again, "*Matita Rossa,* a kind of soft stone, brought to us in pieces, which are sawn with an iron saw, and reduced to a point, which serves to draw upon white and coloured paper. The best comes from Germany.

"*Matita Nera,* a sort of black stone, which comes to us in small pieces, and which are reduced to a point by scraping with a knife; it is used to draw on white and coloured paper. It is also dug in the mountains of France, and other places, but the best comes from Spain."

De Piles, in his Elémens de Peinture, speaking of colours used in fresco, observes,—"*Rouge violet* is a natural earth, produced in England, and employed in fresco painting instead of lake: and the fresher the mortar is, on which this pigment is used, the more beautiful is the colour. The ancients had another colour, which was very proper for this kind of work and which very nearly approached *lake,* but its composition is unknown to us. Some think that it was a kind of minium."

The Spanish painter and author, Pacheco (page 366), speaks of the red pigment used instead of lake in fresco, by the name of "Albin." This author says, "The *Almagre de Levante* supplies the place of vermilion, in flesh and light red draperies, and *Albin* the place of carmine.

The next author I shall quote, is the Spanish author Palomino, who, in vol. 2, page 148-149, says, "*Albin* and *Pabonazo*[a] are mineral colours, and are used in fresco painting, only tempered with water. *Albin* and *Pabonazo* do not change, and are colours which supply the place of *carmine* so well, that, being used on very fresh stucco, they have sometimes deceived people, appearing to be *carmine;* and, observe, that *Pabonazo* is a degree lower in tone than *Albin,* and this is not sold in shops, but is procured from the mines of copper in the kingdom of Jaen; and there, and in all Andalusia, painters and gilders esteem it much, and it is even sold under the name of Almagre." Again, "The crimson in fresco painting, is to be *Albin* and *Pabonazo.*" II. Palom. page 151.

The last, and in point of date, one of the earliest of the modern writers on the arts, Eraclius,[b] whom I shall quote, and whose work

[a] There are artificial pigments called in Italian *Pavonazzo,* which cannot be used in fresco.

[b] De Artibus Romanorum. Eraclius is supposed to have lived between the 7th and 13th centuries, since the latest author he quotes is Isodorus, who lived in the 7th century. See Raspe on Oil Painting, p. 45.—The copy of this author's work published by Raspe is very imperfect; that which is preserved in the Bibliothéque Royale at Paris, contains many additional chapters and much valuable information on early methods of painting, and substances used in the Art.

is still preserved, mentions the substance as affording a red pigment, although he does not limit its use to fresco painting. In speaking of purpurinus, he says, "And indeed glebæ or flints, that is, stones emitting fire, seem very necessary in painting, when they are heated in the fire, and are quenched by having very strong vinegar poured over them; and they produce a purple colour."

And in chapter 266, Eraclius again mentions the same stone in the following extract:—"How a stone and the tooth of an animal is polished. Take the stone which is called *emantes*, which should not be too hard, nor veined, but very smooth and bright, and go to a workman's grindstone, and make it as flat as you like. And when it seems sufficiently ground, rub it still smoother upon a tile, and then, in order to make it finer, with a whetstone. Afterwards polish it upon a leaden table."—*Extract from a* MS. *of Eraclius in Bib. Royale, Paris.*

It will be observed that there are two kinds of stone noticed in the above extracts, the hard and the soft; I shall endeavour to prove, *firstly*—that the Amatito of Cennino, and the Albin of Palomino, are a variety of the Hæmatite; *secondly*—that the Lapis Amatita was, and is the stone commonly used to burnish gold; *thirdly*—that Amatito is not mineral Cinnabar; and *fourthly*—that Pabonazo is the Matita Rossa. But it will be necessary, previously, to ascertain the properties of these minerals, as described by these authors, and of the Red Hæmatite as described by the writers on mineralogy.

FIRSTLY, THAT ALBIN AND AMATITO ARE A VARIETY OF HÆMATITE.—It appears from the preceding extracts, that Amatito was a natural red pigment, prepared from a very hard and firm stone—that tools were made of it to burnish gold—that it took a good polish—that it had striæ[a] or fibres like Cinnabar—that it was so hard as to require to be broken in a bronze mortar, or calcined before it was ground, lest it should

[a] *Tiglio* and *Vena*, the Italian terms for striæ, although apparently synonymous are not so, since, the Dizionario, of Alberti, does not refer from one to the other and since Cennino uses both. *Tiglio* seems to mean veins or streaks of the same substance, as in wood, ivory, &c., and *vena* has the same meaning, and also signifies veins of other substances, included in a mineral, as veins of gold in Lapis Lazuli, &c. The term *Tiglio* seems to correspond with the term *striæ* rather than *vein*. The stone was to be without veins of other materials.

break the porphyry slab—that it made a lake or crimson colour [a]—that it could only be used in fresco [b]—that the colour was so fine as to be

[a] *Purple.* The terms *Pabonazo*, *Pavonazo*, *Purpura*, *Porpora*, were not used formerly to denote the colour we now call *purple*, but merely a red inclining to blue, namely crimson or lake colour. Pliny, (Nat. Hist. Book 31, chap. 33, Holland's translation,) describing the Syrian purple, says, "It is thought to have a most commendable and excellent dye, when it is as deep a red as blood that is cold and settled, blackish at the first sight; but look between you and the light it carrieth a bright and shining lustre. And hereupon it is that Homer calleth blood, purple." Cennino himself proves that he meant by Amatito, a crimson and lake colour and not a purple, as appears from the preceding quotations from chap. 42 and 136, and also from a passage in chap. 74, where he says, "If you would make a purple colour to be used in fresco, take Indigo, and Amatito, and mix," &c. He uses the word "*bisso*" when he means to express a mixed colour of blue and red. See chap. 74, 78, 79, 145, and the note by Sig. Tambroni, who concludes by observing, "The ancients imitated the *porpora* (dye from the fish called *porpore*), by mixing *porporisso* with blue, and the moderns, to supply the place of porporisso, use lake. See Goethe on Colour, by Eastlake, p. 244, 279. Borgh. Rip. 189.

Albin also was a lake or crimson colour, because Palomino, (vol. 2. p. 150) adds smalt to it to make it a *morella* colour. See also Pach. 366, II. Palom. 151, where he says it is used in fresco instead of Carmine.

[b] It is proper to notice here that Leonardo da Vinci (Trattato della Pittura, Chap. ccclii, Milan edition, by Amoretti,) in describing the method of painting on linen cloth (tela), observes, "The flesh colour should be white lead, lake, and Naples yellow; the shade should be black, majorica, and a little lake, or if you please *lapis duro*." Diego Antonio Rejon de Silva, the Spanish translator of Leonardo's Treatise, who used the edition of Leonardo's work published in France by Du Fresne, calls the colours for the shadows, black and *majorica*, and lake or *lapis roxo*. He observes in a note on this passage, "The signification of the word *majorica* is not to be found in any dictionary." I shall have no difficulty in proving that this *majorica* is the soft red hæmatite, and that it derived its name from the Island of Majorca, whence it was brought into Italy. I have now transcribed the passage, for the purpose of shewing that the "lapis duro" or "lapis roxo," which I shall prove to be the *hæmatite*, was used by Leonardo da Vinci in painting on linen. But this is no proof that it was an eligible pigment, and durable in this kind of painting, because Leonardo was fond of making experiments (which there is no doubt the method described in this and the preceding chapters were) and because many of Leonardo's colours were known to have faded considerably. See De Piles, Lives of the Painters, p. 107.

It is somewhat curious to observe the manner in which the passage has been translated in the English edition, by M. Rigaud of the Royal Academy, re-published by Mr. J. W. Brown in 1835, p. 130. "The shades with black, *umber*, distinguished with difficulty from lake and carmine—that it was brittle and should not be suffered to touch iron—that its colour was not injured by fire, since Borghini, and Eraclius, direct it to be calcined, in order to grind it more easily; nor by acetic acid, since the same writers also direct the red hot stone to be quenched in strong red vinegar—that the reasons for discontinuing its use, were, its scarcity in Italy, and the difficulty in grinding it—that this colour is mentioned by almost all the above authors as being very durable.

It also appears, from the preceding extracts, that *Albin* was a mineral, which supplied the place of lake, and was used principally in fresco[a]—that *Matita Rossa* was a soft stone,—that *Pabonazo* was a degree lower in tone than Albin, was procured from copper mines, and was used by painters and gilders, to whom it was known by the name of *Almagre*.

The following extracts are the characteristics of Hæmatite given by mineralogists.

Georgius Agricola gives a minute description of the varieties of the Hæmatite. He says, that the Hæmatite produces the Rubrica, (p. 64. of the Venetian edition in Italian)—that it is of the colour of blood (p. 168),—that being ground on the grindstone it yields a red juice, while the Schist (another variety), gives more frequently

and a little lake, you may if you please, use *black chalk*." Thus getting rid of the incomprehensible word "majorica," (the Pons Asinorum of the Spaniard,) and the *lapis duro;* changing the majorica, which is red, into brown; and the *lapis duro*, which is red also, into black. Umber is always rendered in Italian by "*Terra d' ombra*," and black chalk by *Matita Nera*.

The original passage is expressed thus by Leonardo, "l' ombra sarà nera, majorica, e un poco di lacca, o vuoi lapis duro."

There is no doubt that P. Lomazzo, the personal friend of L. da Vinci, alludes to this practice of da Vinci's in the following extract from the Treatise of the former (Book III, chap. xiv, p. 292), "Per acquerella e per disegnare in carta, per il nero vè l' inchiostro, la pietra tedescha, la terra nera, et il carbone di salce, o' del roncagino; per il rosso, *la pietra rossa detto apisso* la quale era usatissima da Leonardo da Vinci." I have not been able to find in any dictionary or work on art a description of a red stone called "Apissa," but the same word also occurs in the "Idea del Tempio della Pittura," (p. 71,) where Lomazzo calls the stone used for drawing (which other writers call "matita") *Carbone Apissa*.

[a] Pacheco indeed, p. 390, states that some painters used for draperies in oil Almagre de Levante or *Albin*, shading them with carmine and black.

a yellow juice (p. 175),—that it is found also in iron mines, but more frequently in veins alone—that the Hæmatite and the Schist differ in appearance, the latter being easily split in a particular direction, and its fibres being arranged in such a manner as to resemble congealed wood—that the Hæmatite and Schist are produced in many parts of Germany and also in Spain and other places —that where the Hæmatite is found, there is also found the Terra Sinopide. He adds, that the Schist is sometimes dull externally but sparkles internally, like artificial *Minium, and that painters call it also Cinabrio,* and that this kind is found in the Black Forest—that the Schist and the Hæmatite, being like congealed blood, *whenever they are burnt, or calcined, imitate the colour of Cinnabar*—that the Schist has the same colour as the Hæmatite,—that the best Hæmatite is that which has the colour of congealed blood, which is diffusible in water, which is equally coloured throughout, which is pure, (p. 251, 253). By the term *Schist* he evidently designates the *Lapis Amatita,* and by *Hœmatite,* he means the softer kind mentioned in the next chapter.

The French Encyclopædia describes the Hæmatite as "une pierre, ou plutôt une vraie mine de fer dont la figure varie, son tissu est tantôt strié ou par aiguilles, comme l'antimoine; tantôt il est composé de filamens ou de fibres, qui à la couleur pres, la font ressembler à du bois, (wood iron,) tantôt elle est sphérique ou hémisphérique, tantôt elle est en mamelons, et formée par un assemblage de globules qui la font ressembler à une grappe de raisins; tantôt elle est garnie de pyramides et de pointes; tantôt enfin elle parait composée de lames ou de feuillets qui laissent quelquefois des intervalles vuides entr'eux, et la font ressembler à un rayon de miel. L'Hæmatite varie aussi pour la couleur; il y en a de rouge, de pourpre, de jaune, et de noiratre ou couleur de feu, mais lorsqu' on l'ecrase, elle est toujours d' un rouge ou d'un jaune plus ou moins vif. L'Hæmatite, quoique fort chargée de fer, n'est point altérable par l'aimant, le fer qu'elle donne est aigri et il est difficile de lui procurer la ductilite convenable; il y en a dont le quintal contient jusqu 'á 80 livres de ce metal. Voilá pourquoi quelques gens l'appelent *Ferret.*— Encyc. Franc. Art. *Hœmatite.*

Pliny enumerates five kinds.—The five sorts differ chiefly in point of hardness. The best, according to Dioscorides, is that which is friable, hard, black, and smooth, without either gritty parts or veins.

"That commonly used by the painters is factitious, being made of Armenian bole, and other drugs. The common native or the fossil kind comes from Bohemia, &c. This assumes various forms:—spherical, pyramidal or cellular, and is composed of small pyramids; the apices of which appear in a tranverse section in the centre. It contains a large portion of iron, but the iron is obtained with such difficulty and is of so bad a quality, that this ore is not commonly smelted. This stone, when exposed to a moderately strong fire, falls by degrees into scales, and in this state is attracted by the magnet, and gives out its iron to acids. The gilders use it for burnishers to polish their metals. Bauschius has an express treatise, on the *Lapis Hæmatites*."—See Chambers' Dictionary.

The following is Jameson's description of *Red Hœmatite or Fibrous Red Ironstone*. Its colour is usually intermediate between brownish red and dark steel grey. Some varieties incline to blood red, others to dark steel grey, and others to bluish. It occurs most frequently massive and reniform; also botryoidal, stalactitiform and globular. The external surface is generally rough and glimmering, seldom smooth and shining. Internally it is usually glistening, which sometimes passes into glimmering and the lustre is semi-metallic. The fracture is always fibrous, and is straight, delicate and stellular or scopiform. The fragments are commonly cuneiform, seldom as in the coarse sorts, fibrous or splintery.

It generally occurs in distinct concretions, which are large, small or fine, *angular*, granular and traversed by others which are curved, lamellar more rarely, it occurs in cuneiform prismatic concretions. The surface of the concretions is either smooth or streaked, and the colour inclines to iron black, with a shining and metallic lustre. The streak is always blood red; it is hard, passing into semi-hard; it is brittle; it is rather easily frangible; it is heavy, inclining to uncommonly heavy. Specific gravity, 4.740, Gellert; 5.005, Kirwan; 4.8983, Brisson; 4.840, Wiedemann; 5.025, Ullman.

Its constituent parts consist of—Oxide of Iron, 90; Trace of Oxide of Manganese, 0; Silica, 2; Lime, 1; Water, 3;=96.—Daubuisson, Ann. de Chimie, 1810.

It occurs in every situation where the compact subspecies is found, and like it in veins, beds, and lying masses (liegende stocke), that approach in magnitude to mountain-masses; principally in primitive mountains, but also in transition, and floetz mountains. The different subspecies frequently occur together, both in beds and and in veins. In veins it is the compact and ochry that predominate; the hæmatite occurs principally in drusy cavities, the walls of which are encrusted with the scaly subspecies.

It occurs in veins that traverse sand-stone, at Cumberhead, in Lanarkshire; in veins in floetz green stone, at Salisbury-Craigs, near Edinburgh; at Ulverstone, in Lancashire; in Cumberland, and also in Devonshire, and near Bristol, in Gloucestershire. It is found in considerable quantity in Saxony, from Berggieshubel to Voightland; in Bohemia, but not so abundantly as in Saxony; at Bareuth, Wolfstein, in the Palatinate; Silesia, Lauterburgh, Walkenried, Andreasberg, Wernigerode, in the Hartz; and Salzburgh; in Siberia, and in Mexico. It affords excellent malleable and cast iron; and, when ground, it is also used for polishing tin, silver, and gold vessels, and for colouring iron brown.

The name Hæmatite which is derived from the Greek αιμα, sanguis, was given to this ore of iron, from its red colour. With respect to its geographical situation, it is to be observed that it occurs in great quantity in the kingdom of Saxony, less abundantly in the east side of the Hartz and Bohemia; not so abundantly in the Fichtelgebirge, and in considerable quantity in Norway, Sweden, Poland, Hungary, and Russia. In England it occurs particularly abundant in Lancashire. It is found in considerable quantity in Devonshire and Cornwall, and is one of the most common species of iron stone.—See Jameson's Mineralogy, tit. Red Hæmatite.

The description by Phillips and Ure, and other writers of the "Fibrous Red Iron Ore, Hæmatite," and "Compact Red Iron Ore," so closely resemble those which I have extracted from Jameson, that it would be useless to repeat them. It will be sufficient merely to refer to Phillips' Mineralogy, p. 229, 230, third edition, and to Ure's Dictionary of Chemistry and Mineralogy, Art. "Ores," also to the Penny Cyclopœdia, Art. "Iron."

On a careful perusal of these descriptions, it will be seen that the Red Hæmatite resembles in many particulars the pigment described by the various writers on art. Thus it is stated, that Red Hæmatite resembles the Lapis Amatito in the following particulars :—The colour, externally, was bluish, or iron grey, sometimes red, or black, (Phillips, Jameson, Penny Cyclopædia, Cenn. Bald. Agric.).—It was hard, smooth, without veins, or gritty parts, (Dios. Pliny, Jame. Cenn.).—Its structure was fibrous. (Enc. Franc. Phil. Jameson, Penny Cyclopædia, Agric. Cenn.).—When calcined it fell into scales. (Pliny, Borg. Erac.).—It was brittle. (Ure, Jame. Cenn.)—Gilders used it for burnishers to polish their metals. (Jame. Cenn. Bald.)—In this last particular writers on Mineralogy differ from the writers on Art; Phillips and Ure say the powder is used to burnish metals; Jameson does not particularize, but merely observes, of the Red Hæmatite, that "it is used for polishing tin silver and gold vessels, and for colouring iron brown," while the writers on art assert, that the solid stone, when shaped into a tool and polished, was used to burnish metals. It was fibrous like cinnabar, which it resembled in colour, and by which name it was also known.—(Cenn. Agric. Bald. Borg.)

With respect to the *Albin* of Palomino, the description is more indefinite than that of Amatito. In the index of the Terms of Art, added by another writer to the first volume of Palomino's Museo Pictorico, (third edition, 1795,) the following explanation is given of Albin; "a dark crimson colour which is brought in stones (Piedras) from the mines of copper; it serves instead of carmine for painting in fresco." In Gattel's Spanish and French Dictionary, Albin is thus explained, "*Sanguine; pierre de couleur rouge.* Lat. *Lapis Sanguinarius. Couleur rouge faite avec la sanguine.* Lat. *Color ex lapide sanguinario.*" In Pineda's Spanish Dictionary, Albin is translated *Bloodstone.*

It may be proper to mention, that there is a mineral called Albin, mentioned in Phillips' Mineralogy, p. iii, of an opaque *white* colour, from which indeed it derives its name. It has none of the properties of the Albin of Palomino.

Secondly, that Lapis Amatita—Red Hæmatite—was used to burnish gold.—I shall now endeavour to prove that the Lapis Amatita, the Red Hæmatite, was and still is used to burnish metals. It is unnecessary to repeat the extracts already given from Cennino, Borghini, and Baldinucci. These authors have proved that the *Lapis Amatita* was used as a burnishing tool; I shall now prove that the *Hæmatite* was formerly, and is at the present time, used for this purpose, and thus establish their identity.

Eraclius calls the stone used in polishing "*Emantes*." Theophilus, in his Treatise on various Arts, chap. xxxi, says, "polies illud dente vel lapide *sanguinario* diligenter limato et polito super tabulam corneam æqualem ac lucidam,"—translated,—"You must polish it with a tooth, or with a bloodstone, *lapide sanguinario*, carefully filed and polished upon a smooth and shining horn table." The author of the additional chapters appended by Raspe to the first book of Theophilus, directs that gold should be burnished with "*emate*," and in cap. xxxv. says, "Deinde limpidissima petra vel onychino aut *emate* vel simili re convenit scripturam detergere, quod sic et soliditatem accipit et fulgorem vel colorem," i. e.—"It is then proper to clean the writing with a very transparent stone, or with an onyx, or with *emate*, or with some such thing, and thus it receives both solidity and brilliancy or colour." M. Le Comte Charles de L'Escalopier adds by way of note to the first of these passages, "scribendum videtur hic et c. 35 ematite,"—"I think it should be written *ematite* both here and at cap. 35." He also adds in another note on the word *emate* "Nous ne doutons pas qu' il s'agisse de la sanguine, *lapis sanguinarius*, qu' il ne faille lire *ematite*." Hæmatite, (Theoph. p. 290). Benvennto Cellini (Opere, vol. iii. p. 14,) polished gold "pigliando un *amatita* nera (dark) che son quello che adoperano gli spadai metter d' oro." This passage immediately recalls the beforementioned expressions of Borghini and Baldinucci. M. de Brongniart (Traité des Arts Céramiques, &c., p. 646,) informs us that in the manufactory of porcelain at Sevres, gold is still burnished with the "*hæmatite dure*," which the workmen call "*sanguine*." And in the Magazine of Science, vol. i. p. 206, it is said, "Bloodstone [a] is a very hard

[a] There is another mineral called *Bloodstone*, namely the heliotrope or quartz, jaspe-sanguin of Haüy. "It is mostly of a deep green colour, and commonly yellow or blood-red spots are interspersed through its substance. From the latter circumstance it has obtained the name of *Bloodstone*."—Phillips' Min., p. 15. By this colour it is sufficiently distinguished from the Hæmatite.

compact variety of hæmatite iron ore, which, when reduced to a suitable form, fixed into a handle, and well polished, forms the best description of burnisher for producing a high lustre on gilt coat buttons, which is performed in the turning-lathe by the Birmingham manufacturers. The gold on china ware is burnished by its means. Burnishers are likewise formed of agate and flint, the former substance is preferred by bookbinders and the latter for gilding on wood, as picture frames, &c."

Vasari (Intr. chap. XXXII.) likewise mentions the stone by the name of "*Matita dura,*" which when ground, was to be used with the Matita rossa, and another colour prepared from "scaglia di ferro," for painting the shades of flesh on glass.

This certainly does not agree with the assertion of Cennino, that Amatita could not be used in any kind of painting but fresco; but as he does not treat of painting on glass, this does not invalidate his testimony, because this art was not practised to any extent in Italy until the time of Giulio 2. who sent for William of Marseilles to paint windows for him at Rome, (see Seroux d' Agincourt, Histoire de l' Art par ses Monumens, Peinture, vol. 2, p. 143. Le Vieil, De la peinture sur verre, p. 18. Vasari, vol. 5, p. 187). Cennino therefore could not have been acquainted with this description of painting.

Thirdly, that Amatito is not Mineral Cinnabar.—I have now to prove that Amatito is not mineral cinnabar as asserted by Borghini, and as De Piles supposed.

We have already observed, that Geo. Agricola says, that the stone which he calls Schist (after Pliny), resembled in its appearance *minium*, and that the painters called it *cinnabar;* that when calcined it imitated the colour of cinnabar.

Baldinucci, who had seen Cennino's Treatise, probably derived much of his information from that work, and much from common tradition, since, although he was an excellent draftsman, he did not paint. (See Lettere sulla Pittura, vol. 2, p. 392. n.) We have also his distinct assertion, as before quoted, that the true derivation of *lapis amatito* was *lapis hæmatitos*, meaning stone of a blood-colour.

Raphael Borghini, though descended from painters on the mother's side, and intimately connected with the painters and sculptors of his time, was not a painter himself; he was not, therefore, likely to be acquainted with the practical details of painting. In the second book of the Riposo, he has borrowed largely from Cennino. In many cases he has given a literal version of Cennino's text, and in others quite a paraphrase, although without having the honesty to acknowledge whence he derived his information; indeed it is remarkable, as Sig. Tambroni observes in the preface to Cennino's Treatise, that Borghini does not once mention Cennino's name although it is evident, he had read great part of his work. Cennino does not assert that Amatito was mineral cinnabar, his expression is merely, "*ha un tiglio come cinabro.*"

In the note to chap. 42. of my translation of Cennino's Treatise on Painting, I have expressed an opinion, that Amatito was mineral cinnabar, but having since investigated the subject, I am convinced that I was mistaken.

At first sight, the resemblance between the two minerals is sufficiently striking to warrant the conclusion. The colours of both varied between dark grey and red, both are fibrous, and yield a red powder when pulverized; but, there the resemblance ceases; Mineral Cinnabar is soft,[a] Amatito is hard: see the descriptions of native or Mineral Cinnabar in Ure, Phillips, and Jameson. Moreover, Amatito can only be used in fresco, Cinnabar is incompatible with lime.

The best proofs, independently of the direct assertion of Geo. Agricola, before noticed, are, however, to be derived from the works of writers on painting.

Borghini (Riposo p. 167) says, that Cinnabar was first procured from the quicksilver mines of Spain. He afterwards gives a recipe for making artificial Cinnabar. He adds that both kinds were used for painting in *oil.*

Paolo Lomazzo, in his treatise on painting (Lib. 3, Chap. 4) mentions two kinds of Cinnabar, namely, the mineral or native, and the artificial. In the same chapter he enumerates among the artificial pigments, Cinnabar, except the native Cinnabar (il cinabro

[a] Pliny indeed speaks of a kind of native Cinnabar brought from Spain, but he adds, that "it was *hard* and full of sand," and that also brought from Colchis was hard "and not better than that of Spain;" and he evidently disapproved of both kinds.—Book xxxiii, p. 325.

eccetto quello di miniera). In chapter 6, he informs us, hat the artificial Cinnabar was inimical to lime, *(è nemico della calce)*. The only red named by this author, proper to be used in fresco, is Majorica. By this we find, that Amatito was no longer in use. The treatise of Lomazzo was published in 1584, the same year as the Riposo of Borghini.

Palomino, after naming certain colours to be used in fresco, adds, " and vermilion, although the native or mineral, is better than the artificial vermilion." But he says that in uncovered places, and in such as are exposed to the inclemency of the weather, neither the native nor artificial should be used, because in a few days they both lose their beauty and turn to a dull mulberry colour. But in covered situations, and those defended from the weather, it is a beautiful colour and very permanent. But in order to make it more permanent, it should not be laid immediately upon the stucco, which should be previously dead coloured with *tierra roxa,* and the vermilion should be laid over this, making it lighter with white, and darkening it with *albin* and *pabonazo,* and in some of the deepest shadows adding *sombra del viejo* or *tierra negra,* and it will remain so fresh and beautiful, that even with oil colours it could not look better."—2 Palomino, p. 149.

This shews that vermilion and albin were different substances, since the vermilion was to be shaded with albin.

The author of the Vocabulary of Terms of Art, added to the work of Palomino before mentioned, names both the native and artificial vermilion. The native or mineral vermilion, he says, is of a red colour, procured from quicksilver mines.[a] It will perhaps be recollected that he had informed us that albin was procured from copper mines. The former, he says, was good for painting, (using the term generally,)—the latter, for painting in fresco. It is quite evident that he did not consider the terms synonymous.

Alberti (Dizionario Enciclopedico), following Baldinucci, (Tit. Cinabro Minerale,) says "mineral cinnabar is called by some lapis amatita." He adds, of the true native or mineral cinnabar, it is a

[a] Palomino, (vol. 2, p. 340.) also informs us, that native Cinnabar was procured from quicksilver mines.

mineralized ore of mercury, fibrous or smooth, of a red colour and shining."

Vitruvius also remarks that *minium* (cinnabar) would not stand 30 days in places exposed to the light and weather, (Vitruvius Liv. 8. Chap. 9.), and was always covered with wax and oil. In this he has done little more than repeat the words of Pliny (Book 33).

It is unnecessary to quote all the writers on painting who have said that cinnabar is inimical to lime, or to revert to the method adopted by Pozzo to render it permanent in fresco, since he does not mention, whether he used the native or artificial. I cannot discover that any writer on painting, except Pozzo, recommends using cinnabar on the *wet lime* in fresco.

From the foregoing extracts and observations, I trust I have established the fact, that painters formerly possessed a natural red pigment for painting in fresco; and that this pigment was not mineral cinnabar.

FOURTHLY, THAT PABONAZO IS THE SAME AS MATITA ROSSA, and that the names of Sinopia, Majorica, Terra Rossa d'Inghilterra, Bruno d'Inghilterra, Ferretta di Spagna, and Almagra, hereafter mentioned, are only different names for the same mineral colour, which I think will be found fully established in the subsequent part of this work treating of Sinopia.

I shall now show that Amatito and Albin were not the "vetriuolo cotto o abbrucciato" of the Italian writers.

Amatito and Albin were, as I have shown, natural pigments, which required merely to be pulverized to constitute a fine pigment for fresco painting. Vetriuolo cotto or abbrucciato is, on the contrary, an artificial pigment, prepared by calcining sulphate of iron, by which process it acquires its red colour.[a]

It was unknown to or at least not mentioned by Cennino, but is mentioned by Lomazzo and Borghini whose works were published in 1584, and by succeeding writers. It is called *vitriol calciné* by De Piles, (Elémens de Peinture, Jombert's Edition), *vitriolo Romano*

[a] The sulphuric acid is expelled by heat, and a per-oxide of iron remains in the vessels. It has been before observed that the Hæmatite contains in addition to the iron, silica, &c., traces of manganese and lime.

quemado by Palomino; *vitriolo calcinado*, in the Spanish vocabulary of terms of art before mentioned, and *burnt Roman vitriol* by the English.

It is said by Pozzo to be a beautiful colour like lake for fresco, but it is obvious, that if a natural pigment can be procured, the colour of which is equally fine, it must be preferable for painting in fresco.

The Amatito of Cennino was not the amethyst. The lightness and want of body of the colour of the latter, and the fact of that colour being *violet* and not lake, sufficiently prove that the two substances are not synonymous.

It is mentioned in the first Report of the Commissioners on the Fine Arts p. 28, that Prof. Hess uses oxides of iron for red pigments in fresco. It would be desirable to ascertain the exact species.

In conclusion, I would observe, that the red Hæmatite contains nothing in its composition incompatible with lime and with the pigments used in fresco painting; that lime is a constituent part of it; that the ore is found in several parts of England, and in great abundance at Ulverstone, in Lancashire, where it occurs in an enormously thick vein, traversing limestone (see Phillips). That the difficulty of grinding can be no objection to its use, since pigments are now ground in a mill purposely constructed, and that it is most important to the practice of fresco painting, to acquire a permanent pigment of a lake colour; that Amatito is not a new pigment now attempted to be introduced for the first time, but one which has been tried and approved. It may also be observed, that the colours produced from iron are always permanent, the natural more so than the artificial, and that such pigments are of universal application in painting.

I stated the characteristics of Amatito to Mr. Tremayne, of Heligan in Cornwall, and to his kindness, I am indebted for a copious supply of two species of red Hæmatite, from a mine in the parish of Roche in Cornwall, the hard and the soft; and I caused a specimen of the hard Hæmatite to be pulverized, and having washed some of the powder, and poured off the lighter particles, I found a portion of iron had sunk to the bottom, the removal of which seemed to render the colour finer. I also calcined another portion of the stone, and found it separated into scales, in the manner described. The colour of the stone when calcined, varies from lake to violet, according to the length of time it is exposed to the fire; and this agrees with the statement of Dr. Lewis, inserted in the Encyc. Brit. Art. colour-making.[a]

The fibrous red Hæmatite of Ulverstone, has a finer grain than the Cornish.

OF SINOPIA.

Besides the Amatito and Albin before mentioned, writers on art mention other natural red pigments proper to be used in fresco, namely, Rubrica, Sinopia, Cinabrese, Majorica, Terra Rossa d'Inghilterra, Terra Bruna d' Inghilterra, Rouge Violet, Ferretta di Spagna, Almagre, Pabonazo, Tierra Roxa, and Burnt Ochre, are all spoken of by different authors as red colours, or used instead of red colours, and are all ores of iron; and, excepting the last two, are merely different names for the same pigment, differing merely in quality, intensity of colour, or mode of preparation. That this pigment is in fact the Hæmatite or red ochre of the mineralogists.—See Phillips, Jameson, Tit. Red iron ore—Hæmatite.

Sinopia is mentioned or referred to as a red colour by most of the several writers on colours and pigments. It is described by Pliny as a natural pigment, which derived its name from Sinopia a city of Pontus, it was also brought from Egypt; the Balearic Islands, (Majorca, Minorca, &c.) and Africa; but the best was brought from the Isle of Lemnos and Cappadocia, where it was found in certain caves and holes. That which adhered to the rocks was the best, and the pieces of which on being broken, shewed the same colour throughout. There were three sorts differing in colour. The first deep red, the second paler, and the third browner. The Lemnian

[a] His words are as follow:—" The oxides of iron may be made to appear purplish, or inclining to the scarlet, according to the manner in which the calcination is performed. If the matter is perfectly deprived of its phlogiston, and subjected to an intense fire, it always turns out red; but the mixture of a small quantity of inflammable matter, gives it a purplish cast."

It is remarkable that the oxides of iron never shew their proper colour till they are cold.

earth, called also Terra Sigillata, was considered next in value to Minium (vermilion), and none was allowed to be sold without having been previously marked with the seal of Diana (a goat, the Turkish seal was afterwards substituted for this), for which reason it was also called "Sphragis." The painters ordinarily laid a ground of this under vermilion, and sophisticated it in many ways.—See Pliny, Book xxxv.

Dioscorides says, this *red ochre of Sinopia* is very fine: it is heavy, dense, and of the colour of liver without any mixture of stone; it is equally coloured throughout, and if put into water diffuses itself equally.

Geo. Agricola says, that the earth which the Greeks call *Milto*, because it is red, is called *Rubrica*. This is found in mines of gold, silver, copper, and iron, as Theophrastus writes; and it is often found in veins by itself. He adds, that the best kind is brought from Sinopia, and next to that is the earth of Lemnos, where, among the three[a] species of earth which (as it is said) were found in a heap, (tumuletto) was the *rubrica fabrile*.[b] He mentions, that in addition to the places named by Pliny and Dioscorides, it is also found in Germany, and according to Strabo, in Spain, and that this last kind was in no degree inferior to Sinopia. That there were three kinds of Rubrica, the first soft, which stained the hands; the second less soft, which stained less; the third was hard, and was called stone (sasso), which did not stain the hands unless they were wet. This last, I consider to be the Lapis Amatita, the fibrous red Hæmatite, the Glebæ of Eraclius, the Albin of the Spaniards. He adds, that all three kinds were used by painters. (Book II. p. 202.) The pale coloured Rubrica is probably Armenian Bole.

Cennino says, "there is a natural red pigment called Sinopia or porphyry, that this colour is naturally transparent and drying. It bears grinding well, and the more it is ground the better it is. It is good for painting either on pictures or walls in fresco or in secco." Cenn. Chap. 38.

[a] One species of earth appears to have been the Rubrica, another Bole, the third white, the last two were Argillaceous.

[b] *Rubrica fabrile.* This proves the pigment to have been an ore of iron, since the term *fabbrile* or *fabrile* is applied to working in iron—which is called *L'Arte fabbrile.*

Sinopia is mentioned by Borghini (Riposo p. 166), incidentally, when speaking of *cinabrese.* He describes it nearly in the words of Cennino, who mentions it as a red colour called light cinabrese, and composed of two parts of Sinopia and one of Bianco Sangiovanni, (a white made of very white and pure lime.) These two pigments were therefore prepared from the same mineral.

Requeno, a learned Spaniard resident at Rome, in his work written in Italian, entitled Saggio Storico sul Ristabilimento dell' Antica Arte de' Greci e Romani Pittori, (vol. I. p. 258.) commenting on the colours used by the ancients, observes respecting Rubrica, that "this was our mineral red earth. Vitruvius cites that of the Island of Majorca in Spain among the finest sorts, and I have always thought that the ancient Rubrica might be the fine Spanish Almagre."

The only red pigment mentioned by Paul Lomazzo (Trattato della Pittura, p. 191, 192.) as proper to be used in fresco was *terra rossa detta Majorica.*[a] The descriptions of Pliny, Theophrastus, and Geo. Agricola, prove that Sinopia was brought from Majorca, one of the Balearic Islands.

The terms *Rosso d' Inghilterra, Bruno d' Inghilterra, and Rouge Violet* appear synonymous, or nearly so. Pozzo says that this colour (always supposing them synonymous), when used on very wet lime, appears like lake when dry. Malvasia (Felsina Pittrice, vol. i. p. 349) says, that Bruno d' Inghilterra was much used then, i. e. in the latter part of the seventeenth century, in fresco, instead of lake.

Pacheco (Tratado de la Pintura, p. 366) directs Almagre de Levante to be used instead of Vermilion for flesh tints and light draperies in fresco. In p. 350 he says, that this colour is admirable in all kinds of painting. It will be observed this author calls the pigment " Almagre de Levante," an additional reason for supposing it to be Sinopia.

Palomino (vol 2, p. 149) enumerates among the mineral colours used in fresco painting, Albin and Pabonazo, which he says do not change, and supply the place of carmine so well, that when used on

[a] The beautiful vases of Majolica, of which Cennino speaks, (c. 107.) were probably so called from their having been formed, or at least, principally coloured with this mineral.—See "Traité des Arts Céramiques par. M. de Brongniart." Vol. II. Page 55-59.

very wet stucco, they have often deceived people, appearing to be carmine. He adds that Pabonazo is one degree lower in tone than Albin, and that it is not sold in shops, but is brought from the copper mines in the kingdom of Jaen, and there, and in all Andalusia, it is much valued by painters and gilders, and is even sold under the name of Almagre. This passage identifies Pabonazo with Almagre.

I think it will appear, from the preceding extracts, that the pigments called Majorica, or Majolica and Almagre, are of the same nature as Sinopia. But it is probable the latter was the finer colour; since Pacheco always distinguished it by the name of Almagre de Levante, thus shewing the similarity of its nature, and a preference for the oriental pigment, although, as before mentioned, Strabo says, that the kind produced in Spain was not inferior to the true Sinopia. Palomino has distinctly informed us that Pabonazo was also called by the Arabic name Almagre. It is probable that Sinopia was superseded by Terra Rossa d' Inghilterra in Italy, since P. Lomazzo does not mention Sinopia, and by Pabonazo or Almagre in Spain. Georgius Agricola, speaking of the colour called Armenian blue, observes, that it had been very scarce since the Turks had been masters of the country. The same influence may also have prevented the introduction of Sinopia into Europe in sufficient quantities for the use of painters, and occasioned them to have recourse to the productions of other countries for their pigments.

The French translator of Pliny mentions that a kind of Bol d' Espagne, called vermilion, was sold about 1725. Benvenuto Cellini mentions (Opere. vol. iii. p. 145.) among ingredients used to give a colour to gold, "Ferretta di Spagna;" now Ferretta di Spagna, or Ferretta simply, is a kind of Hæmatite which is a true ore of iron (see Alberti Diz. Enc.) There is also an artificial kind described by Neri, (Art. Vit.) made by calcining copper with sulphur. I merely mention this fact to shew that the two were not synonymous. The appellation *Ferret* was applied by the French to the Hæmatite.

The soft species from Cornwall, which appears to be formed from the decomposition of the harder species, and which I have examined, is heavy, dense, of the colour of liver, without any strong or gritty particles, equally coloured throughout, and when put into water, diffuses itself equally, but afterwards settles at the bottom of the vessel. It will be observed that the several kinds of Hæmatite are found generally together; on referring to the description of Albin and Pabonazo, we shall find that both pigments are classed together by Palomino as well as by Pacheco.

The purple tinge, observable in the colour of the Hæmatite, is to be attributed to the presence of a small portion of manganese, which is wanting in the ochres. The colour of the pigment, when washed and ground, is scarcely to be distinguished from Indian red.

The soft red Hæmatite is the mineral from which the Matita Rossa is prepared. This is proved by the following passage from Baldinucci's Life of Cennini, (Opere vol. 4, p. 485).—" Among other things that I observed cursorily, Cennini, mentioning that stone with which we draw, and which we call 'Matita,' gives it the name of *Lapis Amatito*, agreeably to its true origin *Lapis Hæmatitos*, meaning stone of a blood colour." The red chalk crayons, as they are called, now in use in England, are prepared by grinding Hæmatite to an impalpable powder in a porphyry mortar, and making the powder into pastiles with gum or isinglass (Mag. Science, vol. i. p. 349).

The *Tierra Roxa* of Palomino must have been different from the Pabonazo, since that author says its tint is deepened by time (en fortalecerse), whereas the Pabonazo did not change, (Pabonazo y Albin no hacen mudanza). It has been observed by many writers on colours, that ochres, whether raw or burnt, have a tendency to darken in time.

The red ore of iron, commonly called red chalk, or ruddle, is of a brick red, or brownish red colour, massive, and with an earthy fracture, is dull, soft, meagre to the touch, stains the fingers, writes easily, and adheres to the tongue. It is found in clay slate, in sandstone and in lime-stone. Phill. Min. Tit. Red Iron Ore,—Sub Tit. Red Chalk.

Sinopia is often confounded with Armenian Bole; so it is translated by Dr. Holland the translator of Pliny. Geo. Agricola, who appears to have studied mineralogy so deeply, remarks that the colour of his Armenian Bole is " pallido," whereas he says that of

Sinopia is of the colour of liver, and when prepared is a pigment blood-red.

Cennino also appears to have well understood the difference between these minerals. He used the Sinopia in painting, but Armenian Bole in gilding.

Sinopia and Pabonazo, as we have observed, are ores of iron, but Bole is classed by Phillips (Min. p. 53.) among the clays ; in the Treatise on Mineralogy, in the Encyc. Britann. it is placed in the Magnesian Genus. It is described as follows :—

Magnesian Genus, 2. Species *Bole.* Id. Kirw. I. 190. Le Bol, Broch. I. 459. Argile Ochreuse. Haüy. 445.—Exter. Char. Found massive and disseminated; surface dull, sometimes a little glimmering; fracture conchoidal, fragment sharp edged, colour yellowish brown or reddish, with spots and dentritical figures of black; opaque, rarely translucent at the edges ; very soft; easily frangible ; adheres to the tongue; feels greasy; streak shining; sp. grav. 1.4 to 2.

Chem. Char. Before the blow-pipe it becomes black or gray, and melts into a greenish gray slag. Falls to pieces in water with a crackling noise, and without forming a paste. Its constituent parts are stated by Bergman to consist of—Silica 47, Alumina 19, Magnesia 6.2, Lime 5.4, Oxide of Iron 5.4, Water 17=100.

The chief places which yield Bole, are the Islands of Lemnos,—hence called Lemnian earth—Sienna in Italy, and Strigan in Silesia, in which latter place it is deposited on indurated clay; in Upper Lusatia, it forms nests in Basalt. Bole and similar earths were formerly employed in medicine ; they are now only used in the preparation of colours.—Encyc. Brit. Tit. Mineralogy.

I consider that it may be collected from the above extracts, that Sinopia is that species of Red Iron Ore called red ochre by Phillips and other mineralogists. This mineral will require the same preparation as a pigment as other earths; namely, careful washing and grinding.

BLUE COLOURS.

Palomino was right when he said that blue pigments were the Scylla of fresco painting. He had doubtless seen many instances of their want of durability and of their discordance with the other colours of the picture.

The remarks of Mr. Wilson and Mr. Hart, in the II. Report of the Commissioners on the Fine Arts, are a commentary on this passage. "The blue of the skies has either partially changed or entirely faded, whilst that of the drapery is comparatively well preserved. In the School of Athens he (Raphael) has painted the blues in fresco, and they have perished or nearly so, as they have, in most instances, in every part of Italy, where blue has been thus used; both in pictures of this and previous times. In the great works which Raphael subsequently painted in the Stanze, he returned to the old practice of painting the blues above red, probably dissatisfied with the crudeness which was the result of using them on the wet plaster. The blue that has thus been generally used seems to have been of a vegetable nature, as in many instances it has changed to a brilliant green. It may be urged that the use of ultramarine or cobalt, may obviate all necessity for such preparations, and secure the pictures against change; but whilst the former is by far too expensive a colour, the latter is crude and harsh in fresco. It seems to have been the blue which was used by the Carracci, and in their pictures, as in those of Guido, it will be found to be frequently out of harmony with the other colours; either these have in some degree faded, the blue remaining the same, or the blue has increased in intensity. Domenichino used distemper extensively in his works; but in those of Guercino will be found a triumphant solution of the difficulty; his blues are put in in fresco, and yet are in fine harmony with the other tones; they have generally a warm purple hue, and may be either smalt, or cobalt tempered with red, such as colcothar of vitriol. This is strongly exemplified in the Zampieri Palace at Bologna, where the harmony apparent in a fresco of Guercino is an agreeable relief, after the crudity which offends in those of his masters in other rooms of the same palace: a comparison between the Aurora of Guido in the Rospigliosi at Rome (all the blues of which are not retouched), and that by Guercino in the Ludovisi, further corroborates the above observations,"—Rep. 27. Again, Mr. Wilson observes, "The blue has come off entirely in some parts, and has evidently been laid on when the figures were finished, and the lime too dry, so that not being incorporated, it has come off in powder; in other parts where the artist has evidently been obliged to use it first, it is perfectly preserved." Again, "The blues have been scraped off for the value of the ultramarine." "The skies and water have faded to the usual blackish or slate colour." "The nitre has almost entirely eaten up all the greens and blues." "The blue backgrounds, on which the figures are relieved, are either turned black or purple, or have disappeared." See II. Rep. pp. 36, 37, 42, 43, 44.

The "vivid blue," in the church of St. Sigismond, at Cremona, and the blues in the pictures of Guercino, and the school of Carracci generally are almost the only exceptions to the general decay of the blue pigments in fresco. The colour is however more durable when applied in distemper.

It will be proper, in the first place, to enquire what blue pigments have been used, in painting on walls, by artists, and then to ascertain whether they can be employed with propriety in fresco.

The blue pigments mentioned by writers on art to have been used in painting on walls, are as follows :—

PIGMENTS.	NAMES OF AUTHORS.
Cœruleum or Vestorian Azure. .	Pliny, Vitruvius.
Azzurro di Smalto	Borghini.
Smaltino	Pozzo, Orsini trans. of Vitruvius, Galliani, same.
Esmalte	Pacheco, Palomino.
Smalto	Lomazzo, Armenino.
Azzurro della Magna	Cennino, Borghini, Benozzo Gozzoli, Books of the Duomo of Pisa.
Azzurro Oltramarino	Lomazzo, Borghini, Vasari, Cennino, Pozzo, Palomino.
Azzurro di vena naturale . .	Malvasio, Borghini, Baldinucci.
Azul fino,.	Palomino.
Azul di san Domingo	Palomino.

The preparation of the artificial pigment called Cœruleum, Vestorian Azure, and Vestorianum, is described by Vitruvius in the following terms :

"The composition of blue (Azzurro) was first discovered at Alexandria, and subsequently Vestorius established a factory of it at

Puteoli. The manner of making it, and the ingredients of which it is composed, are rather remarkable. Sand is ground up so fine with flour of nitre, as almost to resemble wheat flour, and being mixed with copper filings, made with a coarse file like a rasp, the whole is sprinkled with water, that it may adhere together. It is then made into balls, by working it with the hands, and these balls are laid aside to dry. When dry, they are put into an earthen jar and the jar is put into the fire. And then, when the copper and the sand have united, boiling together by the vehemence of the fire, giving and receiving vapours from each other, they lose their own properties, and being united altogether by the force of the fire, they become of a blue colour.

"Similarly, on account of the scarcity of the colour Indigo, they make an imitation of that colour by mixing *Selinusian* or *Anularian* chalk, with the glass, which the Greeks call ὑαλον *(hyalon).*"

Sir Humphrey Davy observes,[a] "That this colour can be easily and cheaply made. I find that fifteen parts by weight of carbonate of soda, twenty parts of powdered opaque flint, and three parts of copper filings, strongly heated together for two hours, gave a substance of exactly the same tint, and nearly the same degree of fusibility, and which, when powdered, produced a fine deep blue." The ingredients meant by Sir H. Davy, are nearly the same as those mentioned by Vitruvius, except that the latter mentions nitre, instead of carbonate of soda, and sand instead of flint, the difference in the latter, being merely nominal, since pure sand consists of silica almost in the state of powder, and flint also consists of silica in a consolidated form. Volumes have been written to ascertain what the nitre of the ancients really was, but the inquiry is unnecessary here. It is sufficient for our purpose to shew that the Vestorian Azure was a *blue glass.* I think I shall be able to prove that the blue pigment used in Italy and Spain during the latter half of the 16th century, and the whole of the 17th and 18th centuries, was of the same nature as this Vestorian Azure.

Bald. Orsini, the Translator of Vitruvius (Ed. of 1802), speaking of the Vestorianum, says, "this glass is synonymous with what

[a] On the Colours used by the Ancients.—Phil. Trans. 1815. See also Chaptal's "La Chimie appliquée aux Arts."

the Italians call *Smaltino,* which was and still is used in fresco painting in Italy." Orsini also remarks, (note to p. 96), "It is sufficiently clear that the Cœruleum of Vitruvius, is the same as Smaltino which is used in fresco painting, distempering it with milk, or with ox gall; that being mixed it may spread better because it is composed of a fine coloured glass. It must be spread with a brush over the *intonaco* before it hardens, and under it should be a coat of *terre verte,*[a] which serves for a ground *(letto)* for it. But Vitruvius says nothing respecting the manner of using it."

The Marchese Galliani also, (trans. of Vitruv., edition of Naples), observes, in a note on this blue pigment of Vitruvius, "Blue in this passage does not mean the fine blue which is also called ultramarine, and which is made from Lapis Lazuli, ground to powder, but the other common sort of blue, which we call Smaltino." Again, he says in another note on the "glass" mentioned by Vitruvius, "The blue colour made in this manner, is nearly the same as what is now used in fresco under the name of Smaltino.

Borghini remarks, (page 173), "There are many blue pigments, such as *Azzurro di Smalto,* which is made of *glass,* and is used in fresco." He afterwards mentions *Azzurro della Magna,* thus proving that these pigments were not synonymous.

The only blue pigment mentioned by Armenino is *Smalto*; Lomazzo mentions *Smalto,* which he always distinguishes from the other *azzurri* amongst which he classes *Ultramarine.*

The Spanish painter Pacheco says, "*Esmalte* is the blue pigment best adapted for fresco painting, *because it is glass,*" &c. Palomino expresses himself nearly in the same terms with respect to this pigment; his words are, "The blue is the rock of this kind of painting; but fortune has not given us our choice in this matter, obliging us to use *Esmalte, which is in substance ground glass.*"

Pozzo mentions *Smaltino* as the blue pigment to be used in fresco. The directions for preparing various colours added to the Abecedario Pittorico (Naples, 1731), shew that Smaltino was prepared by mixing

[a] Mr. Wilson was informed by some Italian artists (See I. Rep. p. 27,) that a coat of *Terra verte* was laid at times as a preparation for blue, but I was told by Mr. Wilson himself that he had never found an instance of terra verte having been laid under blue.

Zaffre with a salt instead of copper, and then of calcining the mixture.

It is impossible to decide whether the colouring material of the blue glass generally used in Italy was copper or Zaffre. The latter which is a mixture of cobalt with glass, now known by the name of Smalt,[a] was in use in Italy, where it was brought from Germany, before anything was known in the former country of its nature. Georgius Agricola, who was a German, does not mention it in his work, De Metallicis, published 1549. Neri (Arte Vitraia, p. 317-369, Florence, 1612), says its nature was unknown. It is probable that about this period smaltino made from Zaffre superseded that of which copper was the base. Lomazzo (Book III, chap. 4) enumerating the pigments used in painting, says "Gli smalti, come quelle di Fiandra che è il migliore di gl' altri tutti,"—"The smalti, such as that of Flanders, which is better than all the others." From this passage we may infer that more than one sort of *smalto* was in use in Italy, and that one of these was of the same nature as the Vestorian Azure.

This vitrified pigment, then, which is known by the various designations of *Smalto, Azzurro di Smalto, Smaltino and Esmalte* was used on the wet lime, and, according to the before-mentioned writers, the wetter the lime was when the colour was applied, the better. I shall now remind the readers of the general state of the blue colours in the Italian fresco paintings as described by Mr. Wilson and Mr. Hart, and then state my opinion that this pigment is the one that was generally employed in Italy and Spain for above two hundred years, and that it is quite unfit for the purpose, as is proved by the present state of the frescoes. I have not been able to discover when this colour was first introduced into modern painting, but I consider it probable that its introduction took place when the work of Vitruvius first began to be studied and translated in Italy.[b] It is to be

[a] The meaning of the word "Smalto" varies according to its use. It may mean enamel, mortar, cement, basis, ground, pavement, or floor; no conjecture therefore respecting its nature can be formed from its name.

[b] The first edition of Vitruvius, without a date, appears to have been published about 1486. Two others were published in 1496 and 1497. (D'Agincourt, Architecture, p. 90, n.) The first Italian translation of Vitruvius by Cesariano was published in 1521, the second by Durantino in 1524, the third by Caporale in 1535, and the fourth by Barbaro in 1556. Perhaps this pigment was introduced during the life of Raphael, since Mr. Wilson mentions that he

observed that Vitruvius does not distinguish between such colours as were to be applied on the wet lime, and such as were to be used in *secco* (except in the case of lamp black, which he says was to be tempered with glue for painting on walls); but Pliny says decidedly (Book xxxv). of the Cœruleum, "*Usus in creta; calcis impatiens,*"—"It is useful on chalk, but is incompatible with lime." He also includes this colour among those which cannot be used on a damp wall. The marginal note is as follows:—"*Qui colores udo illini recusant,*"—"Which colours cannot be laid on in fresco." The text says, "*Ex omnibus coloribus cretulam amant, udoque inlini recusant, Purpurissum, Indicum, Cœruleum, &c.*"—"Out of all the colours, Purpurissum, Indicum, Cœruleum, &c. prefer chalk, and cannot be laid on in fresco."

It is quite clear, therefore, that the Romans did not use it in fresco and the nature of the pigment proves it to have been unfit for this kind of painting. It was an artificial pigment, and it contained potash or soda, either of which would be a sufficient reason for refusing it a place among pigments to be used on lime.

It has been observed by Mr. Wilson and Mr. Hart, that "the blues and greens were eaten up with nitre." Palomino also states that Luca Giordano retouched with the egg tempera those parts in which the nitre had appeared. Mr. Smith in his able paper on the Causes of and Means of Prevention of Saltpetre on the Surface of Walls, (II. Rep. p. 53-55.) observes that "salts will always make their way to the surface," and that "lime, mortar, or some other sort of calcareous earth, seems to act as a vivifying principle to set the molecules of salt and water in action." M. Durosiez also is of opinion that the presence of all alkalies in the substance of pictures is injurious, (III. Rep. 49). This then will be sufficient to account for the presence of nitre on the blue pigments in fresco paintings, where that pigment has been smaltino, and whether the colouring ingredient in that vitrified pigment be copper filings, or zaffre.

There is no doubt that it was the practice of the Greek or Byzantine school, and that of Giotto, and of the Italians generally, until

had painted the blues in fresco in the School of Athens, and that they had turned green, for we know that he, Michael Angelo, and other artists of that period were in the habit of laying on the blue in distemper.—(See Merimée de la Peinture à l'huile, p. 173.)

after the death of Raphael, to add the blue pigments, in distemper, over a ground of black and red, or black only, or red only, or black and white.

Theophilus, who professes to teach all the Greeks knew respecting colours, in Chap. xv. of Book 1st of his Treatise on divers arts directs, that " on walls a coat of *Veneda,* that is, black mixed with lime, is to be laid as a ground; and upon this colour, when dry, must be laid, in the proper place, a thin coat of Ultramarine tempered with yolk of egg, mixed with plenty of water ; and after this a thicker coat, to make it look well." Cennino also directs both Ultramarine and *Azzurro de la magna* to be tempered with egg, or glue. See Chap. 60, 72, 74, 83.

The blue commonly used by the early Florentine painters was called " Azzurro della Magna," because it was brought from Germany, and sometimes "Azzurro" only. The colour used by Titian and the Venetians, was called by the latter name, and was brought to Venice from the East, as will be hereafter mentioned. I shall first give some early historical notices respecting these pigments, and shall then endeavour to ascertain their nature.

The following notice is extracted from the books of expenses incurred in the construction of the Duomo of Pisa.

" Anno 1392, de lib. M. Mag. Pierus, Pictor, de urbe veteri, habuit et recepit a d. operaris, pro una libra *Azurri de la Magna,* pro ystoria Ginesis de Campo Sancto, quod azurrum emptum fuit," &c.— " In the year 1392, book M. Messer Piero, artist, of Civita Vecchia, had and received fron the Master of the Works, for one pound of *Azzurro della magna,* for the historical picture from Genesis, in the Campo Santo, which azure was bought, &c."

The following extracts from letters written by Benozzo Gozzoli to Pietro de Medici, and preserved in the archives of the family of the Medici, throw much light on the manner of painting on walls at this period. He is speaking of the picture of the Three Magi, in the chapel of the Medici.[a]

" I should have come to speak to you, but I have begun this

[a] In the palace now called the Palazzo Riccardi at Florence. The chapel is now so built up that it can only be viewed by torch-light.

morning to put on the blue (*Azzurro*) and I cannot leave it. The heat is great and the glue spoils directly. I think by next week I shall have completed this piece (*Pontata*). I think you would like to see it before I take down the scaffolding." Dated Florence, 10th July, 1459. Again, "I remind you to send to Venice for the blue (*Azzurro*) because by this day week, this side (*Facciata*) will be completed and I want the blue for the other." 11th Sept. 1459. "I had from the Jesuits two ounces of blue (*Azzurro*) of that kind which is three great florins per ounce." 25th Sept. 1459.

Dr. Gaye, the editor of the "Carteggio inedito d'artisti dei secoli XIV. XV. XVI," (from which these extracts are taken), Vol I. p. 193, observes, "the price of three great florins the ounce for *Azzurro della Magna* is much greater than has hitherto been considered the average price in the fifteenth century."

From these extracts we learn the important fact, that the blue was applied *in secco* when the picture was nearly completed, and that it was mixed with glue.

Giovanni Liombani in a letter to Francesco Gonzaga, Marchese di Mantova, dated 22nd February, 1491, requests the Marchese "to cause a letter to be written to the respectable Zorzo Broguolo at Venice, ordering him to supply me with as much gold, silver, azurro, and other colours as shall amount to the sum of 200 ducats." The artist, as appears from the same letter, was then going to paint in the palace in Marmirolo, of which no vestiges now remain.—See the same work. Vol. I. p. 306.

It was the custom for the person who ordered the picture to supply the blue pigments as well as the gold. Even Titian observed this practice. He writes thus to the Doge of Venice, "Nor do I wish any other payment in advance than colours to the value of 10 ducats and 3oz. of that Azzurro, if there be any, in the Offitio del Sal," &c. By a decree dated the 28th January, 1515, the Council order, among other particulars, "that Titian shall have only colours to the amount of 10 ducats and 3oz. of Azzurro."

Modern writers have supposed that Azzurro della Magna was cobalt blue; but I apprehend without sufficient reason. The principal reason seems to be, that both pigments were produced in Germany. Georgius Agricola does not appear to have been aware that cobalt could be used as a pigment; he describes (p. 466) three kinds, differing principally in colour; the first was black, the second grey, and the third the colour of iron. He says that cobalt corrodes and consumes the hands and feet of those who work it, if they are not careful to defend themselves from it. Matthioli, (Comm. on Diosc. p. 1395) observes, that "Kobolt is a corrosive substance, that frequently ulcerates the hands and feet of those who dig it, nor is this to be wondered at, since it kills like deadly poison." He adds, that in Bohemia it is used to kill flies, but he says nothing of its being used as a pigment. The art of purifying and preparing cobalt as a pigment, is of comparatively modern invention, at least in Europe, and it is extremely probable, indeed almost certain, that it was used in the form of Zaffre as a pigment, long before the art of preparing a pigment of a pure blue colour from it was known; Zaffre not being a pure blue, but inclining to red. It appears also, that the process described by Cennino (chap. 60) for preparing Azzurro della Magna for use, is not applicable to the mineral cobalt, which requires chemical preparation before it can be used as a pigment; for we have seen that the natural colours of this mineral are black, grey, and the colour of iron, and not blue. The simple process of grinding and washing it with water, would not be sufficient to develope the blue colour of cobalt; if it were, it is quite clear, the long and troublesome processes, now in use for purifying this mineral, are unnecessary; besides, if cobalt required chemical preparation, it could scarcely be included with propriety in Cennino's list of natural pigments. (See Cenn. chap. 60, and for the modern method of purifying cobalt, see Ure's Dict. of Chemistry and Mineralogy, Chaptal's Chimie appliquée aux Arts, M. de Brongniart's Traité des Arts Céramiques, Merimée, De la peinture à l'huile, Marcucci Saggio Analitico dei Colori, &c.)

The ancients possessed some native blue and green pigments, to which they gave the names of Chrysocola, Lapis Armenus, Cœruleum, and Cyaneum, (see Pliny, Lib. xxxv. Chap. 6). The first is green, the second greenish-blue or blue, the third and fourth blue. Geo. Agricola, Matthioli, and Laguna, mention pigments of the same name. All agree in the general description, but vary in their account of the colour. They also agree in stating that they were found in copper and silver mines, and sometimes in gold mines, frequently close together, and even adhering to the same piece of ore, and that they were a certain criterion of the presence of copper. The fact is, that they were all native carbonates of copper, changing their name according to the prevalence of the blue, or green, or greenish-blue colour. The first (Chrysocola) will again be noticed. The Armenian Stone is by most writers described to be of a greenish blue colour, and this corresponds, as I shall prove, with the Azul Verde of Palomino, and the Verde Azzurro of the Italians. The Cœrulea is the native blue carbonate of copper, of which there are two species, the earthy and the indurated; the last was frequently mistaken for the Lapis Lazuli, from which ultramarine is prepared.

I shall give, concisely, Agricola's description of the pigment he calls Cœruleo. He says, (p. 219, 221) there were two kinds known in his time, the native and the artificial; that the native was often attached to the same ores as Chrysocola, namely, copper ores; that it was found not only in copper mines, but in those of silver and gold, and that it always shewed the presence of copper; that it was brought from Spain, Germany, Noricum, Dacia, Rhætia, &c., but was scarce because the factitious was more in use. He adds (p. 452), "now this is the Cœruleo which the vulgar call azzurro, which, together with the Chrysocola, is attached to the ore," (or matrix). He says also, that it resembled a hard sand, and is scraped off the ore like sand. And see also Matthioli (p. 1412), who agrees in the general description. The mineral here described is clearly the earthy blue carbonate of copper, of which the following description is given in the Encyc. Brit. Art. Mineralogy.

Subspecies I. Earthy Azure Copper Ore.—*Exter. Char.* Rarely found massive, usually disseminated or superficial; composed of fine particles, which are dull and somewhat coherent; fracture earthy.

Colour, smalt blue, sometimes sky blue; opaque; stains a little; soft or friable.

The earthy variety is found in superficial layers on a slaty marl in Hessia, and it is also found superficial on sandstone in Thuringia. Sometimes the whole of the sandstone is impregnated with this earthy carbonate of copper, there called copper sand earth or copper sand stone. A similar sand stone, at Gourock near Greenock, in Scotland, was, a few years ago, dug out for the purpose of extracting copper.—(Enc. Brit. Art. Mineralogy.)

The resemblance between this species, and the mineral described by Agricola, is obvious. The indurated species is rare. Azure copper ore is found in veins of primitive and secondary mountains, chiefly with the green carbonate of copper and red oxide of copper, in Chili, Bohemia, the Hartz, Saxony, the Uralian mountains, and in Thuringia, at Chessy in France, &c.

In Cornwall, sparingly in Huel Muttrell and Huel Gorland, Huel Unity, Huel Virgin and Carbarack. In the Buckingham mine, near Bridgewater, Somersetshire. At Alderley Edge, in Cheshire, in sandstone with yellow copper and barytes. In Durham, at Wassinghope lead mine near Stanhope, in small nodules imbedded in sulphate of barytes. In Scotland, at Wanlock Head, and the lead hills in Lanarkshire. (Phillips' Mineralogy, p. 310). Phillips classes this mineral under the head " Native Metal and Metalliferous Minerals."

Modern writers on the composition of colours, call this pigment Bleu de Montagne—Mountain Blue—Blue ochre of copper.—Lomazzo mentions the colour under the name Ongaro.[a]

With regard to the last appellation, Ongaro, Pacheco (p. 373) relates a circumstance not generally known. " Philip, Count of Flanders, ordered Michael Coxis of Malines to make a copy for him, of the celebrated picture by Van Eyck at Ghent; he copied it extremely well, and because they could not procure any azure so fine as that used in the original, they sent to Titian, who was at Venice, for some of a natural azure, which is found in Hungary, which was formerly very easy to procure, before the Turks were masters of that province, and the blue for the drapery of the figure cost thirty ducats." Perhaps this was some of the same kind of azure that Titian desired the Doge to send him (if there were any). This anecdote shews, that the blue carbonate of copper was used in oil by Titian, and probably by Van Eyck, since no other blue could be found in Flanders which matched that in the picture.

[a] Because it was brought from Kerhausen in Hungary. Marcucci (p. 70) enumerates it among the *green* pigments, a circumstance which identifies it with the Lapis Armenus which was sometimes blue and sometimes green.

Much confusion has been occasioned by some authors describing the *Lapis Armenus* as a blue stone, while others say it is green. The fact is, that it consists of one of those ores of copper united with other substances, and that it is sometimes blue, sometimes green, and sometimes of a greenish blue. See Pliny, Book xxxv. c. 6. G. Agricola, De Metallicis, 219, 221, 452. Constant de Massoul's Treatise on Painting, and the Composition of Colours, 152, and Bulengerius de Pictura, Sculptura, et Plastice, Lib. II. c. III. Le Vieil (De la Peinture sur Verre, p. 108, n.) says, it is a stone of a lighter colour, not so heavy and more friable than ultramarine; it is found in France, Germany, and especially in the Tyrol. G. Agricola (p. 452) mentions, that "he saw some Armenio in one shop only in Venice, and that the possessor valued it much." The scarcity of the pigment is sufficiently accounted for, by the provinces which produced it being in the hands of the Turks. The Venetians, however, seem to have maintained an intercourse with them, since Gentile Bellini was sent to practise his art, at the court of Mahomet the Second, at Constantinople. As merchandize is generally imported in considerable quantities, the Armenio seen by Agricola at Venice, in one shop, might have been the remains of the old stock imported while the Turks and Venetians had still commercial relations. It is not the blue pigments only which became scarce on account of the wars, the *Sinopia* also fell into disuse about the same period, as Agricola declares, and from the same cause. Another reason also for the scarcity of the carbonates of copper was, as we have before observed, the use of the artificial pigments prepared in imitation of the natural pigments; many recipes for which are to be found in every work on colours.

Matthioli (p. 1412) observes, "Armenian stone is of a bluish colour, although not a pure blue, nor is it so hard as the stone called "Azulo," because the Armenian stone is of a sandy nature, and the painters sometimes use it instead of Azzurro." He says also that the same mineral was found in Germany as well as in Armenia, and he adds that the Armenian stone which the painters use, being taken in the quantity of the twelfth part of a drachm, was useful in removing melancholy. It was also given to children for disorders of the breast, &c. This is sufficient proof that the Armenian Stone was not Cobalt, the poisonous nature of which was well known to Matthioli. In another place (p. 1415, line 58) he gives the name of Verde Azzurro to the Armenian Stone, which sufficiently identifies these minerals. Laguna, the Spanish commentator on Dioscorides, is still more precise, he says, " This kind of stone resembles much in its colour Chrysocola, and that is considered the best which is green with a mixture of blue. From whence I am persuaded that the common stone which is found in so many mines, of which the perfect colour Verde Azul is made, is a species of the Armenian Stone."—p. 539. See, also, Dr. Holland's Translation of Pliny, p. 531, where he calls this pigment Verd' Azzur.

Matthioli observes (p. 1413) that the Arabs confuse the Pietra Cerulea, by which he means Lapis Lazuli, with the Armenian Stone; indeed the resemblance between all these minerals is so great, that they can scarcely be distinguished by inspection. I have a specimen of ore which one mineralogist pronounced to be the Blue Carbonate of Copper, while another to whom it was shewn called it Lapis Lazuli. The only apparent difference between the indurated Blue Carbonate of Copper and Lapis Lazuli appears to be the presence or absence of the spots or veins of gold which are always found in the finest coloured specimens. The Lapis Lazuli may be distinguished from the Carbonate of Copper by subjecting it to the action of fire. The former will be unchanged, but the latter turns black.—See Massoul, pp. 166, 176. Let us hear what Matthioli, speaking of the stone to be used as a medicine, says of the Pietra Cerulea, " It is true that that stone which sparkles with gold should be used; because the others with which the apothecaries, and those who prepare Azzurri in Germany are always provided, are not nearly so beneficial." He also says, " he has seen great quantities of Armenio and Ceruleo in silver mines, in a great many places in Germany, but he never found any which was veined with gold." Cennino (chap. 60) mentions Azzurro della Magna in nearly the same terms. Matthioli continues, " That which is called Ultramarine, and which is made of the true Lapis Lazuli from gold mines, is in great esteem, because it surpasses in goodness and in colour all the Azzurri in the world." The Ceruleo was probably the indurated blue carbonate of copper, which much resembles the Lapis Lazuli.—See Massoul's Art of

Painting, p. 176. Laguna adds that Matthioli was satisfied that the stone called Armenio, was of the same nature as the Cerulea or Cyano (Lapis Lazuli), but that the former was not perfectly formed in the mineral veins; "and in truth we must believe implicitly all he tells us, for he was a most acute and accurate investigator of the nature of all minerals." We may add that the true Lapis Lazuli is not produced in Europe but is brought from Asia, especially from Persia, where it must have been once in great abundance, since we learn from the book of Esther, c. i. v. 6, that the pavement of the palace of Ahasuerus consisted "of red, and *blue*, and white, and black marble." For the description of Lapis Lazuli, see Phillips, Jameson, Ure, Encyc. Brit. Art. Mineralogy, Tit. Lazulite.

I trust I have now proved satisfactorily that the pigments called Azzurro, Azzurro della Magna, Ongaro, and Verde Azzurro were native blue carbonates of copper, and that the latter was the Armenian Stone of Pliny, of Agricola, and of Matthioli. I shall now endeavour to prove that they were also called "Azzurri di Spagna," and "Azzurri di Vena Naturale."

Malvasia mentions (Fels. Pitt. vol. II. p. 349) that he discovered in the studio of Cesare Baglione, many years after his decease, "a chest full of brushes and colours, that is, earths of all sorts, particularly of *verde di miniera*, the most precious which the ancients possessed, the good and genuine sort of which is now lost. Also some fine Verdetto, and some *Azzurri di Spagna*, so bright and fine that even Sirani was deceived by them, and at first mistook them for ultramarine." The reference to this passage in the index is as follows:—"Azzurri e verdetti di Spagna cosi belli anticamente per i frescanti oggi perdutisi, nè più in uso,"—"Spanish blues and greens, anciently so fine for fresco painters, *now* lost and no longer in use." Malvasia says "*now lost*," we must first endeavour to ascertain when they were lost; Sirani, he adds, was deceived by them; now Sirani died in 1670.

These colours were lost, therefore, previous to 1670, and probably some time previous, as Sirani did not appear to know them. Cesare Baglione died in 1590, having the colours in his possession; they were therefore in use in 1590, and must have been lost at some period between 1590 and 1670.

Guercino painted in Bologna in 1618, in the Zampieri Palace in 1631, in the Ludovisi at Rome in 1621, (See Malv. vol. II. p. 363, 365, 368). Mr. Wilson observes, that the blues in his pictures, at these places, are put in in fresco, and are yet in fine harmony with the other tones. Is it not possible he may have used the Azzurri di Spagna?

If, then, this Azzurro di Spagna is so good a colour, it may be asked, why do not the Spanish writers mention it? Palomino, it is true, does not mention the colour, but he does mention a blue stone called "Ignoto" (unknown), which was sometimes used with other blues in fresco, and which is very likely to have been the pigment in question. To account for Palomino's being unacquainted with so valuable a pigment, a production of his native country, we must remember that the Spaniards received the art of fresco painting from the Italians, and adopted their method, and that Palomino died in 1726, fifty-six years at least after we have ascertained the pigment to have been lost. Pacheco's Treatise was published in 1641; he also does not mention the colour; it was therefore unknown or disused in his time in Spain and Rome, for he resided some time at Rome.

Borghini mentions (Riposo, p. 173, published 1585), that "Azzurro di Vena Naturale was useful in all three kinds of painting." Baldinucci observes of the same pigment, that "it was used in painting in *fresco,* in oil, and in distemper." These extracts prove that the pigment *had* been used in Italy in fresco painting, although it is not mentioned by many writers on this subject.

I have proved from Agricola that the mineral which the vulgar call "Azzurro" was produced in Spain in copper and silver mines, and I have shewn that the mineral could not be cobalt, because in its natural state that mineral is not blue. We know the pigment mentioned by Malvasia was not Ultramarine, because that substance is not found in Spain, and because he says the Azzurri di Spagna were lost, whereas Ultramarine was then in use in Italy. We can, therefore, form no other conclusion but that these pigments are native blue carbonates of copper, and of the same nature as Azzurro della Magna, Ceruleo, Mountain Blue, Ongaro, &c.

With regard to the use of Ultramarine in fresco, it appears that this was one of the expensive colours, which were always supplied by the owner of the picture. Pacheco says that in his time it was not used in Spain because it was so scarce and dear; but we find from Laguna's Commentary on Dioscorides (p. 538) that it had been used in Spain prior to 1570, and that its colour was thought so fine that it was used to paint the royal chapels. Palomino, however, gives another reason why it was not used in fresco, namely, "that the lime so acts upon it, that it fades, and after a short time the lights cannot be distinguished from the darks." He directs that for interiors, the Ultramarine is to be laid on in secco, with goat's milk. I have found repeated instances mentioned of the use of Ultramarine *in secco* on fresco paintings, but not one of its use in *buon*-fresco. Palomino mentions yet another pigment used *in secco* on walls, namely, Azul fino, or Azul de Santo Domingo, which appears to have been an artificial pigment made from copper, probably synonymous with the Azurri di Biadetti of Borghini, and the modern "cendres bleues." But it is unnecessary to describe artificial pigments in this place.

French Ultramarine has also been tried in fresco, but I understand from high authority is not approved. Indigo was used occasionally in fresco by Cennino and Palomino, the latter, however, observes, "this colour should never be laid on the lime itself, as it always perishes." Pozzo says, it could be used in fresco during the summer, but not in winter, because it is a bad drier.

To conclude, it is well ascertained that the brothers Campi of Cremona, Bernardino Gatti (Il Sogaro), and Guercino (I. Rep. pp. 27, 40) possessed a blue pigment, which has proved permanent in fresco painting. It appears also that a blue pigment was used in Italy which was lost sometime between 1590 and 1670, and that from the date of Guercino's paintings, it is very probable that he used it, that this pigment was called Azzurro de Vena Naturale, which there is strong reason for supposing to be native blue carbonate of copper.

With regard to this mineral itself it is a natural production said to consist of carbonate of copper, alumina, and lime,[a] and is, I believe, produced in sufficient quantities for use as a pigment in fresco.

[a] According to Pelletier it is composed of oxide of copper 50 parts, carbonic acid 30, oxygen 10, lime 7, water 3, = 100.

It would be desirable to ascertain, by analysis of the blue colours on pictures, what blue pigments have been used in fresco in Italy, in order to select for future use such as have been found durable, and to avoid such as have perished.

The method of preparing the carbonates of copper for use as pigments, is by the simple process mentioned by Cennino, (chap. 60), namely, grinding and washing it, in order to separate the small stones that are sometimes mixed with it.—See Massoul's Treatise on Painting and the Composition of Colours, p. 176. Marcucci Saggio Analitico, &c., p. 70.

GREEN COLOURS.

The employment of green colours in fresco is attended with less difficulty than the blue. This arises from several causes, not altogether depending on the pigment used. I allude in the first place to the mixture of blue pigments with yellow ochres, and to the tendency of blues to become green.

The green pigments used in fresco are *terra verde* (the nature of which is too well known to require any description) *Verde Montaña, Mountain Green, Lapis Armenus,* the *Chrysocolla* of the ancients, a native green pigment supposed to be a mixture of oxide of copper, or, as some say, carbonate of copper with alumina and lime. This mineral is of an emerald green or verdigris green colour, and sometimes a sky blue.—*See Phillips' Min. p.* 309, 313.—*Encyc. Brit. p.* 228, 289.—*G. Agricola de Metal. p.* 219, 221.

Andres de Laguna (Translation of Dioscorides, Salamanca, 1570), observes, the use of the mineral or native chrysocolla was very common centuries ago, for painting the apartments of the superb palaces of princes, on account of its beautiful green colour, which is so agreeable to the eyes. The greenest, and the pleasantest to the sight, is that which is found in the mines of copper.

Another species of copper ore, called *Earthy ferruginous green copper ore,* which is of a light olive green colour, seems to have been used in Spain under the name *Verdacho,* which Pacheco says agreed better with the lime than *Verde Montaña.*

A third species of copper ore, the *Malachite*, is also used in painting.—See Merimée, De la Peinture á l'huile p. 187. De Massoul sur l'art de la Peinture, p. 151, 152.

Verde Granillo is the best sort of Verde Montaña, it was brought from Venice to Spain in pastilles.—Italian writers call Verde Montaña, *Verdetto* and *Verde de Miniera.* This pigment must not however be confounded with the *verdete* of the Spaniards which is verdegris.

Palomino says that *Verde Montaña* should not be used alone on the lime, but that it should be mixed with terra verde, when its colour will be beautiful and durable.

Marcucci directs (p. 71), that the mineral should be ground and made up into small cones. This was the process adopted in Venice, where the pigment was called "Verde Granillo."

Pozzo includes a vegetable green pigment in the list of colours for painting in fresco. The adoption of this colour cannot be recommended.

Mr. Hart observes (II. Rep. p. 43), that the greens in certain frescoes are well preserved; in the Ducal Palace of Mantua, however, he says that they are almost entirely eaten up with nitre.

Now imitations of the native green and blue carbonates of copper have been in use from the earliest times as we learn from Pliny, also from Theophilus and other writers of the middle ages, as well as from G. Agricola and Matthioli, and the more recent Italian and Spanish authors. The use therefore of these pigments in fresco, would be sufficient to account for the appearance of nitre upon the green and blue parts of such paintings. We know from Malvasia's Felsina Pittrice that these native green pigments were lost in Italy previous to 1670.

Lomazzo observes (Trattato p. 194.) that Perino del Vaga invented a colour formed of Verdetto, and bianco secco, that is, lime-white in powder, which he (Lomazzo) remarks had a beautiful effect in fresco, and produced a colour almost resembling Giallorino. Of course, as Lomazzo spoke of a contemporary, he could give no opinion as to the durability of the pigment.

BLACK COLOURS.

Black colours are among those that have been found least durable in fresco.—See II. Rep. p. 42. All writers are unanimous in saying, that none but natural pigments should be used in fresco; therefore carbonaceous blacks, prepared from animal and vegetable substances, should be excluded from this kind of painting.

Native black colours are fortunately abundant. The *Terra Nera de Venezia,* of which Pozzo speaks, is said by Palomino to be a most beautiful colour in every respect. There is also *Terra Nera di Roma, Terra Nera di Piedemonte,* the mineral called *black chalk* (schiste à dessiner, ampelite graphique), which is met with in France, Spain, Italy, Iceland, Wales, Ireland, and the Hebrides, and which is used both in drawing and painting.

Nero di schiuma di ferro, mentioned by Borghini, is an artificial pigment, prepared by mixing the scales from red hot iron with terra verde, and then grinding the mixture to a very fine powder, (*Baldinucci, Voc. Dis. Borghini*). Neither this nor the next can be recommended.

Nero di Terra di Campane, mentioned by Armenino, is prepared from a sort of crust which forms on the moulds in which bells and cannons are cast. It was used in fresco painting, but Baldinucci says, that when exposed to the air, in a short time the colour flies, and spoils the picture.

These black earths are especially useful in making true greys; the extreme darks, every one knows, should be formed of browns, and not of blacks. It is well observed, by the author of an article in the Quarterly Review for December, 1844, entitled "Painting in the 14th Century," that "pure black should never be admitted on walls or canvass, for the simple reason that it hardly exists in any department of nature which can come within the sphere of imitation."

WHITE, YELLOW, AND BROWN COLOURS.

The only *white* pigment that it is necessary to mention here is Bianco Sangiovanni; the others are all fully described by the several authors whose works are translated, and form part of this treatise. Cennino Cennini has left the following directions for preparing Bianco Sangiovanni :—

"Take very white slaked lime; pulverise it, and put it into a little tub for the space of eight days, changing the water every day, and mixing the lime and water well together in order to extract from it all unctuous properties. Then make it into small cakes, put them upon the roof of the house in the sun, and the older these cakes are, the whiter they become. If you wish to hasten the process, and have the white very good, when the cakes are dry, grind them on your slab with water, and then make them again into cakes, and dry them as before. Do this twice, and you will see how perfectly white they will become. This white must be ground thoroughly with water. It is good for working in fresco, that is, on walls, without tempera; and without this colour you can do nothing,—I mean, you cannot paint flesh, or make tints of the other colours which are necessary in painting on walls, namely, in fresco; and it never requires any tempera."—*Cennino, p.* 31.

The *yellow* colours, consisting of ochres of various shades, require no particular notice. Giallorino (Naples yellow) is however sometimes admitted into fresco painting, but it should not be used where the paintings are much exposed to the air.

The *brown colours* are also too well known to need a separate notice. The artist will, of course, remember the tendency of umber to grow darker with time, and will avoid those pigments which contain vegetable matter.

CONCLUDING REMARKS.

Having thus inquired into the nature of the various colours used in fresco painting, I may be allowed to observe in conclusion that all writers are agreed in certain general principles, namely, that none but natural earthy colours can be used with safety and propriety in fresco painting, that these colours are not brilliant, but rather the contrary, and that they derive their beauty from the harmony of the arrangement, and the judicious opposition of the colours. Cennino and others praise certain colours which they say are equal to lake in fresco; they are right, because the colours to which they allude will appear like lake when skilfully contrasted with the other colours used in this kind of painting, but if compared with the colours we call lake and carmine, I have no doubt they would be found very dissimilar. The Amatito and burnt Roman vitriol will harmonize well with the ochres and other earths, but if lake were used, (supposing it could be used in fresco), it would, like the bright blue in the frescoes of Romanelli in the Louvre, and those of the Carracci, be out of harmony with the rest of the picture. If lakes and cobalt be used in fresco, it will be necessary to procure yellows of equal brilliancy, but I apprehend that pictures painted with such colours would lose in harmony what they gained in brilliancy; such colours are too glaring and intrusive for the decorations of buildings. To judge of their effect it is only necessary to compare the ceilings of the Louvre painted by the modern French school, which are as brilliant as the finest lakes, yellows, and blues can make them, with the quiet beauty and mellowness of the frescoes of Romanelli in the Salles des Antiques, (always, however, excepting the blue, which is too powerful for the other colours). It will be remembered that Titian and Raffaello used chiefly earths and common colours even in painting in oil, instead of the more expensive and brilliant colours. No one capable of forming an opinion can suppose they would have preferred the former to the latter, if they had not had the best and most convincing reasons for so doing. We are all too much inclined to seek the perfection of colouring in the pigments themselves instead of in the harmonious combination and opposition of the several colours, and to attribute to the vehicle and colours the effect which the skill of the artist alone can produce.

There is one point, however, on which particular care is required, namely, that the colours used should be the very best of the kind, the brightest, purest, and finest that can be obtained, and besides that, it is necessary, as Armenino observes, to be very clean and careful in using them in order to preserve them pure and distinct, because, by every slight mixture that falls into them, they become soiled and lose a great deal of their brightness.

In conclusion, I may observe that considerable difficulty and much labour has been added to this investigation, arising from the confusion in the names and technical terms, some authors using the names derived from the Greek, others from the Latin, others from the Arabic, and others the names derived from the colloquial language of commerce. In the same language, different terms are used, and different names given to the same substances; and not unfrequently, the same names are given to different substances. It will also be considered that the investigation has been pursued through various languages, written at periods distant from each other, and by authors, some with an extensive, others with a limited knowledge of the subject. These circumstances have added to the difficulties of this inquiry, and with the candid reader will form some excuse for any mistakes that may have occurred in this investigation.

THE ART

OF

FRESCO PAINTING.

PART I.

THE ART

OF

FRESCO PAINTING.

PART I.

CHAPTER I.

THE DIRECTIONS AND OBSERVATIONS OF VITRUVIUS WITH THE COMMENTARY OF GUEVARA.

OF GUEVARA.

THE very interesting work from which the following commentary on part of the seventh book of Vitruvius is translated, was written in Spanish, by Don Felipe de Guevara, who has incorporated in his work all that is material and practical in Vitruvius, on the subject of fresco painting. Guevara occupied the post of *Gentil-hombre de boca* (that is the prince's taster) to the Emperor Charles the Fifth.

The period of his birth is unknown; but he mentions, in the course of the work, that he fought in the celebrated victory at Tunis, and was in the island of Sicily in the year 1535. He travelled over Italy and Flanders, and appears to have been well versed in all that relates to the fine arts, which his situation in the court of Charles the Fifth and Philip the Second gave him ample opportunities of studying. Guevara appears to have been one of the greatest antiquaries of his time, and he possessed a valuable collection of medals and coins. He wrote a work, which has never been published, on the medals and coins of the different cities of Spain, which Ambrosio de Morales (who was personally acquainted with our author,) mentions in his

Spanish antiquities in terms of the highest praise. The manuscript of this work on coins, to which Guevara alludes in his commentaries, (p. 244) is lost.

The present work, which is entitled "Commentaries on Painting," must have been written *after* the year 1550, because the author mentions the work of Vasari which was published in that year, and *before* the commencement of the building of the Escurial, which was undertaken to commemorate the victory of St. Quintin in 1557. The work was dedicated to Philip the Second, but was never presented, nor was it ever published by the author, but was found in a bookseller's shop by Don Josef Alfonso de Roa, a person eminent for his literary attainments and love for the fine arts, by whom it was sent to Don Antonio Ponz, author of the Viage de España, and a friend of Mengs, who published it in 1788, and who wrote the notes appended to the following pages, to which his name is attached.

DIRECTIONS AND OBSERVATIONS FROM THE COMMENTARIES OF GUEVARA.

Of preparing walls and roofs.—It appears to me, (says Guevara,) that it will not be unseasonable, but on the contrary, necessary, since I have treated of the origin and beginning of painting in fresco,[a] to show on what kind of walls and roofs the ancients adopted this method of painting, and how they prepared these walls, as well as what whitewashings and preparations they employed in order to make this kind of painting firm, so that it may last long, be agreeable and durable. The method is that described by Vitruvius, Book vii. c. iii., but from the style in which it is written I suspect it has been noticed but by few: at least, we see the use of what the Italians now call *stucco*, much changed and corrupted. This I think must have occasioned new inventions for facilitating works of this description, that they might resemble those which were more ancient and perfect, although they were not equal to them in reality; and as there are perhaps but few who have a real knowledge of antiquities, these works are passed off for antiques, by persons of

[a] The following is the passage alluded to in the text; "Ludius invented and taught how to paint on uncovered places in maritime cities, with little expense, and in a most agreeable manner. This is the kind of painting which in Italy is termed *fresco*, and with which are painted what the Italians call façades, and we the exterior of houses; it is understood that, in the opinion of Pliny, Ludius was the inventor of this kind of painting at Rome." Page 49. It is unnecessary to observe, that the passage in Pliny is considered, by many writers, to refer to *distemper painting*, and not to *fresco*.—Ed.

indifferent reputation who authorize such practices. Vitruvius contrives the roof (of the apartment) that is to be covered with what is now called by the new term *stucco,* in the following manner: he says, that after having fixed the timbers of the room, they are to be morticed with cross pieces, made of timber which has the property of not warping, as that of box, oak, cypress, juniper, and the olive. The holm oak *(encida)* is to be avoided because it is apt to warp, and occasion cracks which injure the stucco. In our Spain the pine of Cuenca[a] and Balsain,[b] when old and dry is good, because this wood is solid and durable.

These cross pieces are to be nailed with strong nails, which will hold them firmly and prevent warping. But it must be observed, as we learn from Vitruvius, that these are not so durable and safe on flat roofs, as on those that are somewhat vaulted and curved, that in such walls this kind of work, which is called stucco, has great solidity; and if the vault or ceiling of the apartment be made of bricks or other similar materials, many inconveniences would be avoided, and many things would be unnecessary that wooden roofs require, without covering the roof immediately with the first coating of mortar, as is usual in walls of stones and bricks.

Vitruvius next directs, that in roofs constructed of timber, the cross-pieces being first fixed and firmly nailed, reeds are to be bruised and split, and fastened to the roof (as the curve requires) with rushes[c] or slips of Spanish broom tied firmly, as is now done when roofs are to be covered with gesso, and as was anciently the custom in Spain, and is still in Andalusia and the kingdom of Grenada, on account of the deficiency of wood in some places for this purpose.

The rushes or broom should be fastened to the reeds with great care and skill, for in this operation consists a great part of the perfection of the work, and they should be fastened with nails[d] between the rushes. This being done, Vitruvius says, "*trusilar* the roof." This word "*trusilar,*" which neither the Italian nor the Latin interpreters of

[a] A city of New Castile situated between the rivers Xucar and Huescar—Ed.

[b] A forest near the city of Segovia, where the Kings of Spain formerly diverted themselves with hunting.—Ed.

[c] In Italian, called *cannegreche* (large rushes), as contradistinguished from the smaller reeds found in marshes. They are also called *stuoje. See Italian translation of Vitruvius by B. Orsini, page* 69.—Ed.

[d] Vitruvius says, the nails should be of wood.—Ed.

Vitruvius have explained throws confusion on this part of the treatise.[a] It appears to me that *trusilar* has the same meaning as our Spanish term *xaharrar,* which is the first coat of mortar given to the walls in order to prepare them to receive the whiter coats *(blanqueada).*

But although the signification of the word "*trusilar*" may be what I have said, and which I dare affirm, there arises a new doubt as to the nature of the mixture with which the roof has to be plastered; for it appears clear from Vitruvius, that the word "*trusilar*" does not describe either of the three sand coats, or either of the three marble coats, but is a distinct and separate process. Filandro, the interpreter of Vitruvius, suspects that "*trusilar*" means a coat of gesso, and Budeo affirms that this is the true signification of the word "*trusilar.*"

My opinion is, that "*trusilar*" always signifies the first preparation which we call "*exaharrar,*" and that it consists sometimes of gesso, and sometimes of other materials, as this does of which Vitruvius now treats; for he expressly directs, that on no consideration should gesso be mixed with this coat of plaster which the moderns call stucco, and he condemns such a mixture as bad and injurious.[b] I think that this word *trusilar* or *xaharrar,* of which we are speaking, applies to a coat of lime, with which, instead of sand, pulverised bricks or tiles,[c] or other similar substances are mixed, for it is well known that such a mixture works better and sets more firmly than one of chalk and sand.

My opinion is confirmed by the authority of Vitruvius himself, who in Book v. chap. x. speaking of roofs of vaults, says, *inferior*

[a] The word used in the Italian translation of Baldassare Orsini, (1802) is *Rinzaffare,* the Florentine term for the first coat of mortar. L. B. Alberti likewise gives this name to the first coat of mortar.—Ed.

[b] It is said, it was this mixture of gesso with the ground of Giotto's pictures in the Campo Santo of Pisa, that caused their destruction. Vasari gives this reason for their perishing, but he does not allude to the work of Vitruvius. In the Art Union for March 1842, it is stated that Anthony Gegenbauer has painted at Rome some movable frescoes on canvass, upon a ground composed of *lime and gypsum.* It is much to be feared the advantage obtained in painting from damping the back of the canvass, (by which the artist was enabled to work for two or three days on the same picture) will be more than counterbalanced by the want of durability in the picture, occasioned by the incompatibility of the materials of the ground.—Ed.

[c] Vitruvius used this mixture of lime and pounded brick in places exposed to damp. Book vii. c. iii.—Ed.

autem pars, quæ ad pavimentum spectat, testa primum cum calce trussiletur, deinde opere tectorio sive albario poliatur. The meaning of these words is, that the front part of the roof that corresponds with the floor, should be first plastered with lime and the powder of baked pottery, such as bricks, tiles, &c., and afterwards the whitewash should be applied. This coat of lime and powdered brick having been applied, the roof should receive three other coats of lime and sand.[a] After having applied the first, time should be given for it to dry, then the second should be applied and suffered to dry, and then the third coat should be given, so that after the first coat of plaster there should be three coats of lime and sand. These having been applied and suffered to dry, three other coats of lime and marble dust should be given, the first thick, the second thinner, and the third thinner still.[b] After the application of these three coats, the wall should be smoothed or polished with pieces of smooth wood or other instrument used for burnishing, not liable to injure the surface. All these coats of plaster should be applied by rule and plummet, that no difficulties should afterwards arise when the wall has to be painted.

The plastering, says Vitruvius, which has been applied with care, will be firm and durable, and will never crack, because the burnishing will have given it great firmness and a polish of wonderful brilliancy, and the colours which are applied on it will be very bright and beautiful; for colours which are employed and used upon roofs and walls that are fresh and just finished will last for ever, and will not fade, because the moisture which was in the lime when it was burnt in the kiln, is dried up and consumed in such a manner that it remains porous, and ready to receive and absorb anything added to it; and thus mixed and united with substances possessing other properties, and the materials and principles of the one being united with those of the others, when dry, the whole solidifies and hardens in such a manner after the mixture, that the lime seems to have recovered its peculiar properties and pristine hardness.

For this reason walls that are well finished, neither become soiled by age, nor, if rubbed or cleaned, do the colours come off or fade,

[a] The sand coat, (for one only is applied,) is called in Italian, *Arricciato*, in Spanish, *Arenado*.—Ed.

[b] The *Intonaco*. One coat only is applied in modern fresco painting. Mr. Wilson (II. Rep. p. 38,) thinks that lime with marble dust does not make a good intonaco; and he cites the arabesques, painted by Giovanni da Udina in the upper Loggia of the Vatican, in support of his opinion.—Ed.

unless they have been applied carelessly or in *secco;* so that if the coats of plaster have been applied in the manner described, they will be firm and bright, and have the property of resisting the ravages of time, for when only one covering of lime and sand, and another of lime and marble dust is applied, this weak crust cracks and spoils easily, nor does it, from its want of solidity, preserve the polish given to it by friction.

The same thing happens to plastering that is deficient in thickness as to a mirror which is too thin, and which therefore reflects but weak and uncertain images: on the contrary, the wall that has received a thick coat of plaster takes a durable polish, and presents to the spectators distinct and bright images; consequently, thin coats of plaster, which cover the surface but imperfectly, are not only liable to crack, but soon decay, whereas those that are prepared solidly with sand coats and marble coats of good thickness and which are afterwards well polished and burnished, not only cause the colours to appear lively and brilliant, but they present true images to the spectators.

This is in part what Vitruvius has written concerning the plastering of walls; and from this author's description, we learn that the true stucco consists of a coat of lime and brick, the proportions of which should be two parts of lime and one of pounded brick, and of three coats of lime and sand; the first of which should consist of common and coarse sand, the second should be finer and should generally be sifted, but sometimes this is unnecessary. Upon these sand coats should be applied three other coats of marble and lime.

The marble is prepared in the following manner; after being ground it should be passed through sieves of three different sizes; that which passes through the coarsest sieve is to be used for the first coat of lime and marble dust, the second size for the second coat, and the finest for the third coat; and I must inform you that there are two kinds of marble; in some quarries are found lumps only of marble, and these will do for the stucco; the other is more perfect and in larger masses, the dust of which will answer the purpose.

It is proper to observe, that where marble cannot be obtained, the white pebbles found near the rivers in Spain, if burnt, ground, and sifted, as in the glass furnaces, are well adapted for this purpose; and even, if there should be sufficient marble, these white pebbles should be mixed with the stucco, in order to render the work more brilliant. Pliny praises the stucco, which consisted of three sand coats and two marble coats, and adds that Panæus the brother of Phidias, covered the walls of the temple of Minerva, in Elis, with lime and marble, mixed with milk and saffron.

Milk communicates great solidity and whiteness to the lime,[a] and this secret is known in some places, where it is worked up with the lime instead of water. Pliny says, that in his time these walls were rubbed with a moistened finger that merely smelled of saffron; whence we understand that the addition of the saffron was merely for the pleasant smell.

We should not omit to say, that the Greeks were accustomed to plaster the wall in the manner we have described,[b] and moreover, for the purpose of increasing their solidity, after having mixed the lime with the marble, they put it mixed into large mortars, and, by force of labour and blows, ground the mixture thoroughly, that the ingredients might incorporate into a tough and viscous substance, and afterwards, with the same industry and diligence, they plastered the wall. It is said also, treating of the good properties which the lime for this kind of plastering should possess, that there was an old law, forbidding the use of lime that was less than three years old in plastering buildings, and this, they say, was one of the reasons why it never cracked: at the present time, however, no

[a] As to mixing the lime with milk instead of water, it is certain that it gives more consistency to the lime and produces a more mellow white colour. The Spanish word, *encañar*, signifies to apply the whitewash with a brush, in the manner of the whitewashers by profession. In several provinces of Spain, particularly in Estremadura, Tierra de Campos, Valencia, &c., the female servants, and wives of the labourers, are accustomed to whitewash with rags put into a large reed, and this process is called "*enjalvegar*" (*enxalvegar*), whitewashing. It is usually done with white earth.—*Ponz*.

[b] To make the viscous mixture which results from the mixture of lime and pulverized marble or white pebbles with milk, the lime should be steeped some years in water, taking care to stir it every day. When there is occasion to use it, the necessary quantity is taken out with a piece of board with a handle, called in Spanish a *paleta*, and thrown into the mortar with the powder of marble or pebbles, and also the milk; the whole is to be beaten with the pestle until it is of the consistence of glue. A coat of the requisite thickness is then to be applied with the *paleta*, and afterwards it is washed with a wet cloth, and if it should crack it must be smoothed and polished with the same *paleta*, or with spatulas made on purpose.—*Ponz*. The *paleta* appears to be a float of wood.

attention is paid to this subject, to the great prejudice of the proprietors of the work.[a]

To proceed: the ancients, after plastering the roofs, ornamented them in various ways, making the roofs of winter rooms plain and smooth, that they might be easily cleaned from the smoke of fire and candles. In summer apartments they were accustomed to use ornaments in relievo, to which they gave the form of wreaths and compartments, in the same manner as the plaster mouldings now used in alcoves, cabinets, and oratories; and this composition may be moulded with the honey[b] of the plasterers; for Vitruvius says, that the roofs being finished, the cornices should be added, and these should be narrow and of light weight, because heavy cornices could not well be supported, and they would fall down from their own weight.[c]

For this reason, it is evident that the ancients composed first the cornices, compartments, wreaths of flowers, and similar works, and then fixed them up to the roof with glue[d] or with the same stucco, or any other thing that would hold them firmly, as is now done by our modellers in plaster. So that from my description may be understood what kind of stucco used by the ancients, and in our own times in many parts of Italy, is best adapted to secure durability.

Of the Colours.—Having now described the manner in which the ancients plastered their walls, and prepared them for painting, it seems proper also to describe the colours which are used in painting in fresco. Vitruvius mentions two kinds of colours, namely, natural and artificial or compound colours. Among the natural colours he reckons ochre, the *sil atticum*,[e] which some say should be of a purplish crimson colour, and *almagra*. He praises that of Sinope, of Egypt

[a] It cannot be denied that in order for the lime to acquire all the good qualities described, it should remain in water for two or three years; it will after this period be found excellent for the construction of brick vaults, purified, firm, and of the finest quality.—*Ponz.*

[b] The honey of the plasterers is apparently that soft mass of gesso which the plasterers and whitewashers use for the last coating on mouldings.—*Ponz.* This is probably the same as the *gesso da oro* of the Italians.—Ed.

[c] Vitruvius also cautions us against using gesso in these cornices, but desires us to use the same materials throughout, because, as the gesso sets sooner than the other mixture, the work would dry unevenly.—Ed.

[d] The word "*betun*" here used signifies any glutinous matter, and seems to be synonymous with the Italian word *mastrice.*—Ed.

[e] It appears quite clear that Vitruvius meant yellow ochre, which he called "light yellow earth."—Ed.

and of Spain, and that of the isles of Mallorca (Majorca)[a] and Lemnos. He also enumerates among the natural colours the Paretonium, thus called from the place whence it is brought. Pliny says, that Paretonium[b] is produced from the froth of the sea mixed with potter's clay, and that it had more body than any other kind of white. He also mentions Melinum, which is brought from the isle of Melos, which is of an agreeable colour like that of a quince.[c] He also names *creta verde,* which may readily be supposed to be the Verde Terra now in use; and Orpiment; and natural Sandarac which differs from the artificial, that is called by some persons burnt arsenic.[d] He mentions also Vermilion, which he admits, if used in places exposed to the sun, air, and moon, in a few days perishes and turns black.[e] He also names Chrysocola, (which some say is borax) which the same Vitruvius, Book VII. chap. XIV, gives us to understand is a natural green pigment procured from mines of gold and silver.[f] He also enumerates among the colours Indico (which the Venetians call Endigo) the colour of which is a dark blue inclining to black.

These are the natural colours which Vitruvius enumerates among those used in painting on walls. Among the artificial colours he includes *atramentum,*[g] which is a black colour composed of the smoke of pitch, and resin, and other ingredients; he also includes *sil,* lumps of which being made red hot and quenched in vinegar, become of a red colour.[h] The ancients also used white lead burnt, which we call

[a] From this it will be seen that the *Sinopia* of the ancients was identical with the *Almagra* of the Arabs and Spaniards, and also with *Majorica.*—Ed.

[b] Pliny, book XXXV. chap. 6. Probably the variety of carbonate of magnesia, called "Meerschaum," or Ecume de Mer.—See Phillip's Mineralogy, page 180. —Ed.

[c] Pliny says it was *white* in colour, and that it could not be used in fresco.—Ed.

[d] Native Red Orpiment. Baldassare Orsini, the Italian translator of Vitruvius, observes that all the natural colours mentioned by Vitruvius are not proper for painting in fresco, neither are the artificial, with the exception of cœruleo or smaltino and black.—Ed.

[e] Baldassare Orsini says, there is no doubt that native Cinnabar may be used in fresco, but the other kind cannot, unless it be prepared after the manner of Pozzo.—Ed.

[f] This must be Malachite or native carbonate of copper, page 94.—See Treatise on Colours, prefixed to this work.—It is necessary to remark that borax is colourless, and cannot therefore be used as a green pigment.—Ed.

[g] As this colour is to be used with glue, it must be used when painting in secco, and not in fresco: because in painting in fresco, the colours are tempered with pure water or lime water.—See Baldassare Orsini's notes to his translation of Vitruvius.—Ed.

[h] Burnt ochre.—Ed.

Azarcon.[a] He also names Æruca (Ærugo), which is called in our language *Verde Cardenillo.*[b]

He also mentions Ostrum,[c] which he says is the most excellent of all artificial colours; in our language it is called carmine or crimson; and finally, as he reckons purple among these colours, he observes, respecting its composition, that if chalk be mixed with the roots of the rubia[d] and *ysgino*, that the produce is a purple (or crimson) colour. He says that ysgino is the same as vaccinium or hyacinth, which is a kind of violet or purple gilliflower, and that if this vaccinium be mixed with milk, it produces a fine purple or crimson colour; and in default of attic ochre, if dried yellow violets be put into water and afterwards well boiled, strained through a cloth, and well squeezed between the hands into a mortar, a coloured liquor will flow, which, being afterwards mixed with *Terra Eretria* and well ground, imitates the colour of attic ochre.

Also, those persons who are prevented from purchasing natural Chrysocola on account of its dearness, take the yellow *herb* lutea,[e] which is of the same colour as the yolk of an egg and mix it with blue, and the two colours compose a bright green. Also, if Indico cannot be obtained, an imitation is made by mixing Terra Selemnusia, which is white, and glass,[f] and grinding them together. Pliny adds, that the dung of doves mixed with glass produces the same colour. With this colour, says Pliny, are painted the bodies of women.[g]

[a] Red lead.—Ed. [b] Verdigris.—Ed.

[c] The Tyrian purple, prepared from a fish found in the Mediterranean.—Ed.

[d] *Rubia tinctoria*, madder.—Ed.

[e] The Italian translators render the term *lutea* by *guado*, woad; but this plant yields a *blue* dye. It is probably the *Reseda luteola*, a native of Europe, which yields a very fine yellow dye.—The pigment, called *Dutch pink*, is made from this plant.—Ed.

[f] Vitruvius says, "with the glass which the Greeks call ὕαλον (hyalon,) or Vestorianum." Galliani and Orsini, the Italian translators say, "this glass is synonymous with what the Italians call 'smaltino,' which was and is used still in fresco painting in Italy."—Ed.

[g] The author has made a strange mistake. Pliny, book xxxv. chap. 6, in describing the colour called *Annularia*, says, it was used for painting the carnations in *pictures* of women, and is made of a white chalk or earth mixed with a common kind of glass, of which rings were made for the common people; whence its name.—Ed.

These are the colours,[a] according to Vitruvius, with which, in his time, perfect and agreeable pictures were painted on walls, and I have mentioned them, not because we are at the present time in want of colours, for these are well known to those who take an interest in antiquities, but because the colours which were anciently used upon those walls, may also be used at the present day. Finally, from this description, we learn how to prepare walls for painting on in a perfect and durable manner. We have proofs of the durability of this kind of painting, in the pictures which have been found in the ruins of Rome and other parts of Italy, and which, after having been exposed to the air, and afterwards covered with earth, are still bright, sound, and beautiful.[b]

We also learn the advantage of employing this stucco instead of gesso on the walls of houses, even where it is not intended to paint them, and of using relievos of stucco instead of those of gesso, and how easy it is to do so, since the mountains of Toledo furnish sufficient marble, and the rivers supply white pebbles in abundance, while the "honey" of the modellers[c] before mentioned, serves to fill the moulds for moulding friezes and cornices, and similar things in stucco, in the same manner as until the present time has been done with gesso.

Vitruvius appears to have omitted two things, which would have completed his description of the manner in which the ancients plastered the walls and painted on them. The first is, how they kept the wall damp, after having burnished it in order to paint on it, and how they finished the painting before the wall dried, for he says that the colours should be applied before the wall dried. The second question is, how they used the colours, and how they tempered the colours for painting on walls. Since, then, he does not tell us, what must have been notorious to every one, it appears to me that I am justified in conjecturing how they should be applied, if not in describing the process.

[a] Guevara has omitted to notice the blue pigment cœruleum, mentioned by Vitruvius. The description by Vitruvius of the composition of this colour is given in the Treatise on Colours, ante.

[b] The moderns have superseded the tedious and careful preparations of the ancients with regard to their fresco paintings, with much saving of time, by employing only one sand coat or application of lime and sand. The process has been well explained by Don Ant. Palomino in the second vol. of the *Museo Pictorico*, page 98 and following pages. *Ponz.*

[c] "Gesso da Oro."—Ed.

For this purpose, it is necessary to suppose that the present method is incorrect and badly conducted, because the artists of these times plaster a portion of the wall, (assuming that the plaster that is used is recent) and then paint it: they then add another portion of plastering and paint it in the same manner. In fact, this plastering is done piece-meal and not in a whole or a mass, which is attended with great inconvenience; for plastering, executed in this manner, can neither be perfect nor durable, and will have cracks and other defects; for it is evident the portion of plaster which is added to the first piece which is quite dry, cannot unite or incorporate with it as firmly as it would have done if the plastering had all been completed at once.[a] Whence it appears that this manner of plastering has imperfections which time will shew us every day. Besides this, the wall that has been plastered by portions, will not allow of the polishing mentioned by Vitruvius, as an essential requisite for perfecting the work, and for ensuring the durability and beauty of the walls; for if we wish to work quickly on those walls plastered in portions, we can neither do it well nor even moderately well, because the painting in fresco is injured in the parts where it joins the new plastering. Moreover, such walls cannot be constructed properly, by rule and plummet, but must of necessity be full of hard lumps and hollows on account of the joinings of the different masses, at the time of uniting the fresh plastering with that which is dry.[b]

[a] The durability of the fresco paintings of the moderns, since the time Guevara wrote his work, is proved by their having lasted some centuries. Those by Luca Cambiaso, in the roof of the choir of the Escurial, and in the Presbytery, and those of Peregrino Tibaldi in that of the Library, and in the walls of the choir of the Royal Monastery, which are all in perfect preservation, have lasted more than two centuries. This durability, I have said, may be continued some centuries, provided, that the roofs and walls of these edifices can be preserved from the penetration of rain, and other inclemencies of the weather, which destroy them in the same manner as conflagrations, earthquakes and similar things. —*Ponz.*

[b] The works of Giordano in the Escurial in Madrid, and in Toledo, do not exhibit these defects, and the junctions of the *tareas* (day's work) are scarcely visible, neither are there prominences nor hollows. These pictures will doubtless last like those by Palomino in Valencia, Granada, el Paular, &c., as fresh as we now see them and equal to those above-mentioned, and also to those of the ancients, if the same precautions be observed, provided the buildings in which they are contained be preserved. Mengs, who was a great investigator of the arts of the ancients, painted his works in fresco, according to the modern practice,

Having mentioned the inconveniences, let us now speak of the remedy. For this purpose we must suppose that the ancient painters were very diligent and prudent; I therefore consider it certain that they did not plaster the wall in portions, but that, whether it was large or small, they finished plastering the whole at one time, and then painted it with such expedition and diligence, that the painting and the wall dried together;[a] not taking into consideration that they knew how to keep the wall damp for some days.

in the royal palace and other places. Perhaps if these pictures were buried and then exposed to the sun, air, and water, they might not last so long as those of the ancients referred to by Don Felipe de Guevara, and it is certain that the preservation of the paintings found in the sepulchres, and those covered with the burning lavas of Vesuvius in the excavations of Caserta and of Herculaneum, is really wonderful. *Ponz.*

[a] Sig. Requeno (Saggio sul Ristabilimento, &c.) is of opinion that the ancients did not really paint in *buon-fresco* as the Italians do, but that they coloured the walls in fresco, with a single colour, and then painted the figures on them in secco.—In the note to vol. 1, page 190, he says, "In the work of Vitruvius there is no mention made of painting, as is generally believed, but only of the preparation of the *intonaco* for painting, in Chap. 3, '*De tectoriis operibus.*' The preparation of the *intonaco* was formerly made, as Vitruvius says, firstly—with six coats of *intonaco*; secondly—staining the intonaco, while still wet, with one colour, sometimes red, sometimes black, sometimes blue, &c. It was not every colour that was used on this occasion, on the wet lime and marble dust. Pliny expressly tells us, '*udo illini recusant purpurinum, indacum,*' *&c.* (Purpurinum, indigo, &c. cannot be used in fresco;) and of another colour he tells us, that it is '*calcis impatiens,*' (that it cannot bear lime). The words of Vitruvius, '*colores udo tectorio cum diligenter sunt inducti, &c.*' (when the colours are carefully laid on the wet plaster,) must undoubtedly be understood of the various colours with which the *intonachi*, while still wet, were stained. Then that the preparation of the *intonaco* for painting on, of which alone Vitruvius speaks in this chapter, formerly included the operation of colouring the intonaco, before it was dry, with red or yellow, or with some other colour, which, besides what Vitruvius tells us in this third chapter of his '*De tectoriis operibus,*' is proved by the ancient pictures of Herculaneum. When, by any accident, the colours of these scale off, the uniform colour of the ground beneath the elegant figures with which they are painted is seen. As authorities, I cite Winckelmann, and the academicians of Herculaneum, who, observing that when some of the pictures were cleaned with water, all the colours of the figures washed off, and there remained a ground, uniform in colour, smooth, fair, and polished, upon the ancient walls, concluded that the pictures of Herculaneum were painted by the Romans, in *secco*, upon an *intonaco*, stained in fresco. The authority of Vitruvius, chapter III., must therefore be understood of the preparation of the coloured *intonachi*, intended to be painted with figures, landscapes, or ornaments; and the text, '*Colores udo*

I have, however, thought of two plans, by which a fresh plastered wall may be kept moist, so that it may be finished with all the expedition which Vitruvius directs. One is, that the plastering being finished, the whole of it (except such parts as the artist is painting)

tectorio cum diligenter sunt inducti, ideo non remittunt, sed sunt perpetuo permanentes,'—(When the colours are carefully laid on the wet plaster, they do not on that account fade, but are eternally permanent,)—and the other text, '*Itaque tectoria, quæ recte sunt facta, neque vetustatibus fiunt horrida, neque cum extergentur remittunt colores, nisi si parum diligenter et in arido fuerint inducti,*' —(Therefore the plasterings which are properly done, neither become rough with age, nor, when washed, do their colours fade, unless laid on with little care, and when the plaster was dry,)—must be understood of the colours, sometimes yellow, sometimes black, sometimes blue, with which the wet *intonachi* were anciently covered. Moreover, Vitruvius, as we have already mentioned, orders the glue to be mixed with the colours for painting on the above mentioned *intonachi;* he also directs white lead, made from lead and vinegar, to be used; all which things are incompatible with true fresco painting.

" Hence it follows, that the Marchese Berardo Galliani was mistaken in his interpretation of this third chapter of Vitruvius, when he wrote (note IV.) 'The ancients had two methods of painting on walls: one in fresco, *udo tectorio;* the other in *secco* in *arido.*' Vitruvius nowhere speaks of *painting, udo tectorio,* but of *colouring, udo tectorio.* The plasterers sometimes colour with white, sometimes with red, *inducunt colores tectoriis*; but they do not paint.

" Hence it follows, that the person who continued the '*Memorie per le belle arti,*' printed at Rome, in July, 1785, had no cause for his astonishment at my denial that the ancients possessed our method of fresco painting, properly so called. 'The denial,' says he, 'that the ancients painted in fresco, seems to us rather extraordinary, and not agreeable to what Vitruvius says about painting *udo tectorio;* and moreover that this painting is seized by the mortar, and is not destroyed by washing.' This modest and genteel Sig. Diarista will not find the words *pictura* or *pingere* in the passage of Vitruvius, for Vitruvius never speaks of painting *udo tectorio;* '*Colores,*' says Vitruvius, '*udo tectorio cum diligenter sunt inducti,*'—(when the colours are carefully laid on the wet plaster;) an expression which indicates only the practice of staining the wet intonaco, sometimes with red, and sometimes with some other colour. So also, Vitruvius never says that this *painting* is seized by the lime; but that the colours with which the wet intonaco was stained, became incorporated with the intonaco, the plaster seizing and retaining them, so that when washed with water, they do not separate from the wall, which is exemplified in the walls of Herculaneum, on which the red or yellow colour of the intonaco is not affected by the water with which they are rubbed, but the painting does not stand; on the contrary, it yields to the water and washes off.* The paintings at the

* The Arabesques by Giovanni da Udina, in the upper Loggia of the Vatican, were painted in the manner here described.—See II. Report, page 38.

should be covered with linen soaked in very pure water;[a] for this linen cloth, besides preserving the moisture of the plastering, will moreover prevent the air from drying it; and as to the parts on which the artist is painting, he should proceed as follows. Clean sponges should be steeped in very pure water, and partially squeezed, and then applied to the parts of the plastering most necessary to be kept moist, and this process being repeated frequently and with proper care, the wall may be kept moist a sufficient time, and thus we shall attain the end desired; namely, to have old walls painted with great firmness and in the most perfect manner.

It remains to be noticed, that Vitruvius has not informed us with what the colours employed on such walls were tempered. The moderns have remedied this by using lime-water; and as this has been found successful in painting, we believe that the ancients used the same, and if they did not, that this is sufficient, even if the ancients did not use it. However, I must remark, that the moderns

Thermæ, and at the sepulchres of the ancient Romans, must also be considered as painted in *secco;* so that the theory of the chemist, (which may be seen in the '*Effemeridi Letterarie di Roma*,') a theory consisting in applying phlogiston, and by that means restoring to their former splendour the colouring of the ancient pictures, is liable to some exceptions. This theory supposes, firstly, that the pictures on intonaco, found in the excavations at Rome, were painted in true fresco; secondly, that the colors were all mineral colours. I consider, that according to the authority of Vitruvius, both these propositions are equally false. I grant that the colours on the ancient intonachi may be revived by phlogiston; but I deny the truth of the arguments which induced them to try this.

"The reason, however, why the ancients did not paint in fresco, when they well knew that the plaster of the *intonaco* seized the colours, and that the colours so applied, resisted the inclemency of the weather, is a very different question from the first. Whether the ancient Romans did or did not employ our method of fresco painting, is a question of fact; and from facts we know that the ancient Romans did not paint in true fresco. The above mentioned question is a speculation.

"Pictures in true fresco require lime, instead of white lead, to mix with the colours; and colours mixed with lime produce a very different effect when dry, to what they do while wet. Painting in true fresco requires such quickness and readiness in the application of the colours, that at present, there are but very few painters in Italy, who both sketch and finish their figures in true fresco."—Ed.

[a] The artists of Munich have a contrivance for arresting the drying of the work, which is somewhat similar to that described by Guevara. See I. Rep. page 18."—Ed.

deceive themselves in thinking that the ancients did not use artificial colours on walls, but natural pigments only, and those chiefly of earths. Of this mistake Vitruvius is sufficient evidence, since he not only gives us an account of the artificial colours they used, but also describes the composition of some of them.[a]

Those persons, then, who profess the art should experiment with the artificial colours, if they would employ them with the same success as the ancients, it being understood that, at the present time, colours of this description are not used in the same manner as they were by the ancients; they should study the subject and seek a remedy for it; for it is not just that noblemen who love such works, and who cause them to be executed, should be deprived of that brilliancy which artificial pigments (of which there are so many) give to the picture by the negligence and insufficiency of the artist; and especially they should work with great care, because the colours of those earthy pigments that they use are extremely harsh and crude, and bring with them an inexpressible feeling of melancholy.[b]

[a] The error appears to be on the part of Guevara. Requeno has proved satisfactorily that the ancients did not use artificial colours on damp walls. See the note, pages 13 and 14, ante.—Ed.

[b] I have spoken of the paintings in fresco of Cincinato and Cambiaso in the Escurial as familiar examples. If we seek for examples at a distance from home, I do not know whether Raffaello da Urbino, Michael Angelo, and other artists of that period in Italy, prepared their walls and roofs in the manner now practised, and as Palomino describes, or whether they observed any other method more consonant with the doctrine of Vitruvius; as some persons think. It is certain that the "Last Judgment" above the altar in the Sistine Chapel in the Vatican, and the roof of that building, have been well preserved for about 300 years; and the same would have happened with the paintings of Raffaello, if it had not been for the continual copying, (tracing,) and handling of them since they were painted, by which they have suffered, and suffer still in some parts: *these* injuries should be carefully repaired. The pictures of these artists are as highly finished as is necessary for the distance at which they are to be viewed.—*Ponz.*

CHAPTER II.

THE DIRECTIONS OF THE MONK THEOPHILUS.

THE earliest writer after Pliny and Vitruvius who mentions painting on walls (for the appellation of fresco was not then applied to it), is Theophilus, the monk, the author of a treatise entitled, "Diversarum Artium Schedula," supposed to have been written in the beginning of the thirteenth century. Very little is known of the author; it however appears from his work, that he was extremely well versed in those branches of the arts of which he treats. The few directions he has left on this subject are merely as to the painting on walls and ceilings; he does not allude to the preparation of the wall, further than to direct that it should be made quite wet before the painting is begun.

He distinguishes between such colours as were proper to be used on walls, and such as were unfit for this purpose. In chapter XIV, he observes, "neither orpiment nor any colour with which it is mixed can be used on walls;" in another place, he says, "Let two lines be made of equal breadth, one of burnt ochre mixed with lime *(calce)*, under vermilion on a wall; but, on a ceiling, use vermilion itself mixed with chalk *(creta)*."

The following are his directions for painting on a wall. He says, "You should fill in the drapery with ochre, mixed with lime, to give it brilliancy, and make the shades in it either with pure burnt ochre, or with *prasinus*,[a] or with *posch*,[b] which must be made of the ochre itself mixed with green. The flesh colour [c] for walls must be made of ochre, and vermilion, and lime; and the *posch*, and *rosa*,[d] and *lumina*,[e] must be made as before. When figures,

[a] This prasinus is a certain preparation having the appearance of green and black. It is prepared by being dissolved in water and strained through a cloth. It is considered useful as a green colour upon a fresh wall.—Theophilus, c. 2.

[b] Posch is the colour for the shades, made by adding prasinus and burnt ochre *(rubrum)* to the flesh colour.

[c] Membrana. [d] Rose colour for lips and cheeks.

[e] Lumina—flesh colour with white.

or birds, or representations of other objects, are drawn on a dry wall, the wall must be immediately sprinkled with water until it is quite wet. And all the colours which are to be put on, must be mixed with lime, and laid on at one wetting, in order that they may dry along with the wall, and may adhere to it. Under ultramarine and green the colour called *veneda,* which is composed of black mixed with lime, must be put as a ground; and upon this colour, when it is dry, must be laid, in the proper place, a thin coat of ultramarine, tempered with the yolk of an egg mixed with plenty of water: and after this a thicker coat must be laid, to make it look well. Green also must be mixed with *succus* [a] and black."—Chap. xv.

From these distinctions it is evident that ceilings were painted in secco, and that paintings on walls were begun in fresco, and finished in distemper or secco.

Theophilus concludes the sixteenth chapter in the following manner:—

"All colours which are placed under others on a wall must be mixed with lime, to give them more firmness; under ultramarine and *menesch* [b] and green, *veneda* must be laid; under vermilion, burnt ochre; under ochre and *folium,*[c] the same colours mixed with lime."

The following summary of these instructions of Theophilus for painting on walls may not be uninteresting to the reader. It is copied from a MS. in the Bibliothèque Royal, at Paris, written by Jehan le Begue, "licentiatum in legibus, Anno Domini, MCCCCXXXI."

"Pour peindre murs, mettez un po de chaux avec ocre pour avoir plus grant clarte, ou vous la mettez avec rouge simple, ou avec prasin, ou avec une couleur qui est nommée posce, qui est faite de ocre vert et de membrayne, ou vous pouvez prandre dune couleur qui soit faite de synople et docre, et de chaux, et de posce, &c.; et doivent estre murs paint plus moiste que autre chose, pour ceque les couleurs se tiennent mieulx ensembles, et soient plus fermes. Et doivent toutes couleurs pour murs estre melles avecques chaux vive."

[a] A green colour prepared from vegetables.

[b] Menesch—The nature of this colour is not known.

[c] A vegetable pigment from which three different colours were prepared.

CHAPTER III.

LEON BATISTA ALBERTI.

Leon Batista Alberti appears, as Mr. Eastlake observes in the First Report, the connecting link between ancient and revived art; and D'Agincourt does not hesitate to attribute the *Renaissance* of architecture, in a great measure, to his exertions, and those of his countryman and contemporary Brunelleschi, the constructor of the Duomo of Florence. He was eminent in all the arts, but attached himself principally to architecture, and applied himself with much assiduity to the study and explanation of the work of Vitruvius, the only one of the ancients whose express treatise on this subject has reached us. His principal work, *De Re Ædificatoria*, from which the following pages are extracted, was completed, and a manuscript copy presented to Pope Nicholas V. in 1452; and was printed at Florence, at the early period of 1485. It contains, observes D'Agincourt, all that could be known, at that time, relative to the art; and, if we confess the truth, almost all that has since been written in the best works on the same subject.

DIRECTIONS AND OBSERVATIONS.

Alberti treats concerning the coats of plaster which should be laid on walls, of the various kinds of *intonachi*, and how the mortar with which they are made is to be prepared, of statues in *basso-rilievo*, and of the pictures with which the walls are adorned.

He observes (Lib. vi. ch. 9.), " that in all plasterings three kinds, at least, of *intonachi* are required. The first is called *rinzaffato*, and its use is to adhere very closely to the wall, and to hold firmly the other two *intonachi* which are laid upon it. The use of the last *intonaco* is to receive the polish, and the colors, and lineaments, which make the work pleasing. The use of the middle *intonaco*, which is now called *arricciato*, is to obviate any defects both in the first and in the last *intonaco*. The defects are as follows:—if the two last coats, namely, the *arricciato* and the *intonaco*, are caustic, and, so to speak, astringent, as the *rinzaffato* ought to be, they will, on account of their crudity, show many cracks as they dry. And if the *rinzaffato* is mild, as the *intonaco* should be, it will not adhere sufficiently to the wall, but will fall off in pieces. The more coats of it are given, the better will the surface receive the polish, and be enabled to withstand the effects of the weather. I have seen some of the more ancient specimens which had nine coats, one upon the other. It is necessary for the first of these to be rough, containing pit sand and pounded brick, the pieces of which should not be too small, but as big as acorns, or in pieces the size of the finger, and sometimes the size of a palm. For the *arricciato*, river sand is best, being less liable to crack; this *arricciato* should also be rough, because the coats which are to be laid on afterwards will not adhere to smooth surfaces. The last coat must be very white, like marble; in fact, very white pounded stone should be used instead of sand, and it will be sufficient for this coat to be half a finger's breadth in thickness; because, if it is made too thick, it dries with difficulty. I have seen some persons, who, in order to save expense, do not make this coat thicker than the sole of a shoe. The *arricciato* must be mixed according as it is nearer to the first, or to the second coat. In the masses of stone, in stone-quarries, there are found certain veins, very much resembling transparent alabaster, which are neither marble nor *gesso;* but of a certain middle nature, between the one and the other, and which are very apt to crumble. When these are pounded, and used instead of sand, they sparkle like shining marble. In many places are seen sharp points projecting from the wall, in order to hold the *intonachi;* and time has shewn us that these are better made of bronze than of iron. I approve very much of those who, instead of nails, insert between the stones certain pieces of stone, or flints, so as to project; but, for this purpose, a wooden mallet must be used, and the fresher and rougher the wall is, the better it will hold the *rinzaffato*, the *arricciato*, and the *intonaco*; therefore, if, while building, and while the work is being done, you apply the *rinzaffato*, although thinly, you will cause the *arricciato* and the *intonaco* to adhere to it very strongly,—so as never to separate. You may carry on any of these processes during the prevalence of the south wind; but if you apply the *intonaco* while the north wind blows, or during severe cold, or great heat, the *intonaco* will immediately become rough or uneven.

"Finally,—the last coats are of two sorts; they are either plastered and spread upon the wall; or they are composed of materials joined and fitted on to it. *Gesso* and lime are spread upon it; but *gesso* is not good, except in very dry places; for the damp which passes down old walls, is very injurious to every kind of coating. The coatings which are joined on to the walls, are stones, glasses, and such things. The coatings which are spread upon walls, are these:—pure white, with figures of stucco, or paintings; but those which are joined on, are wainscoatings, panellings, and inlaid works. We shall now speak of the first sort, for which the mortar must be prepared as follows:—

"Slake the lime with clear water in a covered trough, and with so much water that there may be a great excess above the lime; then stir it well with the spade, kneading and working it thoroughly; and let it be thoroughly slaked and kneaded, which may be known by the spade not meeting with any lumps or clods.[a] The lime is not considered to be mature in less than three months. That which is good, must be very soft and viscid; because, if the trowel put into it comes out dry, it proves that it has not had enough water to slake it completely. When you mix it with the sand, or with any powdered materials, work it again and again with great labor; and continue to work it until it almost froths. The ancients were accustomed to pound in a mortar the materials they required for the *intonachi*; and they tempered the mixture so that it might not adhere to the trowel when they were laying it on the wall. Upon the coat which has just been put on, and while it is still wet and soft, another coat must be laid, and care must be taken that all these coatings may dry together, and at the same instant. They

[a] To this we must add, that much water must not be added to the lime at once when slaking it; but it must be quenched a little at a time, pouring water on it at intervals, until it is completely saturated; then put it in a place rather damp than otherwise, and in the shade, without mixing anything with it; for it should be preserved pure,—covering it only with a little sand, until, by length of time, it is become more liquid. And it has been found that, by this long maceration, the lime has acquired great virtue. I have actually seen some very ancient, and in considerable quantity, which had been abandoned,—as we have good reason to suppose,—for more than 500 years; and, then being discovered, it was found to be moist and liquid, and, as it were, so ripe, that in its consistence, it far surpassed honey and marrow. And there certainly is nothing that can be found more convenient for any purpose whatever than this. If you use it thus, it requires double the quantity of sand. *L. B. Alberti*, Lib. II. c. xi.

must be smoothed and made even with smoothing boards, floats, and other similar things while they are yet soft. If the last coat of pure white be well rubbed, it will shine like a looking glass; and if, when the same is nearly dry, you anoint it with wax and mastic, liquified with a very little oil, and then heat the wall, so anointed, with a chafing dish of lighted charcoal, or with an iron, so that it may soak up the ointment, it will surpass marble in whiteness. I have found by experience that such *intonachi* never cracked, if, in making them, the moment the little cracks begin to appear, they are rubbed down with bundles of twigs of the wild mallow, or of wild broom. But if, on any occasion, you have to apply an *intonaco* in the dog days, or in very hot places, pound and cut up, very finely, some old rope, and mix it with the *intonaco*. Besides this, it will be very delicately polished if you throw on it a little white soap, dissolved in tepid water. If it is too greasy, it will become pale.

"Small figures of stucco may be executed very expeditiously by casting from hollow moulds; and the hollow moulds may be obtained from *rilievos*, by pouring liquid gesso over them. When they are dry, if they are anointed with the composition which I have mentioned, they will have a surface like marble. These figurines are of two sorts, some in entire relief, and some in bas-relief: those in high relief do very well on a flat wall; but, on a vaulted roof, bas-reliefs are better, because those which are in high relief, on account of their weight, being fixed obliquely, easily separate and fall down, and are likely to fall on the heads of those that are beneath. Care must be taken not to put hollow ornaments, or ornaments in high relief, where there is much dust; but let them be flat and in low relief, in order to clean them easily. The painted *intonachi* are sometimes executed in fresco, and sometimes in *secco*. For those which are done in fresco, all natural colours, which are obtained from the earth, or from mines, or from similar places, are proper; but artificial colours, and particularly those which change when exposed to the fire, require very dry things, and dislike lime, moonshine, and the south wind. It has been recently discovered that all colours can be mixed with linseed oil, and will last for ever, provided that the wall, upon which they are put, be very dry and completely free from damp; although I find that the ancient painters were accustomed, in painting the sterns of their ships, to use liquid wax instead of glue. And, if I remember right, I have seen in the works of the ancients, that factitious gems,[a] fastened to the wall, with wax, or perhaps with white stucco, become so hard, in course of time, that they separated neither with fire nor water. You would say that it was burnt glass; and I have seen some who, with the white flower of lime, have fastened colours, particularly vitrified colours, to the walls while still fresh."

[a] The words in the Italian translation of Cosimo Bartoli, which I have used, are, "colore di gemme," by which I think he means the coloured pastes, of which artificial gems are made, like those described by Cennino (translation), p. 74, and by Cicognara. See note to Cennino, p. 149.

CHAPTER IV.

DIRECTIONS OF CENNINO CENNINI.

The work of Cennino Cennini having been so recently published,[a] it is considered necessary only to refer to the leading practical points detailed in it.

Cennino professes to teach the art of fresco painting, as it was practised by Giotto, and by Taddeo Gaddi, his godson and favorite pupil, and by Agnolo, the son of Taddeo, and master of Cennini. He commences by directing the preparation of the mortar, which is to consist of two parts of sand, and one of lime, if the lime be rich and fresh; the lime and sand are to be thoroughly mixed with water, until the lime is quite slaked, for if any heat be left in the lime, it will cause the plaster to crack.

The wall on which the painting is to be executed, is to be first swept, then made very wet, after which the mortar is to be spread over it, and the surface made quite level, although rough. This coat of mortar is generally called the *arricciato;* Cennino applies the term *intonaco,* both to this sand coat and the fine coat of lime on which the painting is executed.

When the surface of the wall is dry, the design is to be drawn upon it with charcoal. It does not appear that the artists of this period used cartoons, but we collect from the text of Cennino, and from certain expressions of Vasari, in the life of Simone Memmi, that they made small drawings, which they copied on an enlarged scale, on the walls, by means of proportional squares, technically called *rete* and *graticola.* The outlines are then to be fixed by marking them over with a pencil, dipped in ochre. The most singular part of the process is, that the whole wall, including the drawing, was then to be covered over with a thin *intonaco.* The

[a] A Treatise on Painting, by Cennino Cennini, translated by Mrs. Merrifield. —Lumley, 56, Chancery Lane, London, 1844.

descriptions by Morrona, of the ancient frescoes in the Campo Santo, at Pisa, noticed hereafter, as well as the remarks of Vasari and Lanzi, leave no room to doubt that the outline was actually covered with the *intonaco*. Such a portion of the picture as the painter considered he could paint in one day, (which Cennino gives us to understand, was *a head only*,) was then to be covered with the *intonaco*, the wall having been previously wetted, and the surface smoothed with a slip of wood. A colour called Verdaccio, was next to be made of ochre, white, and cinabrese (sinopia and white), with which the outlines of the features were to be drawn; necessary corrections might then be made, by washing out any part of the drawing, with a large brush, dipped in water. The shades of the face were next to be put in with verde terra. Cennino then describes the manner in which contemporary artists painted flesh, after which he details the method practised by Giotto. The difference between these different methods, consisted in the use of many tints of flesh colour, (of which every shade was at once laid in its place), by the school of Giotto, while other artists applied a wash of flesh colour over the face, either before or after the shades were laid in. Cennino is very particular as to this point; he says, "If you would have your work appear very brilliant, be careful to keep each tint of flesh colour in its place, and do not mix one with the other." He afterwards makes the same observations with regard to the shades in draperies.

In painting draperies he used four shades of colour, each of which contained white. He then heightened the lights with pure white, and finished the darkest shades with the pure colour, without white. When the figures were finished, they were to be left for the lime and colours to dry thoroughly; and if any drapery remained to be done, it might be finished, when dry, in secco.

Cennino then gives directions for painting on walls, in secco, and begins by naming those colours which cannot be used in fresco: these are orpiment, cinabro, azzurro della magna, minio (red lead), biacca (white lead), verderame (verdigris), and lake. Those which may be used in fresco, are giallorino (Naples yellow), bianco sangiovanni, black, ochre, cinabrese, sinopia, verde terra, and amatito; these are to be made lighter by the addition of the white, (bianco sangiovanni). He then describes two kinds of temperas or vehicles, with which the colours for finishing the draperies are mixed: the first consists of the white and yolk of an egg, into which are put some cuttings from the tender branches of a fig tree, to which a moderate quantity of water is added, and the whole is well beaten together; Cennino adds, "if too much of the tempera is put to the colours, they will crack." The second tempera consists of the yolk of the egg only; "this tempera," he says, "is of universal application, and you cannot use too much of it." Directions for painting various coloured draperies in fresco and secco, then follow; and he concludes by teaching how to colour mountains, trees, plants, and buildings. We must not omit to mention a remark of Cennino's, which conveys much information relative to the practice of painting on walls at that period: "Remember, that everything you paint in fresco, must be finished and re-touched in secco, with tempera."

Another point, worthy the attention of the novice in fresco painting, is, that after having dipped the brush in the liquid colours, it should be squeezed between the thumb and finger of the left hand, before beginning to paint.—See pages 42 and 43.

It seems that in painting blue draperies, it was the practice of the school of Giotto, as well as in that of Sienna, to mark out the large folds with a needle or bodkin of iron, (Cenn. LXXXIII. p. 52,) and to make the light on the knees and other parts, by scratching off the colour with the handle of the brush. The darkest parts were shaded with lake and black, and finished with the iron point.

CHAPTER V.

OF VASARI.

Giorgio Vasari, of Arezzo, was descended from a family friendly to the arts; he was the grand nephew of Lazzaro, and nephew of another Giorgio Vasari, who was skilful in making *terra cotta* vases, after the manner of the ancients. Michael Angelo, Andrea del Sarto, and others, instructed him in design, and Il Rosso taught him painting. But his principal school was Rome, where he accompanied the Cardinal Ippolito de Medici, by whose family he was loaded with riches and honors. After having studied the works of Michael Angelo and Raffaello, he formed a style of his own, in which, however, his partiality for the former was perceptible. Having become a skilful painter of figures, he studied architecture, and became one of the most distinguished architects of his time. He was capable of directing alone the architectural works of a large building, and also of disposing properly the decorative parts, such as figures, ornaments in relief, grotesques, landscapes, gildings, &c. He thus attained reputation in Italy, and was employed to paint in various places in Rome itself, and afterwards in Naples, Ravenna, Perugia, Venice, Pisa, Florence, &c. He was afterwards invited by Cosmo I. to his court, where, among the great works that he conducted, must be mentioned the Uffizi, and the paintings by Vasari and his pupils, in the apartments of the Palazzo Vecchio. He died in 1574.

The following directions and observations of Vasari are taken from his "Introduction to the Three Arts of Design," prefixed to his great work, "The Lives of the Painters."

DIRECTIONS AND OBSERVATIONS OF VASARI.

Of the use of sketches, designs, cartoons, and perspective drawings.—We give the name of *sketches*, (he observes), to those first rough drawings, which we make in order to decide on proper attitudes, and to form the composition of the picture. These are executed in a very slight manner, and only just marked here and there to give us an idea of the whole picture, and are called sketches; because, owing to the haste of the artist to embody his thoughts, they are drawn very quickly with the pen, with charcoal, or any other drawing material, merely to express the ideas of the painter.

From these are afterwards formed *drawings,* which must be done with great neatness of form, and with as much care as possible; and the various parts must be drawn from nature, unless the artist is conscious that he is sufficiently skilful to complete the drawing without a model. Afterwards, by measuring them with the compasses, or with the eye, the lines of the small drawings must be enlarged, according to the intended size. Drawings are executed in various ways, that is, either with *lapis rosso,* which is a stone that comes from the mountains of Germany, and which, being soft, can easily be sawn and reduced into fine points for marking paper, just as you like; or with the (*pietra nera*) black stone, which comes from the mountains of France, which is like the red. Others are made in Chiaro-scuro on tinted paper, which paper serves for the middle tints, and the pen marks the lines, that is, the outline or profile; and, afterwards, the ink, with a little water, makes a soft tint, which glazes and shades it. The lights are then put on the drawing with a fine pencil dipped in white lead tempered with gum. And this method has an excellent effect, and shews better the arrangement of the colouring. Many persons draw with the pen alone, leaving the paper for the lights, which is difficult, but very masterly. There are many other methods of drawing, which it is not necessary for us to mention; because they all represent one and the same thing, namely, the design.

The designs being thus made, whoever wishes to paint in fresco, that is, on a wall, must first make the *cartoons,* and it is customary with some persons, to make cartoons even for painting pictures. The cartoons are thus made. Square sheets of paper are pasted together, with paste, made by boiling flour and water over the fire, and are fastened to the wall by pasting the edges of them for about two fingers in breadth on the side next the wall, with the same paste. They are then wetted by sprinkling fresh water all over them, and then are stretched, while soft, in order that, in drying, the wrinkles may be pulled out. Afterwards, when they are dry, a long cane [a] is taken with a piece of charcoal fixed at the end of it, and with this, everything that is drawn in the small design is reproduced on the cartoon, in the same proportion, in order to judge of the effect at a distance; and so by degrees, first one figure is finished and then another. Here the painter employs all his skill in the art, in drawing naked figures from the life, and draperies from nature, and the perspective is drawn by all those rules, which have been observed in drawing the design on a small scale, observing to enlarge them in proportion to the size of the cartoon. And if there are perspective representations or buildings in the drawing, they are enlarged by means of the *rete*, which is a grating of small squares, enlarged upon the cartoon, by which everything may be copied exactly. Because, the artist having drawn the perspective as ascertained by the plan, elevation, and section, and made the lines diminish towards and vanish in a point, in the small design, must repeat them, in proper proportion, on the cartoon. As for the manner of drawing the perspective, which is tedious and difficult to explain, I will not say anything more about it. It is sufficient to observe, that the perspective is beautiful in proportion as it appears true, and vanishes from the eye in the distance, and when it is composed of a varied and beautiful arrangement of buildings. It is also necessary for the painter to be careful to diminish the force of the colours proportionably to the increase of distance, and this depends on the discretion and good judgment of the artist. The reason for this is the difficulty caused by the confusion of lines obtained from the plan, elevation, and section, and which, by colouring them, is rendered very easy, and the due observance of this art (aerial perspective), causes the artist to be considered as learned and skilful in his profession. Many masters also are accustomed, before they draw the picture on the cartoon, to make a clay model on a flat surface, making all the figures round, in order to see the play of the light, that is to say, the shadows which a light produces

[a] The use of brushes with long handles has the sanction of many of the best masters. Velasquez was accustomed to use brushes, four or five feet long, and he placed his canvass nearly the same distance from him as the person whose likeness he was painting. Gainsborough also adopted the same plan, and it is quite apparent, no practice can be better adapted than this for giving freedom of hand, and avoiding the extreme minuteness of detail, observable in the works of the early painters, who worked with short handles to their brushes, and finished their large pictures with hatchings like a miniature.

on the pictures. The sunshine is generally used for producing these shadows, as it marks the shadow of the figure on the ground with harder outlines than an artificial light would produce, and drawing the whole of their picture from this, they make the shadows which one figure throws upon another, and so the cartoons and the picture, owing to the trouble which is taken in order to give greater perfection and force, are better finished, and have such relief as to appear as if starting from the picture; and this causes the work to appear finer, and more highly finished. When these cartoons are used for painting in fresco or upon walls, a piece must be cut off every day at the joining, and traced upon the wall, which should be plastered over with lime, and made very smooth. This piece of the cartoon is put in the place where the figure is to be painted, and is countersigned in order that, the next day, when another piece is to be joined on to it, its place may be known exactly, and no error may arise. The outlines of this piece are then traced with an iron stile on to the *intonaco* of lime, which, being wet, yields to the paper and thus receives the marks. After this, the cartoon is taken off, and the colours are laid on according to those lines which are traced upon the wall, and the painting in fresco or on walls is executed. For paintings on canvass the same sort of tracing is used, except, that the cartoon is all in one piece, and that it is necessary to cover over the back of the cartoon with charcoal or black powder, in order that afterwards, when it is marked over with the iron stile, it may be drawn or traced on the canvass or panel. And the reason of dividing the cartoons into compartments is, that the work may be true and in the proper proportion. There are many painters who do not use cartoons for oil pictures, but when painting in fresco they cannot be dispensed with.

The author of this invention had certainly a very happy idea, considering that, in the cartoons, we can see the effect of the whole painting, and that they may be corrected and drawn upon until they are approved of, which cannot be done afterwards to the picture itself.

Of painting on walls, and why it is called fresco-painting.—Of every kind of painting practised by artists, painting on walls is the finest and most masterly, because it consists in doing in one day only, that which in other methods can only be accomplished in many. Fresco painting was much in use among the ancients, and the older modern painters have also continued to employ it. The picture must be painted on the lime while it is wet, and the work must not be left until all that is intended to be done that day is finished. Because if the painting be long in hand, a certain thin crust forms on the lime as well from the heat as from the cold, the wind and the frost, which tarnishes and spots all the picture. And therefore the wall which is painted on must be continually wetted; and the colours employed upon it must be all earths, and not minerals, and the white must be calcined Travertine. This kind of painting also requires a firm and quick hand, but above all a good and sound judgment; because, while the wall is soft, the colours appear quite different from what they do when the wall is dry. It is therefore necessary for the artist, while painting in fresco, to use his judgment more than his skill, and to be guided by experience, it being very difficult to paint in fresco well. Many of our artists are very expert in other branches of the art, namely, in oil and distemper painting, but do not succeed in this, because it is indeed the most manly, the most certain, and the most durable of all methods, and by age it continually acquires beauty and harmony in an infinitely greater degree than any of the others. This kind of painting cleans itself in the air, is proof against water, and always resists any blow. But it is necessary to take care not to retouch the painting with parchment glue, yolk of egg, gum, or gum tragacanth, as many painters do; because, while the painting fails to acquire its usual brightness, the colours become tarnished by this, and, in a short space of time, turn black. And therefore let all those who wish to paint upon walls, paint in fresco, like men, without retouching in *secco;* which, besides being a most vile practice, shortens the duration of the pictures, as has been already observed elsewhere.

Of painting on walls in Chiaro-scuro with various kinds of clay; and how bronze is imitated; and of pictures in clay or in earth (Terretta).—Painters call Chiaro-scuro a kind of painting which depends more on design than on colouring, because it had its origin in the imitation of statues of marble, and of figures of bronze and various other stones. This is usually employed in painting historical pictures on the fronts of palaces or houses, so as to imitate and appear like marble or stone, sculptured into these shapes, or really imitating some sorts and kinds of marble an porphyry, and of green stone, and of red and grey granite, or o bronze or other stones, as they think proper; they divide the front of the house into many compartments, in this style of decoration, which is very much in use for painting the fronts of houses and palaces, as well in Rome as throughout all Italy. These pictures are painted in two manners, either in fresco, which is the real method, or on canvass, for the triumphal arches which are made for the entry of princes into cities, and in triumphs, or in the decorations for *fêtes* and comedies, because they produce a beautiful effect. We will first treat of the different kinds and methods of painting them in fresco. For painting with this Terretta, the grounds are made of potter's clay; the darker shades are made by mixing the clay with pounded charcoal, or any other black, and with calcined Travertine for the light tints. The lights must be laid on with pure white, and the extreme shades must be finished with pure black. Pictures of this kind should be executed with design, force, vivacity and skill, and should be expressed with boldness, which shews art and freedom of hand, because they must be seen and looked at from a distance. Bronze figures are also imitated in this way; they are sketched on a ground of yellow ochre and red, the shades are made of black, red, and yellow; the half tints are made with pure yellow, and the lights of yellow and white. Artists also paint house fronts and pictures in this way, with certain statues interspersed between them, which have a very graceful effect.

CHAPTER VI.

DIRECTIONS AND OBSERVATIONS OF RAFFAELLO BORGHINI.

OF BORGHINI.

Although the work of Borghini, entitled "Il Riposo," published for the first time in 1584, has gone through three editions, little is known respecting the history of his life, except that his mother, as he himself mentions in the Riposo, page 399, was the daughter of Ridolfo Ghirlandaio, after whom he was also called Ridolfo. In the preface to the second edition, it is stated, that he understood thoroughly, not only the principles of the arts of painting and sculpture, but also all the arts connected with them. He was personally acquainted with the eminent painters and sculptors of his time, and his work contains many of their *vivâ voce* precepts. Borghini has borrowed many of the recipes contained in the second book of the Riposo from Cennino's treatise, without, however, acknowledging the obligation. Bossi, in his work on the *Cenacolo* of Leonardo da Vinci, says, the Riposo of Borghini is more valuable for the style than the precepts.

DIRECTIONS AND OBSERVATIONS.

Whoever wishes to paint in fresco, must first lay an *intonaco* over so much of the wall as is sufficient for one day's work; because if the colours are not laid upon the lime, while it is fresh, it makes a kind of crust, owing to the heat, or the cold, and the wind, which dulls and spots all the work. It is therefore useful to wet the wall very frequently. Having put on the *intonaco*, which should have its whiteness lowered by means of sand, and a little black, so that it may appear of a neutral tint, the cartoon, or a piece of the cartoon, must then be applied to it. The piece of the cartoon must be marked in order to know which piece comes next to it; then, with a stile of iron, or ivory, or of any hard wood, trace upon it the marks and outlines of the cartoon, and the lime, being damp, will yield to the tracing, and receive all the marks. Then, taking away the cartoon, we must paint upon these with *earthy*, but not *mineral* colours, mixed with clear water; and the white should be calcined Travertine. This kind of painting requires great judgment; because, while the wall is wet, the colours produce a different effect from what they do when it is dry. We must, above all things, abstain from retouching any thing with colours containing parchment-glue, yolk of egg, gum, or gum Tragacanth (*Dragante*), because, then the painting loses its brightness, and the colours become tarnished, and, in a very short space of time, turn black. Therefore, whoever paints in fresco, should, each day, completely finish his day's work, without having to retouch it in *secco;* because thus his pictures will be of longer duration, and he will be considered a better master. Painting in *tempera* can be done upon a dry wall, upon panel, and upon canvass. To paint upon a dry wall, the wall must be rasped, and two coats of hot glue laid over it; afterwards the *tempera* must be made in this manner:—The yolk of an egg is taken and beaten up well, and a tender fig branch is ground up in it, and with this material, colours of all kinds are tempered, because all are good for this kind of painting, except the white made from lime, which is too caustic *(forte)*; and the blues, which would turn green with the above mentioned *tempera* on account of the yolk of the egg. They must therefore be mixed with a vehicle of gum or of size from parchment clippings; this kind of size may also be used for all the colours, as it is now the custom to do in Flanders, whence we receive so many beautiful pictures of landscapes, painted with this vehicle.

CHAPTER VII.

DIRECTIONS AND OBSERVATIONS OF GIOVANNI BATISTA ARMENINO.

OF ARMENINO.

GIOVANNI Batista Armenino was born in Faenza, about 1530. He was destined for the medical profession. He was sent to a public school, where he was taught Latin and Greek. While pursuing his studies, Figurino da Faenza (who had been assisting Giulio Romano at Mantua), returned to his native country, and the young Armenino, captivated by seeing him work, and hearing his encomiums on the art, was immediately siezed with the wish to study painting. It is not known whether he received lessons from Figurino, but when he went to Rome, in 1550, he already drew well and rapidly. At Rome he studied the works of Polidoro da Caravaggio, and the antique, and being seen by two French students of sculpture, copying a frieze of Polidoro's, they took him into their house, in order to make drawings for them. He studied and copied the Last Judgment, of Michael Angelo, in company with Michael Angelo da Norcia and Bartolommeo di Arezzo,[a] with the latter of whom he studied anatomy. He remained in Rome seven years, continually copying the antique and the best pictures. After leaving Rome he went to Milan, where he assisted Bernardino Campi, with whom he remained some months. He afterwards visited Mantua, Parma, Piacenza, Florence, Genoa, Venice, Ferrara, Ravenna, Pesaro, &c. After travelling over Italy, for nine years, and examining all the best works of art, he changed his profession and his dress, and became a friar and a priest. Although he abandoned the practice of the art, he was still useful to those who exercised it, by collecting, in a single volume, all the most important precepts of the art, which he had observed in his travels, or which had been communicated to him by skilful masters. From the period of his becoming a priest, nothing more is known of him, except that it is supposed he was living in 1587, when his "Golden

[a] Probably Bartolommeo Torre, who fell a victim to a contagious disease, caught in the pursuit of his anatomical studies at the age of 25. *Ticozzi.*

Treatise," (as Sig. Ticozzi styles it), "*De Veri Precetti della Pittura,*" was published.—*Abridged from Ticozzi's Introduction to the "Veri Precetti.*"

DIRECTIONS AND OBSERVATIONS.

Of the great importance of making the Cartoons properly.—Of the use and effects of the Cartoons.—In what manner and with what material they are made.—Which are the most expeditious and easy ways of making them.—How they are traced and pounced on to the work without being damaged; and how they are imitated in the picture.—From Book II. Chap. VI. of the "Veri Precetti della Pittura."

Of the use and effect of cartoons.—We have now to treat of cartoons, which among us are considered as the most perfect mode in which, by our skill in design, we are able to express the whole force of the art, and which, to those who set about them in a proper manner, and with diligence, and who are careful and industrious in finishing them, are so useful for the works which they have to execute, that what afterwards remains to be done, appears to give but little trouble. For the sketches, designs, natural models, and in short, all the other labours which the artist had previously undergone, were for the sole use and purpose of uniting them properly together on the surface of the cartoon; and to speak the truth, in order to reprove those who care little to do this, or who, if they do set about it, do it carelessly; for in a well-finished cartoon, it will be observed, that even the most difficult part of every object is pourtrayed, so that by following the outlines, we work without any chance of error, by means of a perfect example and model of all that we intend to do; in fact we may call it the work itself, except for the tints; and hence we see that Michael Angelo, Leonardo da Vinci, Raffaello, Perino,[a] Daniello,[b] and other excellent

[a] Perino del Vaga, (Pièrino Buonacorsi), was considered by Vasari the first of the Florentine School, after Michael Angelo, in design, and the best of those who assisted Raffaello. He died in 1547. *Lanzi.* Vol 1. p. 142. Vol. II. p. 76, 87, 257. Vol. V. p. 243. *Vasari.*—Ed.

[b] Daniele di Volterra (Ricciarelli) imitated Michael Angelo, by whom it is said he was sometimes assisted in his designs. See *Lanzi.* Vol. I. p. 124, 286. Vol. II. p. 88. He died in 1566.—Ed.

painters, always prepared the cartoon with the greatest care and industry.

Of making cartoons, and the materials used.—The usual manner of making cartoons is, first, to measure the height and breadth of the place where the work is to be made, and then to take paper of the same size, which is made by pasting sheets together with flour paste, until the cartoon is of the same size as the before mentioned place; when it is dry, paste should be spread all round it to the breadth of about an inch: it must next be fastened to the smooth wall, and then sprinkling water over it, and pulling and stretching it all round, care must be taken that, as it dries, it may remain smooth and well stretched. It must then be measured out, and divided by faint lines, into the same number of squares, as the small design which is to be imitated; and then, all that is contained in the first design must be copied with great care and skill, until every thing is drawn in its proper place.[a]

Of dividing the cartoon by squares.—There are certain persons who say, that it is a bad plan to use these squares,[b] and allege frivolous reasons in support of their assertion; for example, that a great deal of the first design is lost, which it is impossible to enlarge properly otherwise than by the eye. Now the eye seems to me to have but little to do with it, for, be a man ever so much accustomed to drawing on a large scale, he cannot deny, that when a design is intended to be copied from a piece of paper, which is generally made about the size of the hand, or a little larger, on to a picture of the size of ten or twenty feet, that it is much easier to do it with the squares than without them; besides which, there is the ground plan, the perspective, and the buildings, which in the small design are drawn by measure, and require merely to be copied off and enlarged in the same proportion, almost without trouble. What is the use, therefore, of making any difficulty about this, when, by doing it, we have all the outlines determined? And I say this, not only with regard to the things I have already mentioned, but also relative to the position of the most minute details, being certain at the same

[a] For the modern method of making the cartoon, see I. Rep. p. 22, 25.—Ed.

[b] The technical word for the process of enlarging by squares is *graticolare*. See Pozzo's Treatise.—Ed.

time of not falling into any very great mistake, nor even into a confusion of lines. So that it is quite clear, that by this means, we avoid making a great number of lines, *which are frequently drawn by way of trial,* before we make the right one; and however expert a person may be in design, he cannot help committing such errors, for it is impossible to do otherwise.

But it is necessary, at the same time, to caution persons not to trust too much to these first lines, nor, while placing them on the cartoons, by means of these squares, to throw aside their judgment, which enables them to correct many of these lines in the small design, and copy them afresh in their proper places, or wherever they may seem needful. This is rendered evident by the fact, that great errors may be concealed in small drawings, while in those on a large scale, every slight error is detected; so that a thorough examination is necessary, to change false outlines and to make good ones, without having any regard to the limits given by the squares. And these are the methods which I have frequently observed and considered, in the designs and cartoons of Raffaello, of Perino, of Giulio,[a] of Daniele, and of Taddeo Zuccaro,[b] and of other good painters who are still living, and who all affirm the truth of what I have said.

Of the different modes of preparation.—But to return to the cartoons. These are made in various manners and with various materials, as I have already shewn with regard to the small designs, and although there are but few in water colours, there are some very highly finished in other modes. Those who prepare them upon white paper, after having made the outlines in the above mentioned manner, in order to shorten the trouble of shading, should rub lightly on the parts to be shaded with a rag full either of pounded charcoal or *black lead*[c] in powder, and the darker shades should be pounced

[a] Giulio Romano, the greatest of all the pupils of Raffaello, whose heir he was, conjointly with Gio. Francesco Penni: Giulio's principal works are in fresco. He painted the palace at Mantua and the Palazzo del Tè. Lanzi says, that the beautiful paintings of the story of Psyche, have been painted over by a modern hand. He died in 1546. *Vasari and Lanzi,* Vol. II. p. 74, 75, 87. Vol. IV. p. 12.—Ed.

[b] Taddeo Zuccaro, was of the Roman school, and an imitator of Raffaello. He was born in 1529, and died in 1566. See *Lanzi,* Vol. II. p. 87, 89, 92. *Vasari.*—Ed.

[c] Lapis nero.—Ed.

and beaten again over the first, and this should be continued until more than half appears shaded. The shades should then be lightly hatched, either with charcoal, or a black lead crayon cut to a point, and these hatchings should be continued as far as the extreme edges, and this part of the drawing should be executed with that dexterity and care, which is always practised by clever and skilful artists, so that, by the cartoons, their expertness in drawing will be proved. But besides the sketch, which during this time has been held in the hand as a model, further study is required before it is finished, for all this process must be recommenced from the beginning, in order to obtain greater correctness, by copying from the life and from models, with the assistance of mechanical skill in drawing, as has been before stated; and, when finished, these drawings appear so forcible, and, with such relief, that they seem ready to start from the paper, which proves that these last means are well adapted to give such perfection in drawing, as every person, according to his industry and knowledge, desires to attain.

We should proceed in the same manner with cartoons which are made upon *tinted paper*, which, with less trouble, are much better than making many hatchings, and rubbing them with the fingers or with pieces of wool or tow, as many persons are accustomed to do before finishing them. The cartoon must now be finished by laying on the lights, which we must set about with great judgment and caution, in order that the highest lights may be placed so as best to imitate the object. There are some who, for the lights, take fine fresh gesso,[a] with an equal quantity of Biacca,[b] and mix them together, and make crayons of them; and, with this material, the lights are very bright. Others again use only tailor's *gesso*,[c] and others again mix Biacca also with this in the higher lights; and in these ways all great designs are finished.

Now, to preserve the cartoons uninjured, as the outlines must next be traced from these on to the works which are in hand, the best way is to prick them with a needle, putting another paper under them which is pricked as well as the upper one. This last paper

[a] *Gesso*—gypsum, plaster of Paris.—Ed.

[b] *Biacca*—White lead.—Ed.

[c] *Gesso da Sarti.*—A fine sort of gesso in lumps (query white chalk), so called because it is used by tailors for drawing or marking out their patterns on the cloth. See *Bald. Voc. Dis.*—Ed.

serves for pouncing the outlines on what is to be the ground of the picture, and particularly upon lime, although many persons, caring little about the preservation of their cartoon, trace directly from it; but the first cartoon should always be kept as a model, while painting the coloured picture. The first method is more convenient.

I think I have now treated at sufficient length, and with great clearness and brevity, of all those modes of drawing, of which I had promised to speak, as being the most necessary and easy, for the assistance of those who wish to attain excellence quickly, having told them every convenient remedy for those things which are either uncertain or difficult. We have now, therefore, to take the same course in treating of colours, which is indeed a very laborious and difficult part, and the most necessary part of the work; but I hope in a similar manner to make it clearly and easily understood. We will treat first of the composition of the colours, then of the manner of using, mixing, and uniting them together, so that they may remain bright and clear; the whole being the result of practice and experience, which we have both seen, and been taught by the best and most skilful artists who have preceded us.

Of the different kinds and sorts of colours, and of their particular natures; how they are prepared in different ways to produce a better effect in the work; with what and how many liquids they are used; how the colours are made to obtain any tint that may be wished, and especially flesh colours, with their various tints according to the complexions of the persons, and how they ought to appear when finished. —From Book II. Chap. VII. of Armenino.

Of the colours proper to be used.—I believe it is known, even to the most indifferent painters, that all the colours which are used in painting, must be of two sorts, namely, natural, which are also called mineral, and artificial. These are commonly mixed for working with three liquids, which are water, glue and oil: the first is called painting in fresco, the second painting in distemper (or secco), and the third painting in oil. But it is well known, that artificial colours never do well in fresco, nor can any art make them last long without changing, and particularly in the open air; and this because they require a very dry situation, and a very dry ground for the picture; but we shall treat of the qualities of each more clearly in their proper places. Now, be it known, that all colours, unless flat tints of them are to be laid, are mixed in various modes, because some of them are made light and some dark, so that from one single colour are made different colours of the same kind, according as white or black is mixed with them all. But as this depends entirely upon the skill of the artist; so the errors arising from it, are caused either by the colours being badly mixed and badly united, or by the hand of the artist not being firm or practised in managing and harmonizing them, so that they may remain pure, clean, and properly united together: for which reasons I shall always exhort young men, to practise these things continually, in order to gain experience, and know their effects, that they may afterwards carry them out in practice with confidence. For as one of the principal intentions of the poet, is to give delight by continually diversifying his poem with various episodes, so in painting, the same variety should be sought by different and gay colours. Although the subject and the composition may be pleasing in themselves, yet, if the colouring, which is the manner of explaining them, is not agreeable to the eyes of the spectators, it will be impossible to produce a good effect; because, by colours well united and harmonized, is produced that beauty, which catches the eyes of the ignorant, and enters imperceptibly into the minds of the wise. It will be seen, that true resemblance arises from the proper use of the colours, which, the more lively they are, the more they strike and please persons, and particularly the nobility, the greater number of whom use them for embellishing their houses. This shews that they are more affected by the pleasure which they receive from the variety and gayness of the colours, than by their admiration for the design of the picture; thus pursuing rather the gratification of the eye, than the improvement of the mind, because a beautiful and harmonious variety of colour, produces the same effect on the eyes as is produced on the ears by harmonious music, when the bass notes correspond to the high notes, and the middle notes also sound in concord; so that from this variety is made a sonorous and almost wonderful union of measures, which fills the mind with admiration.

But the whole science of colouring may be reduced to this, that, when a picture is composed with regularity, of various sorts of colours, both mixed and pure, there will arise a well devised and harmonious composition, no part of which, however insignificant it may be, will be discordant from the rest; and therefore the composition will not then be glaring and disagreeable, and appear like coloured tapestry, nor yet so much sobered down and shaded that the flesh is scarcely distinguishable from the other objects near it. The best plan will be to observe a medium between the glaring and the dull; and to let the colours and mixtures be neither too bright nor too languid, but pure and clean, softly and delicately united with each other, so as to produce a pure and exquisite beauty. We shall not stop to consider the nature of the colours one by one, nor give an account of the different sorts and qualities of them, because these are supposed to be known to every one, but we shall speak of some of their particular properties, and give other cautions concerning their effects, on account of some contrarieties among them which are not to be despised.

Of the purity of colours and mode of preparation.—All the colours therefore, should, as much as possible, be used bright, pure, and fine; and besides this, it is necessary to be very clean and careful about them, in order to preserve them pure and distinct, because, by every slight mixture that falls into them, and which generally consists of the dust of other colours, they become soiled, and lose a great part of their purity and brightness. There is also much practice and diligence required in applying them properly, but in using colours in fresco, we must remember that, as has been before remarked, the wall will not take any other than the natural colours which are found in the ground, and which consist of earths of several colours, which, I think, must be well known, since they are common enough in all parts of Italy; these are, for the most part, ground with pure water, excepting smalt and other similar blues. For the white which is used in fresco, they take, as is well known, the powder of very white lime, such as that of Genoa, Milan, and Ravenna, which, before it is used, must be well purified, and this purification is performed in different ways by different painters; there are some who make it first boil well on the fire, keeping it clear from scum, which is done to get rid of the saline parts, and which prevents its settling and drying too fast when applied to the wall; they then let it cool in the open air, and pouring off the water from it, they put it in the sun on baked bricks and suffer it to dry upon them. The lighter it is, the better it is purified. There are some persons who bury it when they have thus purified it, and so keep it many years before they use it; and others do the same in the open air upon the roof. There are also some persons who add half the quantity of marble dust, which they first pound very fine. It has also been observed, that if the white pigment be put in the open air, in a large vase, and boiled water be thrown into it, at the same time mixing it with a stick, the next day putting it in the sun, it will be sufficiently purified, and may be used the following day for mixtures with other colours, but not for colouring naked bodies.

Of preserving the colours.—Having now prepared and arranged the colours in the manner above-mentioned, and put them in their vases, in order to preserve them uninjured, we must next take shells or small vases, and begin to mix the tints. First put some white into three or four of these shells, and then put some black in just the same number of others, but not in such great quantity; then take the vase of pure colour, either yellow, red, blue, green, or whatever other colour is wanted, pouring it in, and mixing it with this white, which has been put into these shells or vases, so as to make at least three tints, one lighter than the other, by putting less of the pure colour into some than into others. The same colour must also be poured in a similar manner into the shells where the black, or any other dark colour is placed, observing the above directions as to making them one darker than another; so that, by these means, from each pure colour, may be obtained four or six shades, and as many tints as may be wished, and these must correspond with the colours in the design or well finished cartoon. But with regard to the minute differences of the colours which nature presents to us, we shall not enter into any farther description of them, as their number is infinite, which is rendered evident at once by considering the continual variation of colour in fruits and flowers; and if we would imitate these colours, we must make a tint resembling the colour of each.

Of the mixture and application of colours.—But of all the usual mixtures for flesh, the lighter ones are always made of red earth *(Terra Rossa)* and white, and that they are made more or less dark in the same manner as other tints; but these are not always the same, because, as regard must be had to the variation of the tints, which always change according to the various sexes, ages, and temperaments of the persons, when you wish to make them match the complexion, it is, generally speaking, necessary to add to the colour sometimes green, and sometimes yellow, and sometimes both together. The complexion of old men is generally different, so that instead of Terra Rossa they generally require burnt yellow earth *(Terra Gialla Abbrucciata)*, and it is better that you should burn it until you see it become of an uniform dark colour, before you take it off the coals, because it changes to a bright mulberry colour, and thus produces the same effect in fresco as the fine lakes do in oil and distemper painting; and, therefore, when we compose the dark colour for the shades in the flesh, we use this earth, which must be mixed with umber, so that the mixture of these two generally serves for all the shades. We then put a little of this into some clean shells, and make two other lighter shades, by pouring into them some of those light flesh coloured mixtures which were before directed to be made; and one is made darker than the other, that we may harmonize them together, by softening them into the lighter one. Black also is frequently added to the above-mentioned shade colour, composed of the two earths; and this is used when it is wished to give greater relief to the figure, or naked body, and to the extremities.

There are some persons, who mix with these shade colours, pure *Terra Verde*, and others burn this colour in the same manner as the yellow earth. There are others who mix with it *Terra di Campane*, and particularly when they wish to imitate the delicate shadows in young women, because in this manner they appear to agree very well together. But as there are some persons, who, in laying on the lights upon the more prominent parts of the flesh, foolishly use pure white in too great abundance, I would advise you to take the lightest flesh tint, and then mix white with it, and lay on the lights in but few places, and with judgment. There are moreover other reddish and bluish tints besides those in the face, which are easily obtained by mixing red or green with the lighter flesh tints; other similar colours are made with the dark flesh tints. Having thus finished mixing the tints in a proper manner, and having arranged them in order upon a smooth board or plank, we must then take the brushes, which must be well made. Old brushes are better than new, and you must have one brush for each colour.

Of preparing the walls.—When these things are all finished, and the colours are all prepared, in the way I have mentioned, and every thing else done that may be necessary, we come to the fine *intonaco,* which, when it is put on the wall, serves as a ground to the colours, and generally causes the picture to produce a different effect from what the artist who painted it expected; this is on account of the difference occasioned by the drying of the colours, which is sometimes so great as to deceive even the most expert artists owing to their not being well acquainted with the changes the materials undergo. It will therefore be proper to speak a little about it, and to give some general advice upon the subject, because very important works, in which an artist runs the risk of losing a great deal of his reputation and credit, if he unfortunately does not succeed, are generally painted in this manner. You must know, therefore, that all kinds of lime which are laid upon walls for painting on, have the property, if well wetted, of receiving all colours well during the whole of one day; and the lime remains for some hours very firm and in such a state, that during that time, those who are accustomed to it, and who understand it, work very easily and with great pleasure upon it. But afterwards, when it begins to lose its moisture and to set, it will be observed, that any colours then laid on will be of a different tint from those which were put on first, and thus the effect of the picture will be spoiled. For this reason, expert artists, before this happens, cover all their work with a good body of colour diligently and quickly, and in a soft, light, and even manner; because if they delay, the *intonaco* acquires a thin crust when it touches the air, and thus makes the picture spotty and dull. Some information is necessary respecting the use of certain colours, such as *smalto* and *pavonazzo,* which, being generally coarser and of less body than the others, the wetter the lime is, when they are applied, the better. In this kind of work, it is necessary to have the hand very firm, bold, and free,—qualities, which result from a clear and sound judgment, that knows how much every individual tint can change, or lose of its brightness; and not only how much each will change during that one day, but also until the *intonaco* is quite dry.

Now the lime must be put upon the damp wall (which should have been well wetted) in such quantity, as will cover the space to be painted that day; and having first drawn the squares, in the proper proportion, on the dry wall, we must again mark them upon the *intonaco,* making the lines agree exactly with those which are upon the wall underneath. Then, taking the small design in our hand, we copy it carefully on the picture, with a paint brush dipped in some water colour, which should be of a reddish tint, because the marks of these tints can easily be removed at pleasure if they are not right; for by dipping the same brush in water they can all be washed out. But if the cartoon be finished, it should either be traced, or pounced on the wall, in the manner before mentioned, and this plan you will certainly find more convenient. Having done this, the outlines must be marked over with a brush, and, if necessary, corrected. We must then take the colours, sketching out and covering everything, taking care to put lights, shades, and middle tints in their proper places according to the sketch; and this must be done in such a manner, that there may be an union and harmony of the colours, which must appear to the eyes, pleasing, bright, and united. Another coat of colour must then be laid evenly over the work while the *intonaco* is still wet. But although this *intonaco* absorbs, for the most part, the colours first laid on, it is necessary for the artist to work and unite them together by putting on another coat in this manner. There are some persons who think to avoid this, by first laying on one or two coats of white, and they say, that this method also makes the colours appear brighter when the *intonaco* is dry. This is sometimes true in painting grotesques and other similar things which are small and of no importance, but it is positively injurious in great historical pictures, because, although this white reflects the colours, it is nevertheless very injurious to the darks, and destroys much of their harmony and force; [a] effects which are very contrary to the intention of a good painter.

As we are now speaking of the tints, I would not have any one think that because they happen to be well mixed in the gallipots, they must produce exactly the same effects on the wall, because this requires a familiarity with the colours found in nature. There are some artists, who, in order that they may not have to correct their painting on the wall, first imitate the colours correctly with crayons, and others with oil colours; because the colours are thinner in some kinds of painting than in others; and there are reddish and greenish touches scattered over various parts, with which the

[a] It will be observed, that Pacheco and Borghini recommend mixing a little colour with the *intonaco*.—Ed.

before-mentioned tints may not exactly agree in colour, and therefore there must prevail, as it were, a controlling harmony, which must be conceived in the mind of the artist; and this is particularly necessary to be observed in flesh tints where large masses of naked bodies are introduced in pictures, in which the lights, and the brightness of the colours, should diminish with such skill and dexterity, as to appear to die away into the shade, and to lose their brilliancy by degrees, so that it may be seen that the light does not produce the colours, but only makes them visible, for where the least light comes, there the shadows are the deepest and the darkest. We must also observe, that the colour must not be changed, on account of the shadow, but that we must retain the same colour, only making it deeper, because, as has been before observed, darkness is want of light, and not an effect of the colour black; although it is true that draperies and many other things can be made to harmonize with the rest of the picture, and can be finished easily, by means of well selected tints.

But with regard to naked bodies, we have seen some painters of the present day, who had such skill in managing the colours, that with three mixtures alone, they have painted a naked body, having all the half-tints and gradations of colour, which are visible in the natural body. The tints are, one light tint and two dark ones. They lay on a great many shades with the lighter shade colour, and touch all the half-shades and dark shadows. They then take the light tint, with which they cover the whole of the lighter parts, and go over the raw shades, which had previously been put on, even to the extremities, so that the half-tints appear very soft through this from underneath; and those shades, which before, were too raw, being thus softened down, they pass over them again, with the above mentioned shade colour, in order to bring the shades, half-shades, and half-lights, to their right tone. They next take the other tint, which is the darkest shade tint, with which they give the figure relief in all its parts; so that we may say, that these make their tints upon the wall, in the same way that others do in their gallipots. Among those whom I knew, there was a certain Luchetto, of Genoa,[a] who, in my time, painted at S. Matteo, in the church which belonged to the Prince Doria, certain stories of this saint, in competition with a very good painter of Bergamo. I really

[a] Luca or Luchetto Cambiaso, born 1527, died about 1585.—*Mariet. Descript.*—Ed.

have seen wonderful things by him, in that city; he paints with both hands, holding a brush full of colour in each, and is so expert and dexterous, that he does his work with great quickness; and I have seen more pictures in fresco by him, than by any ten others together. His figures are painted with wonderful force, besides which, there is that freedom, that grace and skill, which the greatest conceptions of men of genius rarely display, and which always require the greatest skill and labour. Giacomo Tintoretto,[a] the Venetian, paints in nearly the same manner, and there are some persons who consider him the most rapid painter, but he is inferior in design, and is less careful than Luca; and, as his colouring is softer, his pictures have less relief and force. He has frequently painted very important pictures, without any design, leaving the sketches for finished pictures, and so roughly painted, that one may see the very marks of the brush, from his too great haste and impetuosity. These pictures, therefore, will not bear very close inspection. But it is enough, that they astonish many of our artists at first sight; so that those men who used solid colour, by adopting this manner, and finishing their labours quickly, cause their pictures to remain very fresh, delicate, and gay; and it makes no difference to them, although it does to doubtful or irresolute persons, or bad painters, whether they put on the light colours before the dark, or the reds before the flesh tints. But the tints, and all the other colours, are laid on with the same paint brush which the artist happens to have in his hand, because, by washing it in water and squeezing it a little, it answers his purpose very well.

Having now brought your picture into this state, it is nearly finished, because, when you begin to find that the lime is going to set, and that it does not absorb the colour with the same force as before, you must then finish it off with moist and dark shade tints, working it up in this way quite to the extremities. But the muscles of naked figures, as being of greater difficulty, are painted by hatching them in different directions with very liquid shade tints, so that they appear of a texture like granite; and there are very brilliant examples of this, painted by the hand of Michael Angelo, of Daniello, and of Francesco

[a] Giacomo Robusto, called Il Tintoretto, born at Venice in 1512, died in 1594. *Lanzi.* Vol. III. p. 116. &c.—Ed.

Salviati,[a] who are very celebrated for their works. The lights must then be laid on, in the manner which we have already mentioned.

Now this mode of painting soon betrays the ignorance of those who are but little accustomed to it, because, all that has been badly done, either through timidity, or by the ground being badly covered, or the work being badly finished, begins to shew itself the next day; and it should be known, that when the wall and the picture are quite dry, every little defect will clearly appear, and such will be all retouchings, spots, and colours laid one over another, and badly covered over, or badly united together; so that it is always well to work cautiously, in order not to fall into these great faults. Then, at the end of the day, when all the part that has been plastered is finished, the remainder is cut off carefully, on account of the rough edge, in order that, the next day, fresh *intonaco* may be joined on to it, without shewing the least mark of the joining, as piece is joined on to piece, while the work is going on. The boys will then take care to wash the brushes with clean water, and to arrange their points, and to repair them well: and they must do the same thing with the mixed tints, and the other colours, by pouring water into them all, and particularly into the white which has been purified, of which, as being the principal colour among them, greater care must be taken not to let it dry. Having thus put all the things into their proper places, the wall must be wetted again in the evening, and must be soaked several times against the next morning, particularly when it is very hot weather, in order that the *intonaco* may be kept well wetted during the time you are at work, until all that you wish to paint upon it is finished.

This is the method which is to be observed concerning painting in fresco, and which, together with the above advice, should be, so to speak, the foundation of all the pictures you paint. And you may leave to foolish painters those secrets of theirs, which no one envies them, of using vermilions and fine lakes; because, although they make grounds for them, with various kinds of white, it is, nevertheless, well known that, in the long run, their pictures become ugly daubs, because they employ these colours solely to attract the eyes

[a] Francesco de Rossi, who assumed the name of his protectors, the Salviati, was the condisciple of Vasari, under Andrea del Sarto and under Baccio Bandinelli. He was an excellent sculptor, and a teacher of drawing to students in painting, an art which he cultivated for his amusement. See *Lanzi*, Vol. I. p. 167, 168. He was born in 1510, and died in 1563.

of the vulgar, at first sight, and we cannot consider those persons who have thus employed them, altogether blameless.

To make pictures in Chiaro-scuro, the same means are used, as have been just mentioned; for, having pounded the charcoal, and washed the white, of these two extremes, at least, three tints must be made, one lighter than the other; and then, in order to judge of their effect, while they are being mixed, they must be tried on a brick which has been baked, but not wetted. Some persons mix potter's clay with them; and there are others, who lay a coat of it underneath, for a ground, which answers the same purpose.

A similar method is used for painting pictures to imitate bronze, using mixtures of these colours, namely, yellow earth *(terra gialla)*, and *occheja*[a] for the shadows, for which others mix umber *(terra d'ombra)* with it, and some add *paonazzo*, and others black. In short, any kind of picture can be painted well in this way. But we have said enough on this subject.

Of retouching fresco paintings in secco.—But, to follow out our subject, as regards the manner of painting, this last harmonizing is considered to be, and really is, very difficult in fresco paintings, particularly in those which are not under cover. This arises from the effect of the lime on the colours, for as the lime dries very quickly, nothing can be done after the first day on which you paint upon it. For this reason, I approve of those painters who provide for this, by means of cartoons, which are well finished by their own hands, because, when the tints and the shades have been put in their proper places at first, the finishing touches are then given with the delicate and liquid shades.

But as for those which are in covered places, they can be perfectly harmonized by retouching them in *secco*, because, when the first colours have been painted in solidly, while the lime is very wet, afterwards, when it is dry, it can be brought to whatever degree of perfection is thought proper, with the finest colours, it being allowable to do so, without any injury to the colours, which, however, have been seen to fail after a length of time. In retouching the dark parts in this manner, there are some painters, who make a water-colour tint of black and fine lake, mixed together, with which

[a] *Occheja.* The name and nature of this pigment is quite unknown, unless it be a typical error for *ocrea arsa*, burnt ochre. See Lomazzo, Trattato. p. 196.

they retouch the naked figures, and produce a most beautiful effect, because they make hatchings upon the painting, as it is usual to do, while drawing upon paper with black lead. And for this purpose they use a rather large hair pencil of minever, with which they work carefully and gradually, in the way in which granite is painted. Some persons temper these dark tints with gum, some with thin glue, and some with yolk of egg *(tempera)*, with which latter vehicle they are darker and more permanent than with the others. This I affirm from what I have both seen and done, and also what I have been told by the best painters. And, therefore, pictures painted in *secco* upon canvass, should be retouched in this same manner. *Armenino, De Veri Precetti. p.* 147. *Ed. Pisa,* 1823.

CHAPTER VIII.

OF ANDREA POZZO.

Andrea Pozzo was native of Trent, and a Jesuit. He became an architect and a painter, rather by the force of his own genius than the instructions of a master. The practice of copying the pictures of the best Venetian and Lombard masters, had given him a good style in colouring and design, which he improved in Rome, where he remained many years. He went also to Genoa and Turin, and in both these states may be seen many of his pictures, the best of which are those that most resemble the manner of Rubens, to imitate whose style he aspired. His pictures in oil are rare, for he finished but few. He was always a skilful painter, was judicious in his composition, select in the choice of his forms, his colouring agreeable and lively, his handling free and expeditious. His celerity was surprising; he finished a portrait in four hours, which he had been required to paint by a person who was going to leave Italy for Germany the same day.

He occupied an honourable rank among those who decorated buildings. The roof of the church of St. Ignatius, at Rome, is his principal work, and that is sufficient to establish his fame, if he had painted nothing else. This work combines novelty of invention with harmony of colouring, and picturesque fire, which is admired both by Maratti and Carlo Ferri; the latter of whom was astonished, that in so few years, Andrea had, as he said, with such a masterly hand, filled the Piazza Navona with figures. He concluded by observing, that if the horses of other painters walked, those of Pozzo galloped.

In perspective, he ranks among the most eminent; and, even on concave surfaces, he was able to make all the parts appear convex; as, for instance, the paintings on the Tribune at Frascati, where he pourtrayed the circumcision, and in the Corridor of Jesus at Rome. He however obtained most reputation, by deceiving the eye with imaginary cupolas in many churches belonging to his order: he also painted theatrical scenes, introducing colonnades and buildings with such an imitation of truth, as to render credible what Vitruvius, Book VII. c. 5. and Pliny, Book LXXXV. c. 4. wrote respecting the skill of the ancients in this respect. Although well acquainted with the theory of optics, as is proved by his two volumes on perspective, he accustomed himself never to draw, without having previously made models, and distributed the lights and shades. When he had to paint on canvass, he gave it a thin couch of glue, without gesso, which he would not use, because it appeared to him, that when the colours were applied, it prevented the proper blending of the lights and shades. He was born in 1642 and died 1709. *Lanzi.*—The following precepts on fresco painting were appended to his great work, familiarly called the "Jesuit's Perspective."

DIRECTIONS AND OBSERVATIONS OF ANDREA POZZO.

OF THE PREPARATION OF THE WALL. ARRICCIATO AND INTONACO. —The *arricciato* is the first coat of mortar which is given to a wall or place on which it is required to paint; this should be rather rough. The painter must take care never to begin his painting on walls on which the rough-cast has been recently applied, particularly if in interiors; because, besides the damp, which is very injurious to the health, the lime exhales a bad smell, which is equally prejudicial.

When the *arricciato* is laid upon the wall, and so free from all dampness, as to appear quite dry, it is necessary to wet it sufficiently and to give it a thin coat of mortar, which is laid evenly over the wall, and this is called laying on the *intonaco*. The lime selected for this purpose, should have been slaked for a year, or at least six months, in countries where the lime is strong; but where the lime is milder, it can be used sooner. It must be mixed with river sand, not too coarse, nor yet excessively fine. At Rome, the painters use Pozzolana, but as the grains of this are of very unequal size, it is extremely difficult to levigate mortar composed of it, and still more difficult to work out the cracks and crevices which appear, if it stand for some hours; it is therefore necessary to stir it continually with the trowel. The mortar should be laid on by an expert and active mason, in order that the *intonaco* may be spread evenly, and that the painter may have sufficient time to paint upon it during the whole of that day, or more, according as the weather is hot or cold, or the place damp or dry.

The *intonaco* being equally spread, it will be proper to raise up the small grains of sand with a brush, that the colours may adhere more easily. This is called *granire*, and is especially necessary on large works which are to be seen from a distance. The same preparation can also be used for those which are to be seen close, but, in that case, the roughness and inequality of the grain must be removed, by laying a sheet of strong paper over the *intonaco*, and pressing it moderately with the hand or a trowel, in order to press in the most prominent grains of sand, and to flatten the surface.

Of the designs and cartoons.—Before beginning to paint, it is necessary to prepare a small drawing or well-studied coloured sketch, which the painter should always keep before him, that he may have nothing to think of but the execution. A cartoon should also be made as large as the picture intended to be painted, which should be fixed against the wall in the place the picture is to occupy, in order to detect the errors (if there be any) from a distance, and to correct them.

Graticolare, or enlarging by squares.—When the places to be painted are large, such as churches or saloons, or curved or irregular vaulted ceilings, for which either the cartoons cannot be made sufficiently large, or upon which they cannot be spread without difficulty, it is necessary to use the *grata*,[a] which is very useful for enlarging designs. The *grata* is particularly useful in perspective drawing, especially on vaulted ceilings, and irregular surfaces, to make an architectural design in perspective appear straight, flat, or upright. The small design must first be divided into squares, and then the picture must be divided into the same number of larger squares.[b] After this, the painter, having considered what number of squares he can paint in one day, as was said before, must cause the wall to be carefully covered with the *intonaco*, marking the *grata* (which had been covered over),[c] again on the fresh *intonaco*, that it may guide him in drawing the outlines of the painting. If, after

[a] Vasari calls this *rete*, *Malvasia*, *Graticola*.

[b] The contents of each of the small squares are then copied into the corresponding squares of the large cartoon.

[c] This was the usual practice of the school of Giotto, which does not appear to have used large cartoons. See Cennino, Vasari, *passim*.

having finished painting for that day, any part of the *intonaco* should be still unpainted, which would dry before the next day, it must be cut away,[a] taking care not to make the cuttings in the middle of the carnations, but only in their outlines, or in the draperies. The *intonaco* must thus be put on piece by piece; and the mason must take care to do this well, so as not to daub the outlines of the picture, nor to splash it, and therefore, in order to obviate all dangers of this kind, it will be better to begin painting at the top of the picture.

Of tracing.—When the outlines of the design have been drawn on large paper, as is mentioned before, the cartoon must be laid upon the *intonaco*, the wetness of which will allow it to receive any impression, and then the outlines must be traced over lightly with an iron stile. For small pictures, it will be sufficient to pounce the outlines.

On the preparation of the colours.—Before begining to paint, it is necessary to prepare the colours, and the various tints, such, at least, as will be required for one figure; indeed, if a mass of architecture is to be painted, it will be necessary to prepare a general tint for the whole work; otherwise, it would be difficult, if obliged to mix additional quantities, to match the colours. It is not necessary to speak of the other usual preparations, as thay are common to oil painting.

The manner of painting.—Painting in *fresco* is not different from oil painting, except that it requires greater quickness and celerity, from the difficulty caused by the necessity of the artist accomodating himself to the situation in which the picture is to be painted. Therefore, besides arranging the colours in order, in separate gallipots, it is also proper to be provided with a palette of copper, tin, or wood,[b] with a raised edge all round, in order that the more liquid colours may not be spilled, with a small jar in the middle for holding pure water, that there may be some near at hand with which to wet the colours. A sponge soaked in water will do as well. Care must also be taken not to begin the painting, until the lime

[a] As to cuttings and joinings see II. Rep. page 23.

[b] Palomino recommends a palette of canvass.

has sufficient consistence not to receive the impression of the fingers, because if the *intonaco* be painted on while too wet, the free play of the brush will be impeded, and the whole work will be weak, and only serve for a first painting.

Impastare, e caricare, or solid painting.—Fresco painting has this peculiarity, that the first colours which touch the lime, soon become faint, and lose a great deal of their brilliancy. On this account it is necessary to go over the work again with a greater body of the same colours, and never to leave, for a moment, the part on which the painter is engaged, until it is quite finished and perfected; otherwise all touches done after a few hours, appear like so many spots or soils on the picture, and, in that case, it is better to wait till the painting is quite dry, and then retouch it in *secco*.

Retouching.—Whoever can finish his painting in buono-fresco, will always have his picture more complete, and the colours more lasting than if retouched in *secco;* but, as the lime almost always makes some change in the colours, particularly in the shades, it can and ought to be retouched, by small hatchings, laid on either with crayons made of egg shells, or with paint brushes half dry, dipped in the necessary colour. This kind of retouching is quite useless when employed upon places which are uncovered and exposed to the air, because the rain will wash them all away. To retouch fresco painting so as to withstand water, wet the fresco several times with water, in which gum arabic has been dissolved, and then cover it with the following varnish :—

Acqua di rasa (spirit of turpentine), 2 oz.
Olio di Abezzo (Venice turpentine), 1 oz.

The whole boiled on a slow fire; when dry, let the painting be retouched with colours ground with oil.

Sfumare or softening.—In softening and uniting the colours, soft brushes of hog's bristles, not too moist, must be used, and sometimes the finger may be employed with effect on heads, hands, and other small parts, particularly when the lime begins to harden. But when it is necessary to soften a large portion, such as a sky, a glory, &c., it should be done at first while the lime is quite wet, or when it is only half dry, with convenient tools and in such a manner as the industry of the painter may suggest.

ALTERATIONS.—It frequently happens, that some figure does not satisfy the expectations of the artist, so that he wishes to alter it. For this purpose it is necessary to remove the *intonaco* from that part, without touching the rest of the picture, and after having well cleaned the place where it stood, to wet it well, and lay on it some fresh *intonaco*. In a covered place, however, the more distant figures may be repainted in *secco* over the first. This we only say incidentally, to relieve the minds of young painters from any scruple on this point.

OF THE COLOURS.—It is necessary to know what colours are good for painting in fresco; for it would be of little use to paint a beautiful picture, if, owing to the incompatibility of one colour with another, or of the colours with the lime, the picture should not last long. The following are some observations concerning them, beginning with those which are the best for our purpose.

WHITE PIGMENTS. WHITE FROM LIME.—The white made from lime is the best of all, for mixing with the colours, as well for the carnations as the draperies, provided the lime has been slaked for a year, or at least for six months as before stated. It must be mixed with water, and strained through coarse silk, allowing it to settle to the bottom, and throwing away the superfluous water, so that it may stand upon the palette.

WHITE FROM CARRARA MARBLE AND EGG SHELLS.—The marble must be reduced to powder, and ground with water, mixing it with lime to give it more body. It is white and a good pigment; but it is useless trouble to prepare this, when well seasoned lime, or prepared egg shells, can be obtained. The *white from egg shells* is also very white, and is good for painting in *fresco* and *secco*, and for making crayons for retouching. A great quantity of egg shells must be collected, and cleaned from the egg by boiling them with some quick lime, having first pounded them a little. They must then be strained and washed with spring water, then pounded finer and washed again; and this must be repeated until the water comes off quite clear. They must next be ground very fine with the muller, and made into small cakes, which, when dried in the sun, can be used for the carnations, or for white draperies, or elsewhere at pleasure. We must observe, however, that if these pounded egg shells are allowed to remain moist for some time, they will give out an insupportable odour, which may be prevented by putting them in an earthen jar, and sending them to the oven to bake.

Red pigments. Vermilion (Cinabro).—This is the most lively colour of any, but is quite incompatible with lime, particularly when exposed to the air. If the painting is under shelter, it can be used, but first it is necessary to prepare it in the following manner. Take the pure vermilion, in powder, and put it in an earthen vessel, and pour over it some water in which lime has been slaked, as clear as it can be obtained. Then pour off the water, and add some fresh lime-water, and repeat this several times; and by this means the vermilion becomes imbued with the qualities of the lime, which it never loses. In purchasing the vermilion, it is better to buy it in the lump, than in powder, because the powdered vermilion is frequently adulterated with minium, and does not produce its proper effect.

Burnt Roman Vitriol.[a]—Roman Vitriol baked in the oven, and then ground with spirit of wine, succeeds admirably upon fresh lime; when alone, it makes a red like lake. It is particularly useful as a ground for vermilion. When both are used on a drapery, they produce a lake colour quite equal to that of lake in oil painting. This colour may be used instead of *Bruno d' Inghilterra.*

Rossetto d'Inghilterra.—Instead of the vitriol, *Rossetto d'Inghilterra* produces nearly the same effect, as it is, itself, of the nature of vitriol. If it is used upon the lime, while quite moist, and then shaded, when dry, it looks like lake.

Red Ochre, (*Terra Rossa*), like all the other earths, is most excellent for painting in fresco. It is used in the carnations, draperies, and wherever it is wanted. *Burnt yellow ochre,* (*Terra Gialla Abbrucciata*), is rather of a pale red, and is good for the dark parts of the carnations, mixed with Venetian *Terra Nera.* It is also used to shade yellow draperies.

Yellow Pigments. Yellow Ochre.—There are two sorts of yellow ochre found at Rome, one light, and the other darker, both beautiful in their kind. If used carefully on draperies, they are quite equal to *Giallolino.* Yellow earths are found in other parts of

[a] Sulphate of iron.

Italy, but they are not equal to the Roman. *Naples Yellow, (Giallolino di Fornace)*, is also called *Giallolino di Napoli*. It is very durable, but should not be used in exposed situations.

Green Pigments.—Sap Green *(Pasta Verde)*, is made from the juice of the Buckthorn *(Spincervino)*; mixed with white lime, it becomes yellow, but the colour is rather fleeting.—Terre Verte. That of Verona is the finest, indeed the only green earth proper for draperies, in fresco, as almost all the others are manufactured, and incompatible with the lime. Other kinds of Terre Verte are also found, but are inferior. Next to this, however, the Terre Verte of Capri, when it is genuine, is the best and finest.

Brown Pigments.—Umber is good for the shades of draperies, particularly yellow ones. It must be used with care, and mixed with white lime, because it always becomes darker and increases in depth. *Burnt Umber* is excellent for the shades of the carnations, when mixed with Venetian *Terra Nera*, and particularly in the deeper shades.

Black Pigments.—Venetian black earth (Terra Nera), is the darkest of all for fresco painting, and is good for the shades of the carnations, and produces the same effect as bistre (*Fuligine*) in *secco*, and bitumen in oil. *Roman black earth* (Terra Nera di Roma), produces the same effect as charcoal black, and is in pretty general use. *Charcoal black* can be made in various ways, namely, with vine wood, burnt, with peach stones, with nut shells, with lees or tartar of wine, or with paper. These must all be burnt, and then ground to powder, with a little water, and made into cakes. In fresco painting, in which bone black cannot be used, charcoal black is good for anything for which black is required.[a]

Blue Pigments.—Smaltino (*glass blue*). This is useful in fresco, and should be laid on before the other colours, while the *intonaco* is still wet, for otherwise it will not incorporate firmly. An hour after, a second coat must be laid on, to make the colour deeper. The pure colour will serve for shades, but charcoal black should be

[a] The distinction seems to be, that the vegetable charcoal may be used in fresco, but not animal charcoal. Black earths are preferable to either.—Ed.

used in the deeper shades. All the above mentioned colours must be mixed with lime white, to produce the light, dark, and middle tints used by painters. *Ultramarine* is as good in fresco as in *secco*, but is not used, as it is of such great value.[a] *Indigo* may be used in summer, as it then dries quickly, but it must not be used in winter.[b]

Morello di Sale, mixed with smaltino, makes a purple, as indeed it does when used alone.

The above are all the colours which can be used for painting in fresco.

Colours incompatible with lime, and which therefore cannot be used for fresco painting.—White lead, Verzino lake, (*i. e.* lake from Brazil wood), fine lake, verdegris, blue green (*Verde Azzurro*), *Verde Poro* (leek green), *Verde in Canna, Giallo Santo* (yellow lake), French *Giallolino*, orpiment, bone-black, biadetto, and indigo, which has been already mentioned.

Painting upon walls in secco.—Walls are frequently painted in *secco*, having a priming of soft *gesso*, mixed with size, laid upon them. In this manner, all colours can be used, without exception. It must be observed, however, that walls which have been white-washed several times, must be scraped; otherwise, in dry weather, the excessive thickness of the white-wash causes the priming to scale off, so as to shew the bare wall, which will spoil the picture. On new walls, a coating of *gesso*, prepared as above mentioned, should be laid on while the mortar is wet, and all kinds of colours can be used upon it.

[a] Palomino says, this pigment cannot be used in fresco because the lime destroys it.—Ed.

[b] This colour also is said to be destroyed by wet lime.—Ed.

CHAPTER IX.

OF PACHECO.

PACHECO was born at Seville, about 1571. He was the pupil of Luis Fernandez, and the master of Alonzo Cano and Velasquez. Carducho and Palomino speak of Pacheco as a scientific painter, and a good instructor, yet, even during his life, he was the subject of severe criticism, as we find by the following epigram, written by a sarcastic Andalusian, at the bottom of a naked figure of Christ, which he had painted :—

"¿Quien os puso asi, señor,
Tan desabrido y tan seco ?
Vos mi direis que el amor,
Mas os digo que Pacheco."

"Who made you thus, Lord, so doleful and so dry ? you will tell me it was love, but I tell you it was Pacheco."

However, to do him justice, we find, in his works, great correctness of design, a pure and noble style, natural attitudes, and a profound knowledge of chiaro-scuro and perspective. If, to these important qualities, he had united a more agreeable and harmonious colouring, and greater freedom of execution, he would, at least, have equalled the best painters of Andalusia, who have frequently sacrificed correctness of outline to splendour of colouring.

His most important literary work is the book, entitled "Arte de la Pintura," which he wrote towards the end of his life, and which was published in 1641. This work, from which the following extracts are selected, comprises all the information on the subject that could be furnished by a long life and long experience. The work is elementary and classical, and is considered, by the Spaniards, as the best written work on the subject in the language. It contains, besides lessons on art, many interesting particulars respecting those who have practised the art, and the works which they have produced.—*Viardot, Notices sur les Pemtres de l' Espagne.* Palomino says that he died in 1654.

DIRECTIONS AND OBSERVATIONS OF PACHECO.

INQUIRY WHETHER THE ANCIENTS PAINTED IN FRESCO.—In treating of fresco painting, and of its antiquity and use, let us hear what Pablo de Cespedes[a] has to say. "I found myself in Rome with very learned and experienced painters, who contended that the ancients were not only unacquainted with oil painting, but with fresco painting also, and that they only practised distemper painting; which was news to me. And it appears to me, that much may be said on both sides of the question. That they were acquainted with fresco

[a] Pablo de Cespedes, born at Cordova, in 1538, died 1608. He was a great and almost universal genius, whose desire for learning extended to the sciences, belles-lettres, and the fine arts, and who only failed of being the first in every study, because he turned from one to the other before he had acquired perfection, and because he divided his genius among several branches of study, instead of centering it in one absorbing taste, one sole study, and one persevering struggle for success. He was the friend of Federigo Zucchero, and worked in his studio. He painted frescoes in the church of Ara-cœli, in the Trinità de Monte, with Zucchero, Julio Romano, Daniel de Volterra, Pelegrino da Bologna, and Perino del Vaga.

He understood well the Italian, Latin, and Greek Languages, and was also acquainted with the Hebrew and Arabic. He was the author of several works on the arts, the best of which is entitled, "*De la comparacion, de la antigua y moderna pintura y escultura.*" Pacheco has preserved some valuable fragments of his poem on painting, which is the best didactic poem in the Spanish language. His works, excepting the frescoes executed during his studies in Italy, are extremely scarce out of Cordova and Seville. Palomino says, he was a great imitator of the works of Correggio, and one of the best colourists of Spain: Don Antonio Ponz adds, "that if Cespedes could have enjoyed the friendship of Raffaello as he did that of Zucchero, he would have been one of the greatest painters in the world, as he was one of the wisest." Cean Bermudez thus eulogises him: "We admire the elegance and grandeur of the forms, the vigour of the figures, the study and knowledge of anatomy, the skilfulness of the foreshortenings, the effect of the chiaro-scuro, the brilliancy of the colouring, the truth of the expression, and, above all, his powers of invention; for he had no occasion to borrow from others." The Chapter of Cordova having requested Zucchero to paint a St. Margeret for them, the Italian artist replied, "Can they ask paintings from Italy in a town where they have Cespedes?"

Carducho (Dial. 2. fol. 31.) says, that he studied much the works of Michael Angelo, and trod in his footsteps, not only in painting and architecture, but in sculpture also.—See also Palomino, Vol. II. p. 406, &c.

Cespedes was accustomed to make cartoons in black and red, as large as he intended to make the painting; and there are many portraits by him done in this manner.—*Viardot's Notices sur les Principaux Peintres de l' Espagne.*

painting is testified by the pictures found in Rome, in grottoes, and subterranean vaults, whence it is called grotesque painting. But it is objected, that these are evidently not fresco, but distemper painting, and, although I have seen several, I cannot tell which they are, though I rather think that they are frescoes, and the state they are in is not sufficiently perfect to enable me to decide.[a] This opinion is confirmed by Pliny, who, speaking of black, and how it was used, says, that when used for writing it was mixed with gum, but when for painting on walls, it was mixed with glue or paste. They called this manner of painting on walls *opus tectorium*. And it is clear that in fresco painting nothing is used with the colours but pure water; and also, that *negro de humo* (lamp black, which is what Pliny means) is not proper for fresco painting.

"That the ancients were acquainted with fresco painting can be collected from what this same Pliny says, in chapter III, speaking of three pictures in the city of Ardea, which, although uncovered by a roof, had lasted many years; and the same in Lanuvium, a city near Rome, so that, being painted on a wall, some without a roof and the others in a ruined temple (according to report), being in such a fresh state of preservation, is an indication that they were not distemper; since, although so old, they still retained their first beauty.

"It may also be observed in chapter IV, that Fabius, a most illustrious Roman (who was called Pictor), painted the Temple of Public Safety, in Rome, and his pictures remainded till the reign of the

[a] From the following description given by Federigo Zucchero ("Idea de Pittore," &c. in the Lett. Pitt. vol. II. p. 142, 143.) of the celebrated ancient picture known by the name of the Aldobrandini Marriage, we may conclude that it is a fresco painting. "It was discovered on the mount of S. Maria Maggiore, in the Orti Mecenati, by those excavators, who are continually at work, examining here and there, under ground, to find statues, marbles and figures, buried in those ruins. They found a room, of which a piece of the wall was left standing, upon which was painted an elegant and beautiful picture in fresco, with figures about three palms high, coloured by the hand of a master. This piece was considered worthy of being sawn off, and brought to light, and placed in the garden of the Cardinal Aldobrandini at Monte Manganopoli, and was so well preserved among these ruins, that it was quite wonderful. And I, who was by chance one of the first to see it, *and wash it, and clean it carefully with my own hand*, observed it was as well preserved, and as fresh as if it had but just been painted; so that it pleased me exceedingly, and I caused it to be brought to light." This picture was a favourite subject of study with Raffaello and Nicholas Poussin; the latter is said to have made an accurate copy of it.

Emperor Claudius, when they were destroyed by fire; so that they lasted at least three hundred years." Thus far Cespedes.

Agreeing in these opinions, I answer to those who wish to make it appear that the ancients painted in distemper only, that under this name is comprehended fresco, as all that is not oil painting, must necessarily be distemper, and in reality, fresco is a particular kind of distemper; and it cannot be denied that the ancients painted in fresco, from the duration of their paintings. Thus Vasari, whose words leave no doubt as to the fact, asserts, "Era degli antichi molto usato il fresco, et i vecchi moderni ancora l' hanno poi seguitato,"—Fresco was much used by the ancients, in which the early masters have followed them.

We now come to the *execution of fresco paintings*. Of all kinds of painting, that of fresco painting is the most masterly, dexterous, and expeditious, completing in one day, what, in any other style, would occupy a long time in painting, and which may be retouched. But fresco painting requires great dexterity and boldness, and the mistakes and faults are irremediable, unless the work be cut out. It is the most manly and lasting kind of painting, therefore, those who practise it ought to be more respected and esteemed than other painters, being considered great masters.

The wall must be very dry, strong, and free from moisture, and must have been plastered a long time previous; and the lime which is to be used must be very mild, it being necessary to keep it in soft water above two years, and it must be mixed with fine sand, in equal proportions, and the mortar must be laid on that part only which can be painted in one day.

The colours must be natural colours, the white pigment must be fine lime either from Portugal, or from Marchena; [a] very white, and of great body, which has lost its causticity by being kept for many days in a large jar with soft water; this white, if made into balls, can be kept many years. It is ground with soft water, and is put into a pot covered with the same water, and is used instead of white lead, mixed with the other colours. The light and dark ochre must be of great body, such as that of Flanders and of Portugal, also of Castelleja de la Cuesta, which Luis de Vargas used in painting the tower.

[a] A town of Andalusia.

Of the colours, cartoons, and painting.—*The light ochre* mixed with lime, serves instead of *genuli* for the yellows; the *almagra de Levante* serves instead of vermilion for the flesh, and for the light draperies; and *Albin* for the crimson of this kind of painting. Of the last are made the rose colours, and the purples, when mixed with esmalte, which is the blue pigment best adapted for fresco painting, because it is glass and incorporates better than other blue pigments with the lime. It is the most difficult colour to use, and should be the first finished. It should be used in this manner:—to make light blue it should be mixed with the liquor that is produced by mixing water with the powdered lime,[a] stirring it about until it is thick and clouded; and the middle and dark tints are made in the same manner; this is the safest method of using it; but some persons who wish to darken the tints with pure esmalte, retouch it the next day, either with egg and water and the leaf of a fig tree, or with the yolk of egg as in distemper painting, or with the milk of goats alone. The same may be done with the green, if it is *verde terra* or *verde montaña.*[b] But *verdacho* [c] agrees better with the lime in fresco, and may be made lighter with it at pleasure, or darkened with black. The common brown is the Italian umber, and the black is the *negro de carbon*; but my master,[d] who was much practised in this kind of painting, used the *negro de baño,* which is not to be found everywhere.

And I must tell you, that in tempering the colours you must consider how much lighter they will appear when mixed with the lime, after the painting is dry, and this can be taught only by experience.[e] Therefore, always mix more colour than you require for the picture, for it will be scarcely possible to match the colour afterwards.

The preparation which is usually made after the lime is spread on the wall, is to bathe it with a large brush dipped in soft and clear water, that the cracks, which are frequently found in the stucco, may be filled up before drawing what is to be painted, or pouncing the cartoon, which last is the best way for producing a good effect.

[a] *i. e.,* Lime water.

[b] See this word in the Treatise on Colours—Green pigments.

[c] Ibid.

[d] Pacheco was the pupil of Luis Fernandez.

[e] I. Rep. 24, 35.

And some persons even keep before them not only highly-finished drawings, but heads painted in oil from nature, that the figures may appear in better relief; for if you draw on the wall with pencil (Lapiz), and paint off hand whatever presents itself, you will not preserve the good opinion of others, nor will your works do you honour.[a]

After the cartoon is pounced or drawn, the wall should have a couch of ground lime with a little almagra, so that it should be of a light flesh colour, except when azure or green is to be used, when lime alone should be employed.[b] And then begin to lay on the various colours, making them very liquid, for upon this (*intonaco*) they may be applied well according to their tints as in painting with water colours.

Retouching in distemper.—As to retouching in distemper after the wall is dry, there is much to be said against it, notwithstanding that many great men practised it,—as Mateo Perez de Alecio,[c] in the San Christoval, and in the door of the Cardinal; Antonio Mohedano,[d] and Alonso Varquez [e] in the cloister of San Francisco; Peregrin[f] in

[a] Pacheco was very careful in the preparation of his works. During a practice of forty years, he never omitted to make, previous to commencing his painting, two or three studied designs; he first painted the heads, separately, and from nature; he also drew, upon coloured paper, and always from nature, the arms, hands, legs, and all the naked parts of the body which he intended to represent; and also the different stuffs and draperies, which he disposed upon a layman; and then he made a general composition of all these prepared fragments.

[b] From this it appears that it was not the practice of the Spanish school to lay a black or red ground under blue.

[c] Mateo Perez de Alecio. A native of Rome who painted the celebrated San Christobal, in the Church of Seville, "a work," says Palomino, "which has no equal either in execution or size; since it is thirty feet high. It is executed in fresco, and with such skill, that *the joinings of the* tareas *are not visible.*" He died about 1600, at Rome.

[d] Antonio Mohedano was the friend of Cespedes, whose school he followed. Palomino says, that "he painted in fresco with such skill, both in design and in colouring, that he was inferior to no painter of his own time, and indeed was never equalled. He learned the art from Cæsar Arbasia of Cordova." He died in 1625.

[e] Alonzo Varquez, of the school of Luis de Vargas in Seville, was an excellent fresco painter, skilful in anatomy and colouring. He died in 1650.

[f] Peregrino di Bologna. One of the most distinguished pupils and followers of the school of Michael Angelo. He painted, in fresco, the roof of the Royal

that of the Escurial, and many others; but he spoke well who said that a fresco, when finished in distemper, was only a sketch. I myself in no wise approve of retouching;—let fresco be fresco, and let distemper be distemper. Besides, the colours which are used in retouching, are sometimes lighter and sometimes darker than the picture. But the writer who reproves this practice most severely, is Vasari, who says, "Those who paint on walls labour in a manly way in fresco, and do not retouch when dry in *secco*, which, besides being a very bad practice, renders the picture less durable."

I finish the chapter by observing, that the pencils must be of hog's bristles, wide and pointed, large or small, because the lime does not destroy them, and the brushes [a] are to be of the same kind, using sometimes common and small ones.

Among those who have painted in this manner, with great skill and approbation in our days, are Cesar Albasia, in the Treasury of Cordova, Mateo Perez de Alecio, Antonio Mohedano, and Alonzo Varquez, and in Castile, Bartolomeo Carducho and his brother,[b] and

Monastery of San Lorenzo, with such skill, that the naked figures which appear to support the roof seem (says Palomino) to be the work of Michael Angelo himself.

[a] The distinction between pencils and brushes is, that the pencils are fastened into quills and the brushes on sticks.

[b] Bartolommeo and Vincenzo Carducci were Italians who settled in Spain. The former studied under Zucchero, and was called into Spain in 1585, to assist in decorating the Escurial. He died in 1608. It is considered that of all the Italian painters Bartolommeo was the most useful to the progress of the fine arts in Spain, not on account of the splendour of his works, but rather for his superior method of instruction, for the wisdom of his maxims, and the good school which he formed, and which his brother Vincenzo continued and rendered illustrious.

Vincenzo accompanied his brother to Spain in 1585, and in 1606 assisted in executing the decorations of the Palace del Pardo, where he painted in fresco the cupola of the chapel.

In 1629, Vincenzo entered into a contract to paint in fresco the grand cloister of the Convent del Paular, by which he agreed to paint fifty-six pictures in four years, fourteen every year, for which he was to receive fifteen hundred ducats a-year. This singular contract was punctually fulfilled. Cean-Bermudez, who relates that he had passed a fortnight in this convent to examine at leisure the work of Vincenzo, affirms, that in this long and uniform series of pictures (representing the life of St. Bruno) in which monotony seemed inevitable, we admire on the contrary, great fertility of invention, an ingenious arrangement of the actions and groups, not less than the anatomical science and the harmony of the colours.

Peregrin, but our Luis de Vargas [a] of Seville is inferior to none in the management of his colours, as is evident in the Arch of the Treasury, the Tower, and *Cristo de gradas,* and we are all much indebted to him, he being the first who introduced fresco painting into Seville, and he painted the first fresco there in the year 1555. It is a picture of the Rosary, in shape a large oval, and is painted on a pillar of the Convent of St. Paul, but it was destroyed by attempting to repair it.

Vincenzo Carducho published in 1633 his "Dialogues on the Theory of Painting," which is considered the best Spanish work on the subject. He died in 1638.

[a] Luis de Vargas, the most ancient of the great painters of Andalusia, was born in 1502; he had the great honour of introducing in his own country the true method of painting in fresco and in oil. It was he who substituted the style of the *Renaissance* for the gothic style which then prevailed in Spain.

The great resemblance between his paintings and those of Perino del Vaga prove that he had chosen this pupil of Raffaello for his master. The fresco which Pacheco calls the "Cristo de gradas,"* was painted in 1563; it is on the steps of the church of San Pablo. Within the short space of thirty years after it was painted, that is, in 1594, the Portuguese painter Vasco Pereyra, who was settled at Seville, was entrusted by the Chapter, to repair this magnificent fresco. Palomino also mentions that this painting had suffered much from the effects of time. The cause of the rapid decay of these frescoes is not assigned by either Pacheco or Palomino. Viardot observes generally, "Unfortunately the greater part of his works were in fresco, and these are so much decayed by time and carelessness that scarcely a vestige remains of them." The last of these, which is nearly effaced, was finished in 1568. The pictures mentioned by Viardot and other writers, seem to have been chiefly external frescoes.

* Those who were condemned to do penance were accustomed to stop and pray before this picture, whence it acquired the popular name of "*Il Cristo de los Azotados,*"—the Christ of the whipped.

CHAPTER X.

OF PALOMINO.

Don Acisclo Antonio Palomino de Castro y Velasco was born in 1563. The numerous works, both in oil and fresco, left by this artist, may be placed in the first rank among those produced at this period of the decline of the art. The design of his pictures is correct, the colouring in harmony with the subject, the draperies appropriate, the arrangement of the composition relieves, as much as possible, the common and ignoble forms of the figures. His pictures shew traces of acquirements not immediately connected with the art; his painting is learned, as is that of all declining schools, while in schools that are beginning or rising into greatness, it appears more ignorant and artless. Palomino lived at a period, parallel to that of the commentators on literature, when much was written on art, although the exercise of it had ceased; when the theory was studied, while the practice was neglected; when it was known accurately why, and how, great masters were produced, but the secret of becoming such was lost. This was the case with Palomino; under the obscure and assuming title of "*Museo pictorico y escala optica,*" he published three large volumes in quarto, the two first of which contain instructions in painting, that is to say, the history, the practice, and rules, of the various parts of the art. The third part bearing the title of "*Parnaso Españole pintoresco laureado,*" contains the biography of the Spanish painters, commencing with the life of old Antonio del Rincon, who died in 1500, to his own friends and contemporaries.

When Luca Giordano, who was but an indifferent theologian, was ordered to paint the ceilings of the Escurial (soon after 1692) he found himself much at a loss to execute the subject which the monks desired, the king therefore desired Palomino to assist him with the designs. Palomino executed this delicate mission so well, that the delighted

Giordano, kissed the sketches, exclaiming "they are already painted."

Palomino published the last volume of his work in 1724, and died in 1726.—*Viardot, Notices, &c.*

DIRECTIONS AND OBSERVATIONS OF PALOMINO.

The practice of Fresco Painting.—The practice of fresco painting (observes Palomino), is not adapted for copyists, or timid painters, or irresolute persons, who necessarily avail themselves of the genius of others; for there must always be not only sketches or outlines of the same proportions as the place the painting is to occupy, but also particular studies, both of single figures, and historical groups, and the artist must have sufficient skill to prepare these for himself. By means of these sketches or outlines, the work is carried on with freedom, skill, and power, which this kind of painting requires, because much may be done in one day, and the work will have fewer retouchings and joinings, not to mention other advantages of greater importance, which increase the beauty of the picture.

Now fresco painting is, as I have observed [a] in the first volume,

[a] The following are the observations of Palomino here referred to:—"Finally, the marvellous operation of this kind of painting consists in the attractive virtue of the stucco, formed of lime and sand, which sucks in and drinks up with such seemingly insatiable ardor, and with such violence, the moisture put on with the colours, that it incorporates and unites with itself the said colours, which indeed are homogeneous, or similar to the natural state, since the mineral colours are of the nature of the sand; and the white which is used with them is of the same lime, although some add to it one-half or one-third of alabaster, or white marble, from which combination of the colours and the lime, results another species of stucco, so well united with the other Intonaco which is below it, by virtue of the moisture, that the two form one thing, as they are both inseparable from each other.

"This effect may be prevented from taking place by any one of the three following causes, viz. a very hard frost, an intense heat, or by the work being too long in hand. The hard frost closes the pores of the surface, so that its attractive power ceases, and the whole operation is as useless as if done with ashes; the intense heat dries the lime so rapidly, that it loses that vigor which it should have, and it ceases to possess its former power of combining with the colours; and if the work be too long in hand, the pellicle, or thin skin, which is seen on the top of the water, when the lime is agitated, forms on the surface of the wall, which, closing the pores of the surface, its attractive power ceases, and consequently its effect."

(Book I, chap. 6, s. 8) that kind of painting in which water alone is used, the adhesion of the colours to the wall being occasioned by the attractive power of the fresh stucco, with which the surface to be painted is covered. Hence it is evident, that the subject cannot be sketched on the surface, on which the painting is afterwards to be executed, because, previously to painting, it must be covered with the stucco. It is called fresco painting because the painting must be performed on it while the stucco is still damp; and for this reason, the stucco must not be spread over a larger portion of the surface than can be painted in one day, and this portion is called in Spanish TAREA, and in Italian GIORNATA, which means *a day's work*. Now as in this kind of painting, the first thing to be prepared is the stucco, I shall begin by describing the method of preparing it.

OF PREPARING THE STUCCO.—The stucco should be provided, if possible, four or six months before it is used, and where this is impossible, the architectural part of the picture, and the ornaments, if there be any, should be painted before the historical part and the figures. Now the stucco is made of lime, passed through a cane or open hair sieve, and of sand of good quality, and not argillaceous, which also is to be passed through a hair sieve, in doing which it must be blown with the mouth, otherwise the sieve will be choked up, and the sand will not pass through, and the same will happen in sifting the lime, although, by turning the sieve upside down and rapping it, the lime will fall out.

The proportions of lime and sand must be equal; these are the best proportions, as I have proved by experiments, particularly if the lime is not old enough to have been made mild by time; but if it has been rendered mild by time, the proportions should be three parts of lime and one of sand. It should be mixed with soft water in a very large jar or tub, where it can be beaten and stirred about conveniently; and should be kept well bathed and covered with water. And if the work be on a large scale, there should be two of these jars or tubs, so that when the lime in one is consumed, the other will be ready for use.

The mixture being made in this way, it must be stirred up every day, first taking off with a piece of tile, the skin or pellicle of nitre which will be formed round the edge of the water (it is for this reason that it should be kept covered with water), and when the day's work is finished, the lime should be again just covered with soft water, and so on every day, without suffering it to become too dry. By this means the lime will become so mild, and so purified from all causticity, that it may be used like lard without injuring the colours.

Preparation of the wall.—And although the painter may not be obliged to prepare the lime himself, yet he should know how to do it, that he may instruct the mason, who will be useful for this and other purposes, sometimes to the painters, and sometimes to the master of the work; because every person does not know the qualities or quantities of these things, and still fewer, the mode of preparing them. Before we treat of this latter operation, we must suppose the surface of the wall in a proper state to begin upon. And the first requisite is that it must be quite dry, and free from moisture, because if not, it will be afterwards liable to be spotted with the salt-petre which will appear on the wall when it dries.

The second requisite is that the wall be rough *(i. e. toothed)* but at the same time level; it should be rough, that the stucco may adhere firmly to it, and may not peel or scale off. The reason for its being even and level is, that the stucco may not crack; for as the surface of the plaster must be even in order that the part painted on may not appear out of drawing, if there be any hollows in it, and the stucco be laid on unequally thick, it will swell and crack, and even fall off where it is thickest.

The third requisite is, that the part of the wall which is to be painted the next day be well bathed with soft water the evening before, and the same must be done the next morning, before the stucco is spread, that it may be fresh and moist the whole day, especially in summer; for exactly as the moisture in the interior of the wall is injurious, so that which it receives on the exterior at the time of preparing is beneficial. And I must inform you, that if the wall has been long plastered and is smooth (unless it be of fine white plaster which must be roughened) it will be sufficient to prick the outline well, proceeding in other respects as above mentioned.

Of laying on the intonaco.—The wall being prepared in this manner, and the part over which the stucco is to be spread, (the *tarea i. e.* day's work) being marked out, the mason should take some of the stucco on a wooden trowel or float which he will hold in his left hand and from thence take it with a mason's trowel, such as is used in Valencia or Andalucia, and spread it very evenly on the wall, so that the intonaco (*tunica*) may be about the thickness of a dollar. When this is done and before it is too dry, it must be smoothed with the same trowel, and if the *tarea* be large it should not be spread over the whole at once, but only a piece at a time, and this is important in order that the work may be firm and free from cracks.

This being done, the mason should wash over the *intonaco* with a handful of flax tied up in a linen cloth, well moistened and wetted, for three good reasons; the first is, that it removes the extreme smoothness of the wall, which would prevent the colour from adhering; the second is, that it effaces the marks of the trowel; and the third is, that it disturbs the fine sand and opens the pores of the *intonaco*, after it has been smoothed, so that the colour takes better, incorporates with it more perfectly, and is more easy to work on. This being done, the mason will have done his part of the business.

After this, and without any delay, the *tarea* should be wiped gently with a silk handkerchief, so as to remove the particles of sand from the surface, taking care that they do not fall into the eyes at the time of painting, which frequently happens, particularly when painting a roof or vault, to the painter's great inconvenience; therefore, if on this account only, it would be well for him to wear spectacles.

On using the cartoons.—After this he should fix the cartoon, having first placed it properly, according to the directions already given, on distemper painting,[a] for it will be convenient that the

[a] The observations referred to are as follow:—" And whether the design be drawn on the cartoon or on the intended picture, it must first be drawn with crayons of charcoal, made of the wood of the willow, nut, osier, or pine. These are made by splitting the wood into pieces of the size of an iron tube, or a large cattle bell, (which should be had for this purpose) or at least of the size of the finger, and being tightly jammed into the tube by strokes of a hammer, they should be shut up air tight, then put into the fire, and left there until the tube is of a bright red colour, then taken out and put into cold ashes, covering it well with them, and covering the ashes with a large earthen pot; the whole is then to be left there till quite cold, because the charcoal will fill with air and break easily; then one of the pieces should be put into a piece of cane split into four parts, at the end which is to receive the piece of charcoal, and then tied round

whole cartoon should be fitted on to the wall, in order that the piece that is cut off, should correspond well with the edges and joinings of all the rest, for the right arrangement of the whole depends on the proper placing of this first piece.

This cartoon being fixed, drawn, and pricked in the manner referred to in treating of painting in distemper, and fastened to the wall with nails, it should be pounced with a bag of pulverized charcoal, and the edge where it is intended to be cut off, should also be rubbed with it, that it may serve as a mark where to cut off the *tarea*, and where to begin the next day.

This being done, the cartoon should be taken off, and the edge of the *tarea* where it has been marked with the bag of charcoal should be cut off with a knife or a pointed trowel, cutting it obliquely outwards, that it may not diminish the size of the *tarea*, nor occasion cracks within it, and for this purpose it should always be spread of the breadth of two fingers beyond where it is marked, and that which is beyond the marks, should not be cut off until the *tarea* is

at the part with a thread. It is then to be scraped to a point, and the outline to be drawn with it. When this is all done, the outlines should be fixed, by passing over them a pencil, filled with water colour, and if the drawing be made on the cartoon, the outline may then be pricked through with a large needle or something similar; after that, it should be placed in the site of the painting, and fixed there by means of nails, then it is to be pounced with a bag of ground charcoal, and, after that, outlined with water colour by means of a pencil.

"It will not be useless to describe here the mode of making the cartoons since every person does not know it. In the first place, the paper must be large, (either white or grey), that there may not be too many joinings; the flour paste should be well boiled, and the nails (or tacks) the size of No. 12, or those of Valladolid. This being prepared, if the surface is even, the cartoon is easily made, since the sheets of paper must be pasted together two and two or four and four, letting the edges overlap each other, about the width of the finger. The edges are then pasted with the brush, the cartoon is put in its place, and then the nails should be driven in, so that they will not get in the way afterwards by raising the edge.

"But if the surface be concave and not cylindrical, (for this is the same as a flat surface), it is more difficult, because each sheet has to be nailed in by itself, and even each half sheet, that it may be adjusted to the shape of the surface; and care should be taken in pasting the edges, not to paste the cartoon to the surface, nor should the paste touch the wall, because, besides fixing the cartoon to the wall so as to tear it in taking it off, it is so prejudicial to paste the wall, especially if it be damp, that, when it is moistened, stains appear, which are visible when the painting is finished."

finished in order to keep it moist to the very edges. Afterwards the outlines should be marked over with a pointed black crayon, not very sharp, and the straight lines should be ruled, and if there are any circular curves, they should be drawn with a compass, with a piece of black crayon fastened to one foot of it. This outline should be indented so deeply, that when the black mark is obliterated by the repetition of the tints, the indented line will serve as a guide in painting. Anciently, and even in my recollection, the cartoon was not pricked, but when it was nailed to the wall, the outlines were marked over with the stick of a paint brush cut to a blunt point, with sufficient pressure to indent the stucco; and this alone served for a mark, as may now be seen in the Palazzo del Pardo and other places, by a person who has eyes to see and fingers to feel, although I am far from saying that fresco paintings should be treated with disrespect; that is, they should not be handled. In this manner were done those excellent cartoons in black and white on grey paper, which were always used, and which, after having been used, were held in great estimation by painters, as those of Michael Angelo, Raffaelle, Annibale Caracci, and others, in Italy. But it was found that this tried the patience of the artist so much, that when he came to the execution of the work, he shrunk from such immense labour. More especially when the labour is considered useless, for we have merely to pounce the outline, and mark it with the powdered charcoal, which practice, and that of marking over the outlines with black crayon, has been found in our time much more convenient, easy, and expeditious; advantages not to be despised when they lead to greater perfection in the end, and do not tire the patience of the artist. A light and convenient palette has also been invented, composed of primed canvass, as we have mentioned in the chapter on distemper painting.

The outlines of the design having been completed in the way we have mentioned, the cartoon should be taken off gently, that the charcoal dust may not soil the colours which are to be laid on it, and after that the *tarea* (day's work) should be sprinkled with clean water from a large brush, which may be of *bruised sedge;* for which purpose the painter should have a jar full of clean water, and a brush, which is only fit for sprinkling, and with this the wall is to be sprinkled, and not rubbed, because rubbing would efface the outline while it is so fresh; and this will also be useful for sprinkling it from time to time during the painting, especially in summer. And there should be also another jar full of water, with a brush for moistening, and rubbing from time to time the part which has not been painted, that it may not dry. For after it has been left some time, a film or pellicle forms over the surface of the lime or stucco which fills up the pores, so that it does not absorb the colour which crumbles off like ashes; and the *tarea* should be wetted, although the stucco does not dry, for if it should dry before it is finished, it would be useless and must be cut out, and the stucco must be again spread and the subject drawn on it again; but the water in this second jar will not serve for sprinkling the part that is painted, because by rubbing the plaster with it, it takes up a little of the white, and if this were used for sprinkling, the picture would be spoiled.

This is the process, supposing it fine weather; for if it freezes, (which is the worst weather there can be for this kind of painting), the two vases of water should be put over the fire, that the water may be warm, and with that the surface may be sprinkled or bathed, in the before-mentioned manner; even the water that the mason uses should be warm. All this is necessary during a hard frost, for if the *intonaco* should freeze, it is the worst thing that can happen, as no absorption takes place, and the colours do not incorporate with the *intonaco*, but crumble off like ashes, as I know by experience; and if all these means should not suffice, the work must be left till the weather is milder.

Of the colours used.—Before we proceed further, the colours which are used in fresco painting may be briefly described. They are all mineral,[a] and some are calcined by means of fire. The mineral colours are, Light Ochre, Dark Ochre, Tierra Roxa, Albin, Pavonazo, Sombra de Venecia, Sombre del Viego, Tierra Verde, and Tierra Negra. Those made by means of fire, are Esmalte, Negro de Carbon, Burnt Ochre, Hornaza, Burnt Roman Vitriol, and Vermilion. The best kind of Vermilion is the mineral or native Vermilion, but in uncovered places, neither the mineral nor the artificial is good for

[a] Palomino means to say, that the colours consist of natural pigments only, but of these some merely require to be washed and ground, while others require to be calcined. All the nine pigments of the first class mentioned by the author contain more or less of *iron*, the other ingredients being silica, alumina, magnesia and manganese. These are the pigments, which, in all ages, from the Egyptians and Greeks, to the present time, have been found most permanent.

anything, because in a few days both kinds return to the same colour they had in their natural state, which is a most vile and dirty purple. Therefore, in such places, and in those which are exposed to the inclemency of the weather, Vermilion should not be used at all, either the natural or the artificial. But in covered places, and those defended from the inclemency of the weather, it is a most beautiful pigment, and keeps its colour very well, as I myself have repeatedly experienced. And that it may keep its colour better, it should not be laid on the stucco itself, but the Tierra Roxa should be used first, and over that the Vermilion; making the colour light with white, and darkening it with Albin and Pavonazo, and in some very dark places adding Sombre del Viejo, or Tierra Negra, and it will be as fresh and beautiful as in oil painting.

As to the Ochres, a person need not be afraid of using them; it is only necessary to remark, that ochre which is not mixed with white, darkens much in drying; although that kind which is called "*de Coleteros*,"[a] is more permanent and beautiful than that of Valencia; Tierra Roxa has also the same property of growing darker.

Albin and Pavonazo do not change colour, and they supply the place of carmine so well, that being used while the stucco is fresh, they have sometimes deceived people, who thought they were carmine. And I must tell you that Pavonazo is a degree lower in tone than Albin, and this is not sold in shops, but is obtained from the copper mines in the kingdom of Jaen; and there and in all Andalusia, the painters and gilders esteem it much, and it is even sold under the name of Almagre.

The Sombre de Venecia is not to be depended on, because it loses force, and gets much lighter coloured in drying, appearing, while the stucco is fresh a fine colour, but the artist must beware of it, as it is a deceitful pigment. Therefore, whoever likes may use it, but I consider it as banished from this kind of painting, and in its place, I use the Sombre del Viejo, which is a most beautiful colour, and proper for all things, and as we possess this we shall not miss the other.

The Tierra Verde which is also called Verde de Verona, is of an excellent colour, and if it did not lose its force so much in drying, would be invaluable. However, if used while the stucco is very fresh it keeps its colour better. And it should always be used for green

[a] *Coleteros*—Those who made buff coats.

drapery, mixed with Verde Montaña and a very little ochre, because, as the latter darkens and the former becomes lighter coloured in drying, it will be exactly the same colour as before, when dry. The Verde Montaña cannot be used by itself in fresco, therefore I have not placed it among the colours used in fresco-painting, because, either it does not adhere to the lime, or if it does adhere it burns;[a] however, the first defect may be remedied by using it with milk; but when mixed with Tierra Verde, it keeps its colour well, and is very beautiful, especially if it is of that kind which is brought from Venice in pastilles, when it is called by some Verde Granilla, which is much better than what is sold here in powder. Hornaza mixed with white may also be used for the lights in the green. And for the shadows in covered places, the Tierra Verde may be darkened with indigo and a little ochre or Sombra del Viejo. And if the situation be exposed to the air, it should be darkened with Negro de Carbon, or Sombra del Viejo, or Tierra Negra, which last is a most beautiful colour in every respect, especially if it be that which comes from Venice, and which we get in pellets.

The blue is the Scylla of this kind of painting; but fortune has not given us our choice in this matter, obliging us to use Esmalte, which is in substance ground glass. This pigment may either be used by itself, or mixed with white, and if applied on the wet stucco, it adheres very well when used with lime-water. But if the painting is to be in an uncovered place, I do not think this a secure method of applying the colour, therefore it should be used with goat's milk; and for the dark parts, for which the Esmalte alone would not be sufficient, Negro de Carbon may be used, and it may be finished with Tierra Negra. In covered situations, indigo may be used for the dark parts, but this colour should never be applied on the lime itself, as it perishes; and this is the reason why I have not classed it among the colours used in fresco painting, because it is an intruder. I know by experience, that either pure Esmalte, or Esmalte mixed with indigo, with a little Tierra Verde, or of a blue stone which is called Ignoto,[b] adheres wonderfully well without milk. And in this manner may be made purple colours, mixing with the Esmalte instead of carmine, Albin and Pavonazo in proper proportions; milk should be

[a] "Or destroys;" the expression is used to denote the effect of the sun or frost on flowers.

[b] This word means *unknown*. See Treatise on Colours—Blue pigments.

added to this also, to make it adhere firmly, especially in an exposed situation.

Of black pigments.—With respect to a black colour, that made of burnt oak wood (the bark having been previously taken off) well ground, is excellent if used while the stucco is wet, that it may hold firmly, for the Tierra Negra when mixed with the white of the lime is very grey, but the latter is better than the former for finishing the dark parts.

Of white pigments.—We have now to speak of the white pigment which is used in fresco painting. This is made of the same lime as the stucco, but without sand, for which purpose the whitest quick lime in lumps is chosen; this is slaked in a jar, (which in Castile is called *baño*), pouring water on it from time to time, until it has lost all its causticity, stirring it well until it is thoroughly soaked and covered with soft water. And this must be managed in the same way as the stucco, taking off the pellicle on the surface every day, and this being done, soft water should again be poured over the lime in great abundance, and it should be again well beaten up, and so on every day for four months, if possible; and as the length of time occupied in preparing this pigment is a great inconvenience, it will be proper for those who are accustomed to this kind of work, or even those who are not, to make it in large quantities; and after it has been well purified, it may be kept either in pellets, or in a large jar, leaving it to dry.

But before removing the water, the whole should be strained through a close horse hair sieve, resting the sieve on two sticks laid across the jar into which it is to be strained, and stirring about the thick liquid which is put into the sieve with a brush, that the fine parts may pass through, and tapping it on the outside from time to time, that the thick part which remains in the sieve may subside. And after it has been all strained in this manner, it will be like milk; it should then be left to settle, then the lime water should be poured off; preserving, however, enough for use, if you require it for any purpose, and pour it off gently, that it may not mix with the lime.

But when it is required for use, the lime settled at the bottom of the jar should be taken out with a large wooden spoon, aud then the tints for the buildings, and other general tints, may be made of it in the same manner as the tints are made for painting in distemper, only with this difference, that the white, instead of being gypsum, should be of lime. For crimson, Albin or Pabonazo must be employed, and to use these tints properly, it is not necessary to take them out with a spoon, but the colour in the vase should be previously stirred with a brush, and while it is thus liquid, it should be put into the vase, which is to be held in the hands, for this kind of painting is all done by means of water.

We have now to speak of the white paint for the palette, which may be a portion of the same lime, if it be mild, straining it again through a very close silk sieve, for which purpose it must be diluted with much water, otherwise it will not pass through, and even then it will be necessary to stir it with a brush, and then to remove the refuse from the sieve from time to time. The lime being suffered to settle, there will be found in the bottom of the jar a white coagulum, which is to be used for the palette, taking it out with a spoon which is to be kept for this purpose only.

But if the Blanco de cal (lime white) is of that kind which has been kept in pellets, or dried in a jar, in the manner we have previously mentioned, it will be necessary to break it up, and to put water to it, and after it is well moistened, to grind it again on the stone with the muller.

And if the Blanco de cal cannot be prepared in this way, on account of the length of time occupied in its preparation, it will be necessary to procure some pieces of the purest white marble, and break and grind them in an iron mortar. The powder is then to be sifted ; and after this it should, if possible, be ground in a small mill, which some, and myself among the number, keep for this purpose, as well as for grinding other colours in large quantities for these works, which is a very convenient practice. Some of this powder should be mixed with the lime-white, (blanco de cal) in the proportions of at least one part to three or four of the blanco de cal, and this is very suitable for flesh colours, draperies, flowers, and the most delicate things. And indeed, wherever this can be obtained it should be used, as it is of great importance, even if the lime be purified, although in this case, only one fourth, or even less, of the powdered marble should be used.

Luca Giordano used this white pigment in whatever he painted, and he assured me that it is employed in the same manner throughout Italy. I must also inform you that, for want of marble, you may use alabaster, which gives a great firmness to the white, because, from the lime and marble is formed a kind of stucco, such as is used by modellers in plaster, who with this imitate statues of marble, and other things, which deceive people by their touch, their lustre, their coldness, and their hardness.

Of using the palette, brushes, &c.—These things being prepared, the colours being ground, and each put into its proper vase or saucer, with a spoon for each, in the manner described in the chapter on distemper painting, and supposing the palette unnecessary for general tints, which are prepared in the same way as those used in distemper painting, we are now going to treat of the use of the palette, which may consist of a piece of canvass of the length of a "*vara*,"[a] or at least three-fourths of a *vara*, because there will then be room to mix the tints with the brush, without their running one into another, and a sufficient quantity of each colour should be put on the palette at once, in fact more than is required, that the colour may not dry too soon, and it should even be sprinkled with water from time to time. For cleaning the palette when necessary, the painter should have a sponge as large as his fist, with which, being moistened, the palette should be thoroughly cleaned, and the dirty water should be suffered to run into a large glazed jar full of water, which is held in the hand, and which serves for this purpose, as well as for washing the pencils when the colour is to be changed. There should also be another jar of clean water to dip the pencil in, in order to moisten and dilute the colours and the tints which are made, although this may be dispensed with, by not dipping the pencil to the bottom of the other jar, where all the colours washed off the palette or out of the brushes settle. Thus provided, and with a good stock of large brushes and pencils of the same hair,[b] (which are the only kind of brushes that can be used in fresco painting, because the lime burns all others, except those made of the hair of young hogs, which are useful for some small delicate purposes), the painter may begin to paint, putting in first the back ground or skies, which are behind the figures, and he must always observe this order, beginning with the more distant objects and approaching gradually until at length he reaches the figure or figures in the foreground. For the contrary practice would cost him immense labour, from his having to

[a] A *Vara* is about three feet English.

[b] That is, of hogs' hair. See Palomino, vol. II, p. 42.

observe all the outlines, nor would the aerial perspective be well kept, nor the outlines properly preserved.

I should also inform the fresco painter, that he should not paint all the *tarea* at once, but only what he can complete at one sitting quickly, for having once began to paint any part it must not be left until it is quite finished, because, if it dries, the subsequent paintings will not unite well with, or match the first, except a few fine dark touches (or hatchings), in some parts. But if the work is commenced late in the day, and the weather is dry, it should be sprinkled from time to time with a brush dipped in clean water, and the surface of the stucco should be moistened by rubbing with the other brush; and indeed in dry and hot weather, it will be well for the painter, who begins his work late, before he commences, to wash it with the before mentioned handful of flax, tied up in a linen cloth, (which should be well moistened) and with some of the same stucco, by which means the sand is disturbed, and the pores of that which is already spread are opened. If, in doing this, the outlines of the drawing are very much disturbed, they must be marked over again; and the same may be done in winter, especially if the weather be damp, in order to finish it the next day, if anything remains to be done.

Of laying on the flesh colour.—As to the flesh, after it is outlined with Tierra Roxa or Pabonazo and ochre, the painter should put over it a general middle tint of flesh colour, which must be afterwards lowered in the shadowed parts, using for this purpose a tint made of Esmalte and Tierra Verde, adding ochre and white and red, according to the colour required. Very good tints for the shadows can be made also with Tierra Roxa and green, finishing them with Sombra and Albin, and if the shadows require greater depth with Tierra Negra and Pabonazo. And I must inform you that if the painting is not left to repose, the tints may be united as in oil painting, when the colour is discharged from the brush or pencil. And even without washing the brush, it may be moistened with water and shaken, and the tints may be united and softened very well with it. It will be better to do this with a small and very soft brush. But the painter will adapt the size of the brushes to the proportions of the pictures and the size of the figures, and in this manner will be formed a perfect style with an impasto equal to that in oil painting, without that excessive labour which prevailed in the ancient manner, where every part was hatched like a miniature.

And here I may mention that after having laid on the first colouring of the flesh, which afterwards serves as a sketch, Hornaza may be used, mixing it with white and red, and even with Tierra Verde and vermilion for the reflections of some shadows, and it is a most soft and sweet colour, and is excellent for giving the flesh a good tint; but it should not be used on the bare stucco, but over another colour, to beautify the tints, and should never be exposed to the inclemency of the weather; and it is to be used in the same manner in painting light yellow draperies, which are to be laid on a ground of ochre and white. The Vetriolo-quemado is also very good for darkening some of the carnations and red draperies; but it is not one of the most essential colours, since we possess burnt ochre and the other reds.

Of retouching.—We have now only to speak of retouching fresco paintings when necessary; because, truly it will be all the better if it be not necessary. This is done, especially if it be in an exposed situation, with the same colours which are used in fresco painting, mixed with goat's milk, although in case of necessity, these may be used diluted with water, and in this manner all that requires it, may be retouched, especially the joinings of the *tareas*. The blues (*esmalte*) should be painted over entirely in secco, unless they have been already done in fresco. And in covered situations even the Azul verde and Azul fino which is called *de Santo Domingo* may be used, but never in fresco, which destroys them. Nor can ultramarine be used in fresco, because the lime causes it to become pale, so that there is no distinguishing the light parts from the dark, therefore in a covered situation, after having laid the Esmalte on the fresco, ultramarine may be laid over it with goat's milk, not using the Blanco de cal, but a mixture of white lead and talc white[a] in equal quantities, ground together; and the white will be much better if made of egg shells alone, well ground up; but I must tell you that it cannot be used with gum or glue, because the lime weakens them both. I have heard that Jordan[b] used a tempera of

[a] Blanco de Espejuelo—A sort of mixture in fine mortar, that glitters on the walls when the sun shines on it.—*Pineda's Dictionary*.

[b] Luca Giordano; born at Naples in 1632. He applied himself to painting almost from infancy, and from constant practice acquired such rapidity and facility of execution, that he retained through life the soubriquet of "*Luca fa presto*," which had been given him by his companions when a child. Palomino says he did as much in a day as others do in a week. He painted in fresco at

egg to retouch some places where the salt-petre had appeared; but I have not tried this, although I should think it good if no milk could be obtained.

I must not omit informing you that the ancients gave the intonaco a couch of a general tint of white and Tierra Roxa before beginning to paint, that the surface might be smooth and polished; and even after having finished their painting with that labour which may be seen in the minute feathered style of their paintings, they placed upon it a large sheet of paper, and over that they polished the fresco, until it was smooth and even. Although this appears needless and useless, and may easily be dispensed with, I do not consider it a bad plan, to please the vulgar with this appearance of finish, since the painter should endeavour to adapt his picture to all classes of spectators. For as the Apostle says, "I am a debtor to the wise and to the ignorant." And all should be paid in their own coin. It is for this reason that I said fresco paintings were to be treated with care, and placed at such a distance that they can only be enjoyed by the sight without being profaned by the touch.

Of foreshortening, &c.—It will not be a digression if I now point out to the reader the difference between historical paintings on ceilings, and those which are painted parallel to our sight, or perpendicular to the horizon; although if the first mentioned historical

Rome, with Pietro da Cortona. He went to Spain in 1692, where he painted a great number of pictures both in fresco and oil. He began and finished all the frescoes in the Escurial in two years. Bermudez gives a list of 196 pictures by him, dispersed among the churches and palaces of Spain. He repaired, and almost repainted, the frescoes by Rizi and Carreño in the church of San Antonio de los Portugeses which had suffered much from damp. His fertility of invention was so inexhaustible and his facility of execution so prodigious that he would begin and finish a picture in a day, and counted his paintings by hundreds.

He was the last of that magnificent generation of painters who had followed the masters of Raffaello in Italy and his disciples in Spain. He had a multitude of pupils who could not imitate him in his perilous course: all remained behind, and the most celebrated among them did not rise above mediocrity, and were but the imitators of the imitator. Luca Giordano had destroyed at the impulse, as it were, of a fatal facility of invention and of hand, the last entrenchments of art; he left but a chaos behind him, and his name will remain as the solemn demonstration of this truth, that, besides natural talents, two qualities of the head and heart are necessary for an artist, reflection and dignity.—*Viardot, Notices, &c.*

paintings are executed in compartments with their frames or mouldings either real or counterfeit, they may be conducted in the usual manner. But if they are to be painted on concave surfaces, in ovals, in which we will suppose the story or event is actually to be painted, and not to be merely placed there after having been painted in another place, it is necessary that the figures should be foreshortened, as if they were seen from the feet upwards; although the point of sight should be in the centre of the picture, that the foreshortening may not appear too violent. For this purpose it is necessary to imagine that the scenes represented in these pictures take place in the air, and sometimes even on the clouds, for as we look at them from below, if they were represented on a regular pavement, the pavement would conceal them from our view, unless the figures were placed on the very edge, as for instance on steps. In doing which, it will be necessary particularly to attend to the perspective. We may add, that the model or figure, to be copied, being put on the table, the painter, standing either in the middle, or on one side of it, or above or below, as required, should copy it exactly as it appears to him: then, the drawing being raised in the air, above the eye, it will appear as if the person who drew it had looked at it while raised in the air. I should not omit to add that these paintings on vaults or ceilings should be looked upon with some allowance, for the artist cannot always produce the effect he wishes, on account of the great labour and inconvenience with which they are executed; and sometimes they cannot be seen from a sufficient distance on account of the smallness of the scaffold; and if any one asserts the contrary, it must be because he has not found himself in this predicament; and let the painter be very careful not to paint from the top towards the bottom, that which is to be viewed from the bottom towards the top, especially in concave places, or he will find himself deceived.

Of sketches for a cupola.—It is proper to mention another thing, which perhaps those who are accustomed to these works will deem important, which is, the mode of making the sketches for a cupola, if they cannot be made on a concave surface, which they should be when possible. It is as follows: considering the length of the circumference as equal to three times the diameter and one seventh part more, that is, that the proportion of the diameter to the circumference is as seven to twenty-two. Having ascertained this, we may draw this line on a piece of flat canvass, or paper, of sufficient size, and give it a height, in the middle, of one-fourth of the circumference of the circle whose diameter is equal to the aforesaid line, and from the extremities of this line to the above mentioned height, draw a curved line in the form of a portion of a circle; and in the space contained by these two curved lines, draw your sketch, which will prove admirably adapted for the situation, considering the highest part of the said figure (which is the middle), to be the top of the cupola.

Of constructing scaffolds.—It is also proper to speak of the way of constructing scaffolds, so as to admit the light. They should be made smaller than the cornice of the astragal of the cupola, by at least half a vara, and the same distance from the projection of the cornice. In the middle, should be left an aperture or vacancy of a proper size upon which should be raised another fixed scaffold, leaving the space of seven feet only between its surface and the centre of the cupola.

There should also be a ladder of the same height as this scaffold, which should be movable, and capable of being turned all round it, and, if desirable, some planks may be laid across, from the scaffold to the ladder, for which purpose it must be of the same height as the second scaffolding, and this is used for the concave part of the cupola. Scaffolds for painting arched roofs are made in the same way, except that in the middle, there should be a portable scaffold on trestles.

CHAPTER XI.

DIRECTIONS OF JOHN MARTIN.

THE following extract is taken from a manuscript in Sir John Soane's Museum, which was purchased at the sale of J. Jackson, Esq., R.A., in 1831. It was written by John Martin, and is dated 1699. The original spelling is retained.

FRESCOE, OR PAINTING ON WALLS.—I.—In painting on walls, to make it endure the weather, you must grind your colours with lime water, milk, or whey, mixed in size colour-pots. II.—Then paste or plaister must be made of well-washed lime, mixt with powder of old rubbish stones :[a] the lime must be often washed till fine all its salt is abstracted; and all your work must be done in clear and dry weather. III.—To make the work endure strike into the wall stumps of headed nails, about five or six inches asunder, and by this means you may preserve the plaister from peeling. IV.—Then, with the paste, plaister the wall a pretty thickness, letting it dry (but scratch the first coat with the point of your trowell) longways, and crossways as soon as you have done laying on what plaister or paste you think fit, that the next plaistering you lay upon it may take good key and not come off, nor part from the first coat or plastering, and when the first coate is dry, plaister it over again with the thickness of half a barley corn, very fine and smooth, then your colours being already prepared, work this last plaistering over with the said colours in what draught[b] or de—you please, (History, &c.)

[a] It will be observed that the author recommends " powder of old rubbish-stones" and " ox-hairs" to be mixed with the lime for the *arricciato*. As this was not the practice of the Italian or Spanish schools, or at least as it is mentioned by none of the writers on fresco painting whose works are here translated, it seems probable that the art of fresco painting was still occasionally practised in England by artists unacquainted with the practice of the foreign schools.

[b] So in the original manuscript.

so will your painting write and joyn fast to the plaister, and dry together as a perfect compost. Note, your first coate of plaister or paste must be very hair'd with ox-hair in it, or else your work will crack quite through the second coate of plaistering; and will spoil all your painting that you paint upon the second coate of plaistering; but in the second coate that is laid on of paste, or plaister, there must be no hair in it at all, but made thus,—mix or temper up with well-washed lime, fine powder of old rubbish stones (called finishing stuff) and sharp grit sand, as much as you shall have occasion for, to plaister over your first coat, and plaister it all very smooth and even, that no roughness, hills, nor dales be seen, nor scratches of your trowell. The best way is to float the second coat of plaistering thus, after you have laid it all over the first coat with your trowell as even and smooth as possibly you can. Then take a float made of wood very smooth, about one foot long and seven or eight inches wide, with a handle on the upper side of it to put your hand into, to float your work withall, and this will make your plaistering to lye very even, and lastly with your trowell you may make the said plaistering as smooth as may be. V.—In painting be nimble and free, let your work be bold and strong, but be sure to be exact, for there is no alteration after the first painting, and therefore heighten your paint enough at first, you may deepen at pleasure. VI.—All earthly colours are best, as the Okers, Spanish-white, Spanish-brown, Terra-vert, and the like; mineral colours are naught. VII.—Lastly, let your pencils and brushes be long and soft, otherwise your work will not be smooth, let your colours be full, and flow freely from the pencil or brush; and let your design be perfect at first, for in this, there is no after alteration to be made.

THE ART

OF

FRESCO PAINTING.

PART II.

EXTRACTS

FROM VARIOUS AUTHORS

ILLUSTRATIVE OF THE PRACTICE

OF

FRESCO PAINTING.

PART II.

PRACTICE OF THE EARLY ITALIAN SCHOOL.

THE ancient pictures called *frescoes*, in the Campo Santo at Pisa, are painted on the wall on an intonaco of lime and very fine sand, in that manner which is called " fresco." It appears, at least as far as we can judge, that here (in Pisa) the intonaco was not laid on in such quantities only, as could be painted in one day, which is called " true fresco," and which is very durable and firm. Our old artists in fact were acquainted with no other modes of painting, than the fresco much used by the ancients, and that of using wax dissolved in essential oil. The other mode, of mixing the colours with tempera on canvass, primed with gesso, and stretched upon hard boards, continued until the time of the celebrated Fleming, John Van Eyck, called Giovanni di Bruges, about the year 1410.—II. *Pisa, Illust. by Morrona, p.* 192.

" It will be proper to repeat here the observations on the manner of painting on walls in fresco, adopted by the artists of these times (about 1485), suggested by the examination of pieces of the *intonaco* which had fallen from the wall. It is astonishing that they should have sketched the the subject with a pencil dipped in red, on the wall covered with the *arricciato,* and that they should afterwards have covered their work over with the *intonaco.* The reason given for this by Vasari is not satisfactory ; he says, that this method was the cartoon used by the old masters for painting in fresco with greater expedition, &c. We shall see now whether I can more nearly assign the true cause of this proceeding.—

" I observe in the first place, that they drew the subject on a large scale on the wall, enlarging from the small design on which they had embodied their ideas, and that they sketched in this manner the whole composition of the picture, in order to see the effect of the proportions when enlarged, and to correct the errors. Then it is probable that they traced the outlines, drawn with red, on to paper, which formed the cartoon mentioned by Vasari. This then being applied upon the intonaco composed of lime and fine sand, and on the levigated and smooth surface, corresponds with the drawing beneath ; and if this be not the case in every part, it probably arose from some variation made by the painters, on the cartoons, or on the wall itself."—*II. Pisa, Illust.* 224, *Cennino c.* 67, *and see II. Rep.* 24, 25.

" Simon Memmi had also begun in the middle of the façade of the great refectory of the convent, many small historical pictures, and also a crucifixion in the form of a cross, which remained imperfect, being merely drawn as may be seen even now, with pencil dipped in *rosaccio* upon the *arricciato ;* this mode of painting served instead of a cartoon to some of our old masters, in order to enable them to paint with more expedition, because, having marked out all their work upon the arricciato, they drew it with a pencil, copying from a small design all that they intended to paint, and enlarging it in the proportion required for the picture. There are also many pictures in other places drawn in the same manner as this picture, and many others that have been painted, from which the painting has scaled off, leaving the design in rosaccio still visible."—*Vasari, Vol. II. p.* 177, *and see Lanzi, Vol. I. p.* 31.

The following extract shews a curious contrivance for preserving painted ceilings from being injured by damp : " Earthen vases are placed under the roofs of the churches of S. Erculino and S. Martino, in Milan, in order to preserve the ceiling from being injured by damp." Morelli, Notizie d'opere di disegno. p. 41. " In the

Archiepiscopal Court (Milan), and in St. Zuan de Conca (Milan), the ancient pictures in fresco, which to this day shine like looking glasses, were by the hands of old masters." "The pictures in the Castle (Pavia), in fresco, were by the hand of Pisano, they are so smooth and shining, that, as Cesarino writes, you may see your face in them." [a]—*Id.*43, 46.

Preparation of cartoons.—The following extracts show the importance attached by painters to the careful preparation of cartoons.

" It is said, that, on Perino del Vaga's arrival at Genoa, Girolamo da Trevisi, who was painting one face of it (the D'oria Palace), which fronted the garden, had arrived there before him in order to paint certain things; and while Perino began to make the cartoon for the historical picture of the shipwreck, and while he was enjoying himself very leisurely, and seeing all that was worth seeing at Genoa, he continued preparing the cartoon more or less industriously, so that a great part of it was already finished and the naked figures drawn, some in chiaro-scuro, others with charcoal and *lapis nero*, others only hatched and outlined; while, I say, Perino was going on in this way, not even beginning his picture, Girolamo da Trevisi was murmuring against him, saying, " What is all this about the

[a] The words of Cesariano, (Commentary on Vitruvius, p. 115) when treating of painting in fresco, are these, "While it is yet fresh we can, as Vitruvius says, dispose this composition of lime to receive splendor and brilliancy; like the old pictures in the Archiepiscopal Curia, in Sancto Joanne in Concha, in Milan, also in Pavia, and especially in this Castile, where the noble Pisano painted, and also in Placentia, in paintings by Antonio del Carro."

Morelli supposes this Pisano was Vittore Pisano Veronese, otherwise called Pisanello, who painted in many cities in Italy, at the end of the fourteenth century. These pictures in the castle of Pavia are mentioned in the following terms, in the history of that city by Breventano, written in 1570; " The halls and chambers, as well above as below, are all vaulted, and almost all painted with various fine historical and other paintings; the sky or roof is coloured with very fine azure, in which seem to move a variety of animals in gold, such as lions, leopards, tigers, hounds, stags, wild boars, and others, especially in that part which faces the Parco, (which, as we have said, was ruined by the artillery of Francis, on the 4th of September, 1527), in which was seen a large saloon sixty braccia long and twenty wide, covered with beautiful historical paintings which were perfect in my days, and which represented hunting and fishing, and tilting parties, with various sports of the dukes and duchesses of this state." Morelli, Notizie, p. 180. These extracts should be compared with the observations of Guevara and Alberti relative to the shining surfaces of ancient pictures.

cartoons; I, for my part, have the whole art at the point of my paint brush." And as he frequently grumbled in this manner, it came to the ears of Perino, who, being angry about it, immediately caused his cartoon to be fixed up in the ceiling, where the picture was to be painted; and having, in many places, removed the planks of the scaffolding, in order that it might be seen from below, he opened the room to the public; when this was known every one in Genoa went to see it, and being astonished at the excellent design of Perino, he acquired immortal celebrity. Girolamo da Trevisi went there among others, and when he saw the work of Perino, which so much exceeded his expectations, being alarmed at the effects its beauty might have on his own reputation, he left Genoa, without asking leave of the Prince D'oria, and returned to Bologna, where he lived. So Perino alone remained with the Prince, and finished this room, painting in oil upon the wall. It is considered, as it ought to be, a work quite unique for its beauty, there being, as I have said, in the middle of the ceiling, and even under the *lunettes*, most beautiful stuccoes."—*Vasari, Life of Perino del Vaga.*

" You ask whence it is, that a painter, who has several manners, in a sketch sometimes observes one manner, and sometimes uses several; although afterwards, in finishing the picture he adopts one only. I answer, that this happens according to the degree of enthusiasm with which the painter applies himself to the sketch. When the conception of the work, which is to be executed in this or that manner, is already formed in the mind; if then the painter springs impatiently to his sketch, to finish it at once, it becomes more uniform in that one manner, in which he intends to paint his picture, in perfect concordance with that genius, which at first caused him to conceive and compose it. For example; Correggio thought of representing the nativity of our Lord in that sacred night scene,[a] and setting about it, with that spirited and effective vigour which characterised him, composing the embryo all at once, in the first sketch, he left the whole finished in that one manner and that one tone of colouring, which he had determined on, for painting the entire picture. In this manner is made that real and incontestibly original sketch, in the hands of that good painter and *dilettante*, Signor

[a] This picture is now in the Gallery at Dresden, and is engraved in the second volume of the pictures of that Gallery. It has been varnished, with more harm than advantage to the Painting.

Giuseppe Ghezzi; which throws doubts on the authenticity of another small one, which, at Reggio di Modena, was shown, as a great favour, by torch light, to Signor Passeri, and to myself; particularly as the style of this, is very inferior to that of the large picture, although the figures are exactly the same; while in that belonging to Sig. Ghezzi, the figures are in somewhat different attitudes, but the style is in exact conformity with that of Correggio in the large picture. He adopted the same method in the first sketch on canvass, of the height of four palms, of the Assumption in the Duomo di Parma. He conceived a splendid apparition of heavenly glory, by which the Blessed Virgin might ascend to heaven, and as if too impatient to take the trouble of drawing his design with the *matita,* he sketched that Assumption with oil colours, with the tone and style of colouring which he intended to use in his picture; although he afterwards completed the design for this principal group of the Assumption, as far as related to the design, with separate studies drawn with pencil (matita). I have three of these originals with the Madonna herself surrounded with a crowd of angels, and have caused them to be engraved, as well as other parts of the same cupola."—*Lett. Pitt. Vol.* 3. *p.* 327, 330. *Sebastiano Resta to N. N.*

" The only difficulty he (Annibale Carracci) ever had was sometimes in kneeling attitudes, which embarrassed him, and which he designed ungracefully; this they say was the case with the San Giacinto in the Church of S. Domenico; and also with the Angel in the picture of the Annunciation to the Blessed Virgin in S. Pietro, who looks very uncomfortable, for Annibale did not bestow proper care in the arrangement of his cartoon (if indeed he did so at all), and in giving it exactness by means of the *Graticola.*[a] Not so with Agostino who they say was even more correct than Annibale; it being his practice never to regard trouble, but only to give himself satisfaction. I find that it was his custom, to overcome all the difficulties at first by making separate sketches of each part, and each object that was to enter into the picture, until he had cleared every doubt, and overcome all impediments, that then putting the whole together he formed a very complete and perfect design (which

[a] Namely—proportional squares, or *rete.*

was sometimes painted in oil, with white lead for the lights) from which he did not depart in the slightest degree, in the execution of his picture; and he painted in this manner rapidly, without hesitation, and with great tranquillity, which may be clearly seen in his picture of the Nativity, in the picture of the Children in St Bartholomew, in that of the Flight at Sampieri, and in many others. And this is the true method, although idle persons may say that making so many designs is a tedious operation which fatigues the mind, and causes weakness in the execution of the picture, and that it is an unnecessary labour which is quite thrown away, and that it is better to make the design on the picture itself. I have never seen any picture of Annibale, or even of Ludovico, without having had it in my power to see the designs, either before or after having seen the picture, and they were as elaborate and highly finished, as I said those of Agostino were. This may be easily observed in the famous collections of their most serene Highnesses of Tuscany and Modena; at Rome, in the collection of the learned Bellori; at Bologna, in the collections of the Buonfigliuoli, Pasinelli, Negri, Polazzi, and in my own collection."—*Malv. Fels. Pitt. Vol. I. p.* 484.

The following anecdote shews that large paintings were sometimes successfully executed in fresco without cartoons.

"But those who were not acquainted with his (Cæsare Baglioni) witty and facetious character would have been very likely to have thought him silly, and this actually happened to him the first time that he was called to Parma, to paint some of the rooms of the ducal palace there, when he was observed by the other painters to pass his time as joyfully, and to think no more about the work, than if it had been play, while they were working so hard at theirs. They, as they ought to do, made many sketches, and forming from them a perfect design, prepared from it a cartoon. They then set the cartoon against the place the picture was to occupy, and observing whether it suited, they corrected and adjusted it; while he, laughing and sneering at these preparations of theirs, which he called impediments and annoyances, after playing his flute, boasted that he would begin to scratch the lime at once with a nail without so many sketches and drawings. And it being therefore believed, and told to the Duke, that he was no less silly than rash, the Duke sent for him, and asked him what his intentions were, and whether he chose to paint his two rooms or not. He replied that he had come there for no other purpose than to obey his Highness, and as his Highness seemed to shew a desire to be served quicker than he expected, or than there was any need of, he would satisfy him by shewing him the next day one entire wall painted over; when the painters said this was impossible, he replied that if he did not do it, they might drive him out of the court as a cheat and a scoundrel. So Baglione having sent quickly for a plasterer, and ordered him to plaster the wall, painted it in the following manner. He colored in grey a broad and plain margin all round the wall, and had the rest white-washed, and then painted a curtain, to cover up the empty space, with all its folds, shades, and creases, like one of those curtains which cover up the stage in a theatre until the time for reciting the play; then in one of the upper corners, he painted the head and hands of a labourer, who seemed to be fastening from the inside the said curtain to a large nail. When therefore the Duke and the other painters, being impatient to see what he had done in so short a time, came into the room, they were quite astonished at finding that they had been laughed at; but on the other hand they were surprised at the head and hands which were so well painted, that they proved him to be an excellent painter, whilst these persons, full of astonishment, did not know what to think or say, unless that he was making fun of them, which indeed the Duke seemed to hint. He told his Highness not to doubt but that in proper time the curtain would be let down and all that was under it would be shewn, which, with the whole work, would be completed to his Highness's satisfaction, and that he had played this trick to laugh at those other painters, who were so long about their work, and who completely puzzled themselves with it, which was a manifest sign that nature had not intended them for that art, and that therefore the more they labored at it, the less skill they would have in it; that painting in fresco demanded quickness and freedom of hand, without which it was no use attempting it. And he gave such good reasons for this, that he satisfied his Highness, who could not help praising Baglione for the jocose, and at the same time wise manner, which he had adopted for preserving his freedom of hand and practice, which he knew to be the most valuable part of his art. Baglione afterwards finished that room in eight days. He soon after finished the next room, and acquitted himself so well, and gave so much pleasure not only by his good painting, but also by his good humour and joviality, that his Highness retained him in his service, with a salary of ten *scudi corti* of that coinage per month, and his board, and appointed him his painter."—*Malvasia. Felsina Pittrice, vol. I. p.* 340, 341.

But if such instances are rare, it is still rarer to find painters who painted the pictures first and drew the cartoons afterwards, yet that this was the case we find from the following anecdote of Lorenzo Garbieri.

" He, (Lorenzo Garbieri) was of a rather warm temperament, and sometimes too much so, and was therefore quick in invention, and quicker still in execution; he had not the patience to make sketches or designs which are extremely rare, by his hand; but when he was obliged to make some for any one, whom he could not refuse, he generally copied them from the picture, which he had previously painted and finished, and these he shaded and finished highly, laying gold and silver on the lights, in the same manner as those which he sent to Rome, as a present to his friend the Cardinal Giustiniani, as he had already done with those which he had painted in the Capella di S. Carlo, Bologna, in order to gain the Cardinal's friendship. He therefore desired with great, though reasonable earnestness, however distant the opportunity might seem, to execute some immense painting in fresco, in which he could, for once, (as he used to say) gratify his whims and his caprice, certain, however, that, being rendered more patient by his age, and more cautious by experience, he should not fall into that immoderate fury, which is seen and admired, in his Prophets and Sybils, in the first ceiling of the Capella della Morte, owing to the figures being drawn *off hand,* (as they call it), on the picture itself without cartoons, though it is otherwise very well designed, and with freedom, and wonderful colouring; his usual severity being softened down by the wet lime, which he was obliged to use instead of priming, and the vehicle being water, instead of the colours being mixed with oil."—*Malv. Fels. Pitt. vol. II. p.* 305.

OF THE PAINTING.

The following extracts relate to *Painting*. The first extract, referring to Giotto's method of painting flesh in fresco, should be compared with Cennino's account of the process. The passage (which is from Vasari) is not clearly expressed in the Italian; it will be better understood by comparing it with the extract from Malvasia's Felsina Pittrice immediately following. It is almost unnecessary to observe, that neither Vasari nor Malvasia describe accurately the method of painting flesh practised by Giotto, as described by Cennino.

"He, (Parri Spinelli) coloured very well in distemper, and perfectly in fresco; and he was the first, who left off, in fresco painting, laying *verdaccio* under the flesh colours, and glazing them afterwards with flesh coloured reds, and *chiaro scuro* as in painting with water colours in the manner of Giotto and the other old painters. On the contrary, Parri used solid colours in making the mixtures and tints, laying them judiciously in their proper places, namely, the lighter tints for the most prominent parts, the middle tints for the general colours of the flesh, and the dark tints on the extremities of the outlines. With this manner of painting, he showed greater facility in his pictures, and gave great durability to his fresco paintings, because, having put the colours in their proper places, he united them together with a brush that was rather large and soft, and so well did he execute his pictures that one would never wish to see better, and his colouring is unequalled."—*Vasari, Life of Spinelli.*

"While painting in oil, it was his (Tiarini's) custom, never to mix the colours together with the knife, or on the palette, but to mix them touch by touch and stroke by stroke, with paint brushes for the most part hard and scanty, always dipping them in the same colour. He used to pride himself for this, and laugh at the others, especially Guido, whom he described, as if in derision, as one of those Painters who did not know how to paint without first making the mixtures and compounding them together. He glazed his drapery very much; not only the reds with lake, but also the yellows with *Giallo Santo,* the greens with *Giallo Santo* and ultramarine, and sometimes even the blues, with verdigris, or *Verde Eterno*; so that I have sometimes seen his pictures painted at first entirely with white lead and bone black, as if sketched, and then covered all over with colour, being painted and finished, so as to appear as if covered with a veil, as I observed to be the manner of some of the more ancient painters, and, as Vasari relates of Giotto, that he adopted this practice even in painting figures in fresco and in the flesh colour, which he sketched with a certain *Verdaccio*, and then covered them over with glazings of flesh coloured red, and with chiaro scuro, in the same way as in water colours; this custom, adds Vasari, was afterwards dropped, and painters began to paint with body colours, making the mixtures thick. Except in these glazings, he always abstained from liquid colours; and as with Schiavone, it was also his custom to let the colours sometimes dry on the palette and then to use them hard in that manner, because the colours then remained fresh, and with a good body, and for this reason his early pictures which have as it were been painted twice over, and with a good ground underneath, withstand so much better the injuries of time, than those of other painters."—*Malv. Fels. Pitt. vol. II. p.* 206, 207.

The following are instances of good and rapid painting in fresco buono, shewing the value always attached to such as were painted without retouching in fresco, and the advantages of rapid execution.

" Michael Angelo at first (in 1508) refused to paint the ceiling of the Sistine Chapel, wishing to refer the commission to Raffaello; but being obliged to accept it, and being unaccustomed to painting in fresco, he sent to Florence for some of the best fresco painters, in order to assist, or rather to teach him the art; then he obliterated what they had done and commenced the work alone. Having completed one half, he opened it to public inspection for a short time. Then he began the other half, and proceeded more slowly than was agreeable to the impatience of the Pope, (Giulio II.) who threatened him, if he did not make more haste with the work, he would throw him off the scaffolding. He finished the remaining part alone in twenty months. Alone I say, because his taste was so refined that no one could satisfy it, and as in sculpture, every file and every chisel that he used, he made with his own hand; so in painting, he ***not only made the tints and other necessary preparations and arrangements, but he ground the colours himself, not trusting to artists or boys.*** In this chapel are those grand and varied figures of prophets and sybils, of which Lomazzo, an impartial judge, because he belonged to another school, said ***he considered to be the best in the whole world.***"—*Lanzi. vol. I. p.* 114.

Vasari's account of the painting of the same chapel is more circumstantial: it is as follows:

"Pope Julius was very desirous of seeing the works that he (Michael Angelo) was painting; and his curiosity was the greater because they were concealed from him. And so one day he determined to go and see the chapel, but it was not opened to him, because Michael Angelo would not show it. On this account there arose a quarrel, so that Michael Angelo was obliged to leave Rome, not choosing to show it to the Pope, because, as he told me himself, when the third part of it was finished, there began to appear on it a certain mouldiness one winter while the north wind was blowing. The cause of this was that the Roman lime being white, and made from travertine, does not dry so quickly, and when mixed with *Pozzolana*, which is of a tan colour, makes a dark mixture. If this mixture be liquid, and watery, and the wall be thoroughly wetted, it frequently effloresces as it dries. This was the case, in the present instance, for in many places the salt effloresced, although in lapse of time the air consumed it. Michael Angelo was very much disturbed by this circumstance, and would not go on with the work, and when he excused himself to the Pope saying, that he could not succeed with it, his Holiness sent to him Giuliano da San Gallo, who, having explained the cause of it, encouraged him to go on with the work, and taught him how to get rid of the mouldiness. Having thus half finished it, the Pope, who with the assistance of Michael Angelo, and by means of certain ladders, had already seen some part of the ceiling, insisted on the chapel being thrown open, because he was naturally hasty and impatient, and could not wait until it was perfect, and had received, so to speak, the last touches. The moment it was thrown open, all Rome ran to see it, and the Pope was the first, not even having the patience to wait till the dust, caused by the removal of the scaffolding, had settled; and Raffaello da Urbino, who was an excellent imitator, having seen it, suddenly changed his manner, and immediately, to shew his skill, painted the prophets and the sybils in the chapel of the Chigi in the church of Sta. Maria della Pace. Bramante then tried to induce the Pope to give the painting of the other half of the chapel to Raffaello. When Michael Angelo heard of it, he was angry with Bramante, and, without any consideration for him, told the Pope many of the faults both of his life and of his architectural works. But the Pope appreciating the value of Michael Angelo more and more every day, desired he would go on with the work, and having seen the picture uncovered, considered that Michael Angelo could greatly improve the other half; and thus he completed the whole of the painting entirely by himself, in twenty months, without even the assistance of any one to grind his colours. Michael Angelo has sometimes complained, that, on account of the Pope hurrying him, he was not able to finish it to his own satisfaction, for the Pope was continually asking him, importunately, when he would have finished it. So that, on one occasion, he answered, 'It will be finished when I have satisfied myself in those things that relate to the art.' 'And we desire,' said the Pope, 'that you satisfy our wish, that it should be finished quickly.' The Pope ended by telling him, that if he did not soon finish it, he would have him thrown off the scaffolding. And therefore Michael Angelo, who feared, and had reason to fear, the anger of the Pope, immediately, and without delay, finished what was wanting; and, having taken down the rest of the scaffold, opened it on the morning of All Saint's day, when the Pope went to the chapel there to sing mass, to the satisfaction of the whole city. Michael Angelo desired to retouch some things in *secco*, as the older painters had done in the historical pictures beneath, and to make certain back-grounds, draperies, and skies, of ultramarine, and to place gold ornaments in some places, in order to give the work richness, and a better appearance, because the Pope, having been told that this was wanting, and hearing it so much praised by whoever had seen it, wished him to make the addition, but, as it would have taken up too much of Michael Angelo's time to reconstruct the scaffolding, the painting remained as it was. The Pope, who frequently went to see Michael Angelo, used to say to him, 'Let the chapel be enriched with colours and gold, for the effect is too poor.' And Michael Angelo used to answer him familiarly, 'Holy Father, men in those times did not wear gold about them, and those who are there painted, were never very rich, but on the contrary they were holy men who despised riches.'[a] Michael Angelo was paid by the Pope at different times three hundred scudi (£650 nearly) of which he had to spend twenty-five in colours."—*Vasari, Life of Michael Angelo.*

"Gio. Francesco Barbieri (Guercino) painted in fresco a house of Signor D. Bartolomeo Panini, at Cento, both inside and outside,

[a] Armenino also observes (p. 240) that Michael Angelo painted this chapel *with simple earths, without gold.*

in such a manner that it seems to be painted in oil, and many painters have wished to make themselves certain of it by a very close inspection. He here shewed, besides the strength of his imagination and the sublimity of his genius, his judgment in the disposition of historical and fabulous compositions, having painted with great skill in one room the four seasons, and in the saloon all the actions of Ulysses, and in other rooms the Armida of Tasso, with such beauty and brilliancy of colour that this house has always been the most curious object of visit for princes, and *Virtuosi*, who have even gone to Cento on purpose."—*Malv. Fels. Pitt. vol. I. p.* 362.

" When Il Pomarancio desired to have the services of some youth more intelligent and experienced than those whom he had taken to Rome with him, he wrote to Bologna about it, to Bernardino Baldi, with whom he had, when at Rome, contracted a great friendship, which he continued to preserve by means of letters. Baldi sent Lorenzo Garbieri, who being arrived, began immediately to paint some angels, (which can easily be distinguished) without cartoons or pouncings, looking only at the design, and copying it off on a large scale upon the wet lime with a sharp nail, he began to colour them with so much boldness and facility that while it astonished that great artist, produced much jealousy and envy among the others, so that they leagued together, and beginning to persecute him violently, prevented his remaining there very long."—*Malv. Fels. Pitt. vol. II. p.* 301.

" Amico Aspertino painted with both hands at once, holding in one hand a brush filled with light colour, and in the other, one filled with dark; but what was more remarkable and laughable, was that he bound round his waist a leather strap, to which hung his gallipots of tempered colours; and he looked like the devil of S. Maccario with all his phials hanging round him, and when painting with his spectacles on his nose, it was sufficient to make the very stones laugh, especially when he began to talk, for he talked enough for twenty persons, and he loved to say the strangest things in the world."—*Vasari, Life of Amico Aspertino.*

" In the arches and vaults of the Convent of S. Croce, Lorenzo de Bicci painted in 1418, representations of some of the kings of France, friars, and devotees of St. Francesco, and drew their portraits as well as those of many learned men, and of men remarkable for their dignities, such as, bishops, cardinals, and popes; among which are portraits, from the life, in two circles in the roof, of the popes Nicholas IV and Alexander V. Although Lorenzo gave all these figures grey dresses, yet by the great skill he had acquired by his long experience in painting, he so varied them, that they are all different from each other. Some incline to red, others to blue; some are dark, and others are light, and, in short, they are all different and deserving of approbation. Moreover, he is said to have executed this work with so much quickness and facility, that once when he was sent for by the *frate guardiano* of the convent (who used to procure his dinner) just as he had laid on the *intonaco* for a figure, and begun to paint, he said, 'Put on the saucepans, for I will just finish this figure, and then I will come.' So that it was said with truth, that Lorenzo had greater quickness of hand, greater practice in colours, and greater boldness, than any other person ever possessed."—*Vasari, Life of Lorenzo di Bicci.*

"Domenico Ghirlandaio understood well the method of painting on walls, and worked on them with facility, although his style of composition was somewhat affected. He repainted the Capella Maggiore in Sta. Maria Novella which had been painted by Andrea Orgagna, but which, owing to the bad state of the roof, had been injured by the rain. This chapel was considered most beautiful, being large, and pleasing for the vivacity of its colours, the skill and neatness of the handling upon the wall, and the few retouchings in *secco*, besides the composition and arrangement of the figures. And certainly Domenico deserves great praise, on all accounts, and particularly for the liveliness of the heads, which, being portraits from the life, give excellent likenesses of many distinguished personages. He painted also for Giovanni Tornabuoni, at his villa called Casa Maccherelli, at a short distance from the city, and close to the rivulet Terzolle, a chapel, now half ruined, on account of its being situated so near the torrent. Although this chapel has been for many years uncovered, and continually wetted by the rain, and scorched by the sun, the painting has stood so well, that it would seem to have been always under shelter, such is the durability of fresco paintings, when judiciously painted, and not retouched in *secco*."—*Vasari, Life of Domenico Ghirlandaio.*

" But the most beautiful part of this painting (by Stefano Veronese) is two Prophets, in the middle of the upper part, as large as life, because the heads are the most beautiful and lively that Stefano ever painted; and the colouring of the whole work, having been carefully executed, has remained beautiful even to our times, notwithstanding that it has been much exposed to rain, wind, and frost; and if this painting had been in a covered place, as Stefano did not retouch it in *secco*, but was careful to complete it well in fresco, it would still be as beautiful and lively as when it came out of his hands, whereas, as it now stands, it is a little damaged."—*Vasari, Life of Vittore Scarpaccio.*

" In 1618, Matteo Rosselli painted in fresco another lunette in the Cloister of the Nunziata. This picture proved so beautiful (not so much on account of the invention and colouring, as for the wonderful harmony which it possesses), that Pietro da Cortona was obliged to say that it was the most beautiful picture in the place; and Passignano praised it very highly. Indeed, to tell the truth, Matteo Rosselli had the talent, which none but himself possessed, of uniting and harmonizing his colours perfectly, in fresco-painting, while the lime was fresh. In order to attain this object, he never spared trouble, but was accustomed to begin to work at sunrise, and, taking but very little refreshment while on the scaffold, he used to persevere at his work in the summer until dusk, and in winter until five o'clock in the evening; because he wished to leave the *intonaco*, and not the *intonaco* to leave him. And therefore he never had any occasion to retouch in *secco*, and his pictures look more like oil than fresco paintings."—*Baldinucci, vol. II. p.* 60.

COLOURING AND COLOURS.

" Among all those who have assisted Primaticcio, none have done him more honour than Nicolo da Modena, of whom we have already spoken. For he has excelled all the others by the excellence of his skill, having painted with his own hand, after the designs of the Abbot, a room, called the *Sala del Ballo*, with such a great number of figures, that it seems hardly possible to count them; and they are all as large as life, and coloured in a transparent manner, so that, by the union of the colours of the *fresco* it appears painted in oil.

"After this picture, he painted in the great gallery, also from the designs of the Abbot, sixty historical pictures, taken from the life and actions of Ulysses; but the colouring of them is much darker than that of the *Sala del Ballo*. This is owing to his having used no other colours but earths, just in the state in which they are produced by nature, without, we may almost say, mixing any white with them, but the darkness of the shadows is so intense, that they have excessive force and relief. Besides this, he has united the joinings so well, in every part of it, that it appears as if it had been all painted in one and the same day, and he therefore deserves the highest praise, particularly as he has painted the pictures *entirely* in *fresco*, without having at all retouched them in *secco*, as many are accustomed to do at the present day."—*Malv. Fels. Pitt. vol. I, p.* 153, 154.

"Giacomo Cavidone's *beautiful manner of painting in fresco with so few colours*, pleased Guido so much, that he wished him to teach him his manner of working; and, expecting to have to paint the Cupola at Loretto, he placed all his reliance upon Giacomo, and sent for him to Rome while he was painting the chapel of Monte Cavallo, paying him 30 *scudi* (£7 nearly) a month, as appears from his pocket book." —*Malv. Felsina Pittrice, vol. II, p.* 219.

Of the works of Gio. Carlone and Gio. Batista Carlone, Lanzi says, "It is not easy to find works equally extensive, executed with equal diligence, compositions so fertile in invention and heads so varied and animated; figures with the contours so well defined, and so well detached from the ground, colours so beautiful, so brilliant, so fresh, after the lapse of so many years. There is a red colour (perhaps used too frequently) that appears crimson (porpora) a blue which resembles the sapphire; a green in particular which artists consider quite miraculous, and which looks like an emerald. The brightness of these colours recals to the mind pictures on glass or enamel; and I never remember having seen in the works of any other Italian painter a style of colouring so new, so pleasing, and so flattering. To certain persons who compare these colours with those of Raffaello, Correggio, and Andrea del Sarto, they seem to have a certain rawness; but on subjects of taste, where there are so many ways of pleasing, and so many degrees of merit in artists, who ever succeeded in pleasing every one? The similarity of the style, induced the best informed persons, to consider them the work of one master; but the best judges consider the pictures of Gio. Batista to possess a certain exquisite taste in colour and chiaro scuro, and a greater grandeur of design. It has been endeavoured by a close examination to ascertain the manner in which these pictures were coloured; and it has been found that when painting ceilings and walls of rooms the artist had applied the colours upon the dry wall, after having laid under them a coloured intonaco, which defended them from the action of the lime.[a] They were applied with most delicate gradations and with wonderful uniformity; whence these frescoes appeared as if painted with oil; these are the encomiums of Sig. Ratti and nearly those of Mengs his master."—*Lanzi, vol. V, p.* 269.

"Perhaps the finest works that we have in Venice by this master (Tiepolo) are his pictures in fresco. In this kind of painting which requires both quickness and facility of execution, Tiepolo excelled every other painter; and he introduced with wonderful skill into his pictures, a beauty and sunny brilliancy which are perhaps unparalleled. In order to attain this perfection, other artists have endeavoured to make use of the finest colours in fresco; and have made every effort to discover new ones. Tiepolo, on the contrary, made use of dirty tints and impure colours, and of the most common pigments, and by opposing these tints to others that were pure and bright, with his ready pencil, he produced an effect which is rarely seen in other pictures. In this kind of painting he shewed his great knowledge of the effect of contrasts in colours, and the importance of knowing how to employ them with praiseworthy sagacity."—*See Lanzi, vol. III, p.* 223.

"That the Carracci were not good colourists, although they studied in the Lombard and Venetian schools, is asserted by Mengs and proved by many of their pictures in oil, those of Ludovico especially being discoloured and decayed. This was either occasioned by the

[a] It seems difficult to imagine how colours laid on a dry wall can be said to be painted in fresco. Probably these paintings were executed in the manner described by Mr. Wilson in the II. Rep. p. 40.

The process, whatever it was, must have been good, since the pictures continued to preserved their freshness and brilliancy in the degree mentioned by Lanzi, alter a lapse of 150 years; for Gio. Batista Carlone died in 1680, and Gio. Andrea his son in 1697.

defective priming, or the immoderate use of oil, or by not having suffered a proper time to elapse between the priming and the painting of the picture. This cannot be said of their frescoes. These seen close, exhibit a freedom of handling quite Paolesque, nor did the skill of the Carracci, said Bellori, or that of any other painter of the period, produce specimens of better colouring than the works of the Carracci in the Casa Magnani. They display a truth, a force, a combination, a harmony of colours, which entitled them to be called the reformers of this branch of painting. They abandoned those yellowish and other feeble tints introduced by avarice instead of azures and other more expensive colours; Bellori attributes the greatest merit to Annibale, asserting that through him Ludovico himself renounced his first mode of colouring which was after the manner of Procaccino."—*Lanzi, vol. V. p.* 70.

"Tintoretto used to say that beautiful colours were sold in the shops of the Rialto; but that design was produced from the recesses of the brain with much study and long watchings, and this was the reason why there were so few who understood and practised it." —*Ridolfi, vol. II. p.* 253.

"While Rinaldi was painting the beautiful picture of Bacchus and Ariadne, and Cesarino begged of him to use good and fine colours, he began to laugh heartily, and turned to him and said, 'good design and common colours;' alluding to what, according to Ridolfi, Titian was accustomed to say, that it was not the colours, but the design, that made figures beautiful; and also, that good colours could be bought at the Rialto, but that design was contained in the portfolio of the mind."—*Malv. Fels. Pitt. vol. I. p.* 481.

"The colour (of a Crucifixion by Pietro Cavallini at Assisi) is preserved in a great degree, and especially the azzurro, which here and in other parts of the church forms a sky which is really the colour of the oriental sapphire as our poets say."—*Lanzi, vol. II. p.* 12.

"Pisano, or Pisanello, a Veronese painter, having been many years in Florence with Andrea dal Castagno, and having finished Andrea's pictures after his death, acquired so much credit under the name of Andrea, that the pope Martin V. when he came to Florence, took him away with him to Rome, where he made him paint, in St. John

Lateran, some historical paintings in fresco, which are very pleasing, and as beautiful as possible, because he laid upon them, in great abundance, a sort of *ultramarine,* given to him by this pope, so beautiful and of such a fine colour, that it has never yet been equalled." —*Vasari, Life of Vittore Pisanello.*

"Because it was the custom of Buffalmacco, in order to make the flesh colours easier to paint, to form for the whole of the picture, a ground of *pavonazzo di sale,*[a] which in course of time, produces a saltness that corrodes and consumes the white, and the other colours; therefore it is not surprising that such paintings spoil and corrode, while others, painted much longer, keep in good preservation. I, who thought it was the damp which injured these pictures, have since found, by experience, that it was not owing to the damp, but to this particular custom of Buffalmacco, that they are so much damaged, that we can distinguish neither the design nor anything else; and that where the flesh tints had been formerly, nothing now remained but the *pavonazzo.* This method of painting ought not to be used by any one who wishes his paintings to be durable." —*Vasari, Life of Buonamico Buffalmacco.*

"Among other particulars, I must not omit, that this lady (daughter-in-law of Cæsar Baglione) gave me the keys of a certain small room in the larger house, which had never been opened since the before mentioned Joseph (son of Cæsar Baglione) had left Bologna, and which contained every thing belonging to the studio of his deceased father. I found four chests in it; one of which contained a great number of sketches, and cartoons of many pictures, painted by him on various occasions, and all the most famous engravings which had been published up to that time, by Buonmartino, Albert Durer, Altogravius, Marcantonio, Agostino, and many others who had used the graver, bound up in several volumes. The other chest was full of brushes and colours, that is to say, earths of all sorts, particularly of *verde di miniera,*[b] the most precious which the ancients possessed, the good and genuine sort of which is now lost. There were leather

[a] Many authors mention this "*Pavonazzo di Sale,*" but I cannot find any account of its composition. Its name shows it to have been compounded with some salt or alkali, which has always been found injurious to fresco paintings.

[b] *Verde Montaña*—Native green carbonate of copper.

bags full of English browns[a] (Bruno d'Inghilterra), which were then so much in use, being employed in fresco instead of lake; also some very fine *verdetto* and some *Azzurro di Spagna,*[b] so bright and fine that even Sirani was deceived by them, and at first mistook them for Ultramarine."—*Malv. Fels. Pitt. vol. I.* 348.

"Dario Varatori painted in fresco some sybils and prophets in the Carmine, at Padua, being obliged to complete the work on account of certain festivities, and being at the same time under a course of medicine, he carried his draught with him to the work; he took the bottle in his hand, looked at it, smelled to it several times, then taking a disgust to it from having taken so much, he dipped his pencil into it, and finished with it the drapery of one of the figures, making use of it for the shadows which were of that colour."—*Ridolfi, vol. II. p.* 269.

It will perhaps be recollected that Léon. da Vinci recommended "Aloes Cavallini" as a pigment.

OF THE USE OF GOLD ON FRESCOES.

"The *fresco* by Domenico Ghirlandaio in the Duomo of Pisa is on a gold ground."—*I. Pisa, Illust. p.* 236.

"Girolamo Curti wished to try two inventions of his, which were new at that time, and have certainly not been practised since. The first was to hatch (tratteggiare) his frescoes with gold leaf, by a secret process of mixing together boiled oil, turpentine, and yellow wax, and spreading the composition while hot, with a small brush, wherever the lights occur; because this mordant renders the gold leaf, which is put upon it, somewhat raised and very shining. This mordant pleased him, and it cannot be denied that the rich appearance of it succeeded well, particularly on certain occasions, times and places, as in theatrical scenes, funerals, large buildings and similar things, which are to be seen by torch light, although after-

[a] *Sinopia.*

[b] Native blue carbonate of copper, *Azul Fino*, or of St. Domingo.

wards it began to be employed far too frequently, in great excess, and with intolerable affectation in fresco paintings."—*Malv. Fels. Pitt. vol. I. p.* 160, 161.

"I therefore conclude that it cannot be denied that modern decorations are more sumptuous than the ancient; as well as more pleasing and more varied, perhaps in too great a degree; that they have greater beauty and vivacity, but perhaps less depth and nature; that they please, but I do not know that they instruct; that they attract, but I do not know that they deceive. The profusion of gold hatchings, which is now used so immoderately, makes the work richer, but not more admirable; brighter, but not of better relief; and if the only light adapted to it be wanting, it remains dull, and without the proper brightness; and therefore Giralomo (Curti), although he was the inventor of it,[a] did not care to use it frequently. He employed it at proper times and in proper places, and not always and everywhere; rather for trial than for use; rather as a whim, than a custom; desiring to shew himself a true painter, and not a mere gilder. In his colours also he imitated nature and did not follow fancy. He obtained his colours from *macigno*, travertine, bricks, and marble; not from agates, jaspers, chrysolites, or amethysts.[b] He represented objects that exist or that can exist, not such as never have been nor ever can be. His design also was natural, not ideal; real, not imaginary; according to his own experience, and to reason, not according to caprice or fancy. He painted with body colours, he did not wash with water colours; he painted with a solid *impasto*, and not with his colours too liquid. He studied the durability of his pictures, not their appearance. He was accustomed to make sketches, that he might have an opportunity of correcting his designs, and because he did not trust in the goodness of the white lime, he sometimes increased its density with white marble finely powdered, ground and mixed with it, and which, as may be seen, in the façade of the Grimaldi palace has resisted so well the injuries of time."—*Malv. Fels. Pitt. vol. II. p.* 173.

Jacopo di Pontormo, was commissioned by the Duke Alessandro de Medicis (who was assassinated in 1536), to paint the whole of the

[a] That is hatching the frescoes with gold.

[b] Meaning, that he used common, and not fine, colours.

Capella Maggiore of S. Lorenzo (built by Cosimo Vecchio di Medicis) since called the Capella de Principi.

"Of these frescoes, begun by Jacopo de Pontormo in S. Lorenzo and finished by Bronzino, no traces remain but the *diary* of Pontormo preserved in the Biblioteca Palatina, (segnata, No. 351) which has preserved some curious notices respecting these pictures." They are useful to artists, inasmuch as they shew what portions of the pictures were painted in each day. The diary begins thus,—" On Sunday morning the 11th of March, 1554, I dined with Bronzino, Wednesday evening, the 29th, I ate almonds and painted that figure which is over the bald head.[a]

" On the 9th June, 1554, Marco Moro began to build the wall of the choir and fill up the holes in S. Lorenzo.

" The 30th January 1555, I began the loins of that figure which is lamenting over the child.

" The 31st, I painted the slip of linen which encircles them.

" The 1st February, I painted the drapery above, on the 5th I finished it, and on the 16th I painted those legs of that child which are here represented.—The 4th, I painted the head of the figure above which stands thus.

" March the 4th, Sunday, I painted the *torso* of the figure under this head, and on Monday the arm belonging to the same figure which is raised, as shewn in this sketch.

" On Tuesday and Wednesday I painted the arm of the old man which is like this.

" On Wednesday the 20th, I finished the arm, begun on Friday, the bust of which I painted on Monday. On Tuesday, I painted the head belonging to the arm I have mentioned. On Thursday morning I rose very early, but the weather was so bad, so windy, and cold that I did not work, but remained in the house. On Friday I painted the other arm, which is placed across, and on Saturday the 23rd, a little of the blue ground; in the evening of Sunday I supped on eleven ounces of bread, two eggs and spinach.

"Tuesday, 26th, I painted that head of the boy which is looking down.

" On Wednesday, I painted the rest of the boy; I was so inconvenienced by remaining in a stooping posture all day, that on Thursday

[a] Sketches with the pen are always added; the MS. appears to be a copy of the seventeenth century.

I had a pain in the back, and on Friday I was worse, and was otherwise indisposed, and ate no supper; and on the morning of the 29th, which was Friday, 1555, I painted the hand and half the arm of that large figure, the knee, with a part of the leg where the hand is placed.

"The 3rd April, I painted the leg belonging to the knee with great fatigue on account of the darkness.

"On Friday I began the back of the figure under this.

"On Tuesday I painted the leg with the thigh under, and the back which is below the first mentioned back, thus.

"On Saturday, I painted the rock, and the Duke came to S. Lorenzo, that is to say to the Ufizio. On Thursday I painted those two arms. On Friday I painted the head with the rock below it. On Saturday I did the trunk of the tree, the rock, and the hand. On the 27th I finished only the leg placed thus. Tasso died. On Wednesday and Thursday I finished it. On Tuesday, I begun the torso the head of which is looking thus. On Thursday I did an arm. On Friday, the other arm. On Saturday, the thigh of the figure placed thus. On Monday, the 20th May, I began the arm of this figure. On Tuesday, the other arm. On Friday, I finished the figure. On Wednesday, I did the head below this figure, thus. On Thursday, 30th May, the thigh. On Friday, the back. On Saturday, I finished the figure. On Wednesday, I did the shoulders of the figure. On Thursday, I did the arm. On Friday, I finished it. On Wednesday, I did the head of the dead man with the beard above this figure. On Thursday, I did the head and arm of the figure placed thus. On Friday, the torso. On Saturday, the legs and finished the figure. On Tuesday, unfastened the planks of the scaffolding; on Wednesday, filled up the holes in the wall. On Thursday, 4th July, I began the figure like this. Friday and Saturday, I did as far as the legs. Friday, the 5th, I did one thigh. On Thursday, I did the other thigh.

"On Friday, the 12th, I worked on the long pipe, close to the boarded partition. On Tuesday, 16th, I began this figure. On Thursday I worked in S. Lorenzo a little, and finished the figure. On Friday, I did the head looking this way. On Tuesday, I began the figure. On Wednesday, I did as far as the legs. On Thursday, 1st August, I did the legs. On Friday, I did the arm on which the figure leans. On Saturday, the head of the figure below it, which is thus."—*Carteggio Inedito d' Artisti, vol. III, p.* 166, *&c.*

INSTANCES OF THE DURABILITY OF EXTERNAL FRESCOES.

"Close to this picture he (Lorenzo di Ricci) painted also in fresco a San Cristofano of the height of twelve and a half *braccia* (=25 feet), which was a very extraordinary thing in those times, because up to that time, with the exception of the San Cristofano of Buffalmacco, there had never been seen a larger figure, nor, considering its size, although it is not painted in a good style, a more accurate and well-proportioned figure, in all its parts, than this. Besides which, both of these pictures were painted with such skill, that, although they have been many years in the open air, beaten by the wind and storm, being exposed to the north (Tramontana), they have never lost the brilliancy of their colours, nor have they been ever damaged in any part."—*Vasari, Life of Lorenzo di Ricci.*

"Pietro Perugino was desired to paint a dead Christ with St. John and the Virgin, on the steps of the side door of S. Maria Maggiore, and he painted it in such a manner, that although exposed to the rain and the wind, it has nevertheless retained such freshness, as to appear as if Pietro had just painted it. It is certain that Pietro was well acquainted with the colours, as well in fresco as in oil; so that all skilful artists are under this obligation to him, that through his means, and the study of his works they have obtained much practical information."—*Vasari, Life of Pietro Perugino.*

"The commonalty at Florence, the year that Gabriel Maria (the Master of Pisa) sold that city to the Florentines for 200,000 *scudi* (=£44,444. 9s.) after Giovanni Gambacorta had sustained a siege for thirteen months, and he also had at last agreed to the sale, caused Starnina to paint, in memory of this circumstance, on the Guelfish façade of the palace, a Saint Dennis as bishop, with two angels, and, underneath this, a view of the city of Pisa, in doing which, he took so much care about every thing, and particularly about colouring it in fresco, that, in spite of wind and rain, and notwithstanding its being turned to the north, it has always been and still is considered as being worthy of praise, for having always retained its freshness and beauty so as to appear as if but just painted."—*Vasari, Life of Gherardo Starnina.*

CAUSES OF THE DESTRUCTION OF FRESCOES.

The causes to which writers on Painting commonly attribute the destruction of frescoes, are, damp, and the presence of salts in the substance of the wall, or the plastering or intonaco, or saline particles deposited on the pictures by the sirocco and other winds which blow over the sea; the injuries arising to the paintings from injudicious attempts to repair them, entire neglect, and wilful injuries. Instances of the injuries to frescoes arising from damp are so numerous, that it is useless to enumerate them, particularly as the writers on painting do not mention any particulars relative to the construction of the walls on which they are painted, or the situation of the buildings.

The following extracts shew the opinions entertained by different writers as to the cause of the destruction of certain frescoes.

" In the Church of the Annunciation at Parma, on the left hand as you enter, Correggio painted in fresco the Mystery of the Incarnation; but this picture has been much injured, because it was painted in another place, and the wall being pulled down, the picture was placed in its present situation, and it always happens in similar cases that the humidity of the new wall and salts, arising from the lime, form, on fresco paintings, a kind of tartar which covers and obscures them."—*Mengs. obras, p.* 289.

" A Fresco, by Andrea Comodi in the vestry of S. Carlo a Catinari, at Rome, is become dark and covered with a mist, an unusual thing for so good a colourist."—*Lanzi, vol. I. p.* 193.

" The Cupola of the Duomo of Pisa is not *double,* and consequently is not proof against the humidity that occasions the injuries which are slowly increasing, but which by great good luck, have as yet spared the most essential and beautiful parts."—*Pisa Illust. vol. I. p.* 310.

Lanzi says, that " the master-piece of Cigoli (Peter healing the lame man), for which he received the honor of knighthood, is quite destroyed either from the dampness of the church, or the ignorance of those who undertook to clean it."—*Vol. I. p.* 192.

"The damp of the walls (of the Campo Santo of Pisa) causes the pictures to scale off; and the surrounding air impregnated with damp and saline vapours is equally injurious to them. No great damage will probably ensue for a few years; but we shall see one day, as in the case of *S. Girolamo di Lomi* that the sirocco, prevailing in the plains of Pisa, and confined within these extensive loggie, (besides the injury done by them, and by the violence of men to the intonaco, and the materials of the walls) will commit fresh havoc."—*Il. Pisa Illust. p.* 16.

"So Giotto going to Pisa, executed at the end of one of the façades of the Campo Santo, six large historical pictures in fresco, taken from the history of the patient Job. And as he very judiciously considered that the marble of that part of the building where he had to paint, was turned towards the sea and must therefore be impregnated with salt, from the effects of the *sirocco*, that the wall would damp, and give out a certain efflorescence, as the bricks of Pisa generally do, and that therefore the colours and the pictures would be tarnished and corroded; in order to preserve his pictures as much as possible, he caused to be made, wherever he intended to paint in fresco, an *arricciato* or *intonaco*, or plastering made of lime, *gesso*, and pounded brick, mixed so nicely that the pictures which he painted have been preserved up to this day; and they would have stood better, had it not been for the carelessness of the persons who ought to have taken care of them, in allowing them to be much injured by the damp, because the neglect of any provision against damp, which might easily have been made, was the cause that these pictures, having suffered from the damp, have perished in several places; the carnations have become black, and the intonaco has scaled off; besides which it is the nature of gesso, when mixed with lime, to become wet and corrupted; whence it appears, it must necessarily spoil the colours, although it appears at first to give them a good and firm hold."[a]—*Vasari, Life of Giotto, vol. II, p.* 75.

"With regard to the destruction of the paintings of Giotto in the Campo Santo of Pisa, the Canon Tosti, (MS. Dialoguo Sopra l'istoria

[a] It is rather singular that Vasari should assign the same cause both for the preservation and the decay of the pictures; namely, by the mixture of lime, gesso, and pounded brick. Vitruvius remarks that *gesso* must never be mixed with lime.

del Campo Santo de Pisa. L. L. p. 11), states that while the architect was preparing the roof, the Campo Santo remained for a long time uncovered on account of tedious law-suits, and the damp occasioned by exposure to the rains did great damage to the works and to the memory of Giotto. This is a proof we do not complain without reason against insufficient superintendents of public works."[a]—*II. Pisa Illust. p.* 205.

"The Campo Santo of Pisa is faced with white marble procured chiefly from the neighbouring mountains—*II. Pisa Illustrata, p.* 175. —except on the north side where it joins the city walls."—*P.* 176.

"In the early part of his life, Andrea Schiavone employed himself in painting all subjects for the shops; he also contracted a friendship with masons in order to procure employment, accustoming himself to paint the fronts of houses, the painting of which was frequently intrusted to these workmen; so that his friendship with the masons was the cause of his fortune. And to such a state was the art reduced in Venice that painters were often obliged to carry away the rubbish, as if there were no difference between painting and whitewashing. This practice of fresco painting is disused in Venice, because the frescoes are destroyed by the salt water, which incorporates with the lime, and instead of it, architects introduce the custom of encrusting the walls with marble like a fortress, as if men had to make war with death, not remembering the words of Horace,—

> '*Pallida mors æquo pulsat pede pauperum tabernas,*
> *Regumque turres.*'
>
> 'Pale death, with equal step will soon or late,
> Knock at the cottage and the palace gate.' "

—*I Ridolfi, p.* 320.

"Giorgione, took great pleasure in fresco painting, and, among other things, which he painted, was one whole façade of the Cà Soranzo in the Piazza di S. Paolo, in which, besides many other pictures and stories, and other fantastical ideas of his, there is seen

[a] These pictures were painted previous to the year 1400. The Campo Santo was begun in 1278, and it was finished in 1283, except the Capello Maggiore, which was finished in 1454.—*II. Pisa Illust., p.* 203.—Ed.

a picture painted in oil upon the lime which has withstood rain, sun, and wind, and is preserved even to this day. There is also a figure of Spring, which seems to me, to be one of the most beautiful things that he painted in fresco, and it is a great pity, that the weather should have so much damaged it. And I, for my part, do not know of any thing, that does more injury to fresco paintings, than the *sirocco*, and particularly in the neighbourhood of the sea, where it always brings with it so many saline particles."—*Vasari, Life of Giorgione. Borgh. Rip. p.* 303.

Lanzi, (Vol. III. p. 133) remarks that the climate of Verona is friendly to the preservation of pictures and that "whilst at Venice, the sea air has spoiled the best fresco paintings, the greater part of those painted in Verona have been preserved."

" Francesco Pagani painted two façades of the palace of Giuliano de Ricasole in fresco in chiaro scuro historical subjects from ancient Roman history; among these he painted in yellow, figures of Jupiter and Juno, which were esteemed so fine, that Jacopo da Pontormo, one of the best painters that ever lived in our city of Florence, passing one day that way, said in the presence of many persons, that if he had not known that these figures were by the hand of Francesco, he should have thought them the work of Michael Angelo. But this fine picture, in the course of a few years, perhaps from being exposed to the tempests and winds, especially in that part which faced the sea, became so effaced, that little of it remained in our days."—*Bald. vol. VII, p.* 605.

" Which paintings (an Annunciation and a St. Jacob and St. Philip in the chapel of the Bishop of Arezzo), owing to the back of the wall being turned to the north, were almost entirely spoilt by the damp, when Agnolo di Lorenzo d'Arezzo repainted the Annunciation; and shortly afterwards, Giorgio Vasari, while still young, repainted the St. James and St. Philip which was of great benefit to him, as he learnt a great deal then, not being able to get instruction from other masters, by considering the manner of painting of Giovanni (Tossicani,) and the shading and colouring of this painting decayed as it was."—*Vasari, Life of Tommaso* (*Giottino*).

"The pictures by Pordenone on the exterior of the house of Martino d'Anna a merchant of Venice, have been destroyed by the 'Tramontana' and are scarcely visible; but one representing the rape of Proserpine under the vine arbour is still preserved."—*I. Ridolfi, p.* 153.

We find by the following letter from Nicholas Poussin that the frescoes of Primaticcio at Fontainebleau, painted about 1540, were so much decayed as to require repairing in 1642.

"I was not able to answer your last letter of the 27th June, until I returned from Fontainebleau, where I was gone, as I wrote by my last letter, because M. de Noyer had given me orders to go there, to see if the pictures of Primatticcio, which had been damaged by the injuries of time, could be restored; or at least to discover some means of preserving those which had remained most entire."—*Lettere Pittoriche, vol. I. p.* 299.

OF RETOUCHING, REPAIRING, AND CLEANING FRESCOES.

With respect to cleaning, retouching, and repairing frescoes, different opinions have been entertained by the best writers on the subject. The weight of authority appears to be in favour of cleaning but against retouching and repairing frescoes. In a very learned and argumentative letter from Luigi Canon Crespi to Francesco Count Algorotti, inserted in the third volume of Lettere su la Pittura by Bottari p. 264, ed. Roma, 1759, he strongly condemns the practice of retouching and repairing frescoes, and controverts the opinions and observations of Bellori, by whom the repairs of the gallery of the Caracci in the Palazzo Farnese, and of the Loggia of Raffaello at the Lungara, are much praised. I merely refer to the very long letter of Crespi, not considering his observations of much practical use, but I insert a translation of the observations of Bellori, on account of their practical value, preceding them however, by some extracts from other writers on the subject.

"All those paintings which Antonio Veneziano executed in the Campo Santo, at Pisa, are universally, and with great reason, considered the best of all those which have been painted by many excellent masters, at various times, in that place; because he always painted everything in fresco, never retouching anything in *secco*; and this caused his colours to remain brilliant even to this day. This should be a lesson to artists, to shew them how much the retouching of fresco paintings with other colours, after they are dry, injures the pictures; it being an ascertained fact, that they appear old, and are prevented from being cleaned by the weather, when they are covered over with gum, gum-tragacanth, egg, size, or any similar thing which varnishes *(appanna)* the pictures underneath it, and does not allow time and air, to clean that which is really painted in fresco beneath, upon the wet lime, as would be the case, if other colours, in *secco*, were not put over them."—*Vasari, Life of Antonio Veneziano. See I. Lanzi, p.* 42.

"Luca Signorelli painted in fresco, at Volterra, in the church of San Francesco, over the altar of a fraternity, the circumcision of our Lord, which is considered wonderful; although the infant, having suffered from the damp, was repainted by Il Sodoma, not nearly so well as it was before; indeed, it would be sometimes better, to suffer the pictures, painted by good artists, to remain half spoiled, rather than to have them retouched by inferior painters."—*Vasari, Life of Luca Signorelli.*

"The Madonna in the Campo Santo, said by Vasari and Baldinucci to have been painted by Benozzo Gozzoli, is thought to have been in fact painted by Stefano, and, being damaged, to have been afterwards repainted by Benozzo, as his pictures were by another hand.[a]"—*Pisa, Illust. II*, 214.

The following account of the alteration of a picture in fresco, by painting over part of it in distemper, a proceeding which had escaped the detection of Vasari, will be read with interest.

Fra. Angelico da Fiesole painted under his great work (the crucifixion), in the convent of San Marco, seventeen heads and busts, representing various saints; among which is seen the portrait

[a] These retouchings prove that the pictures soon decayed.

of Saint Antonino, Archbishop of Florence. St. Antonino died in 1459, exactly four years after the death of Fra. Angelico, and the picture was painted while Antonino, neither dead nor canonized, still presided over the Florentine church. The knowledge of this fact induced Baldinucci to make a closer examination of the picture, and he ascertained, that the figure had not been originally painted as a representation of St. Antonino, but that the Fathers, desiring to possess his portrait, caused the name of the figure, which had been painted in fresco, to be coloured over with colours in distemper, and the drapery of the figure to be converted into the robes of the archbishop, to which were added the mitre, and other letters, by which the figure was converted into a portrait of St. Antonino. It is not known by whom this transformation was effected, but, from the antiquity of the painting, it must have been painted shortly after the canonization of the Saint, that is, about A. D. 1510, for the canonization of a saint is not permitted to take place until fifty years after his death, and this we know to be true, because, in addition to its being easily perceived by any one who attentively examines the difference between the two kinds of painting, ancient as they both are, the more ancient may still be seen in parts where the more modern, which is painted in distemper, (a kind of painting not so durable as fresco), has peeled off; the difference also of the style of the new work, although it has been painted in imitation of the ancient, is apparent; and finally, the comparison of the ancient with the modern letters, has cleared up every doubt. "And I," observes Baldinucci, "was desirous of communicating this fact, in order that no confusion may arise in the minds of posterity concerning historical facts, and particularly such as are connected with the arts." He adds, that Vasari was not acquainted with the circumstances, and that he merely observed the portrait in question was not that of St. Antonino, but that of some other saint.—*See Baldinucci, vol. V, p.* 163, 164.

" Alesso Baldovinetti also painted the principal altar, and the chapel of S. Trinità in fresco, for M. Gherardo and M. Bongianni Gianfigliazzi, rich and honourable Florentine gentlemen. The subjects were taken from the Old Testament, which he sketched in fresco and then finished in *secco*, tempering the colours with yolk of egg, mixed with liquid varnish, made over the fire, which vehicle, he thought, would have preserved his pictures from damp; but it was so strong, that, in many places, where it was laid on too thick, it scaled off; and so, while he thought to have found a rare and excellent secret, he was deceived in his expectations."—*Vasari, Life of Alesso Baldovinetti.*

Mr. Wilson, in his report to the commissioners on the fine arts states, that "In the palace at Modena, there is a large hall, the ceiling of which is painted by Franceschini. The wood work in the lower part of the hall was entirely burnt some time ago, and the fresco ceiling was completely blackened by smoke, but was afterwards cleaned with perfect success."—*II Rep. p.* 34.

OF THE REPAIRS OF THE GALLERY OF CARRACCI IN THE PALAZZO FARNESE, AND OF THE LOGGIA OF RAFFAELLO AT THE LUNGARA. —*From "Descrizioni della Immagini Dipinti da Raffaello D'Urbino, Di Gio. Pietro Bellori." Ed. Roma,* 1751.

"The gallery had two notorious defects. The first was a great crack from top to bottom of the vaulted roof, which, cutting it in two transversely, had extended down both walls to the pavement, and had produced a great many smaller cracks, so that almost all the priming of the roof had bulged, and particularly that on the wall facing the south, on which the *Andromeda* was painted, which had already begun to fall off in pieces, and indeed some small pieces had actually fallen from the roof itself.

"The second defect was an efflorescence of nitre, at that part on which the Cephalus and Aurora was painted, which also spread to the medallions, and naked figures contiguous.

"The cause of the first defect was attributed to the weight above, which pushed the wall outward, towards the street; and therefore four chains were fastened down below, upon the pavement, and four more upon the roof, all of which, being extended from the outer wall to the wall of the *loggia* in the courtyard, pulled the wall together, and prevented any similar mischief for the future.

" In the second place, a new and wonderful invention was thought of, for fastening the priming, and re-attaching it to the mortar, so that it might not fall any more. It consisted in nailing the priming to the wall, in the same manner as one would fasten to it a silken or woollen cloth. This being executed, with all necessary patience, by *Sig. Francesco Rossi,* who was in part the inventor of the plan, I think proper to record it here, for public instruction.

" He used a nail similar in shape, to the capital letter T, such as is used by printers, with a number of tacks all along the branches; and sometimes, in order that the upper part of the nail might not extend over the light parts, or the carnations, he had the branches shortened, or used a nail of the shape ⅂ with only one branch. Before putting in the nail, he used to ascertain the place where it was most required by striking the wall with his hand, and listening to the sound and echo of the hollow part, and where the colours were the darkest, he made a hole, with great care, with an auger, penetrating as far as was necessary to make the fastening strong, and then filled it up with *gesso.* Then, choosing a nail, of the length required by the depth of the hole, he drove it in until the head of it reached the surface of the priming, in which he made a groove, to conceal the head, or the lateral branches of the nail. Having done this, he suffered the priming, which the use of the gesso had wetted round the nail, to dry, and then painted it over with certain water colours, in tint exactly resembling what it was before, and corresponding to the parts of the picture which remained; and these tints, when dry, agreed so well, that it was not possible to find the slightest difference in them. This is so true, that *Sig. Carlo Maratti* has told me, that several times, when he has been upon the scaffolding, and examined the work with great attention, he could not find out where the nail had been placed, and that, in fact, when the artist himself wished to point it out, he was sometimes mistaken, and did not know where it was.

" It is really wonderful, and almost incredible, that there should have been fixed in that gallery, for the above mentioned purpose, 1300 nails, and 300 more in the cabinets painted by Annibale, and that no professor whatever, however skilled in these pictures, should be able to discover the slightest injury, or to point out any mark, or to indicate the place, in which one of these nails had been fixed ; so great was the skill with which the operation had been effected : the greatest care had also been taken not to touch even the edges, so to speak, of the priming, by which the nail was surrounded.

"The second defect, arising from the efflorescence, was caused by the starting from the wall of the travertine, which forms the cornice above the four exterior columns, because the wind drove the rain on to this cornice, and the wet insinuating itself into the space behind the cornice, where it had started from the wall, began to wet the wall, and to communicate the moisture to the inner side, and thus to soak the priming and the colouring of the picture. This was provided against for the future, by putting plates of marble upon the travertine of the cornice, reaching half a palm into the wall, care being taken to make them slope outwards, and to lap over one another at the edges. As to the past mischief, the same *Sig. Gio. Francesco de Rossi* had the merit, by virtue of a private secret of his own, of removing the efflorescence, and of restoring the pictures on that side to their former state, as they are now seen, with every hope, after a trial of two years, of their durability.

"The *Loggia of Raffaello*, although more ancient, has been respected more by time, than by the inclemency of the weather; because, although the roof has opened and cracked, and the priming has started in several places, yet, as these cracks have already settled properly, it has not been necessary to compress or restore the walls, but only to re-fasten, and to nail up the priming in the same manner as in the gallery of Annibale, by means of 850 nails.

"The mischief done by the air to this *Loggia*, has been much more considerable, because, having been open for about 140 years, without the protection of the planking and glass, which are now seen in the spaces under the arches, between the pillars, the result has been that it has always been exposed both to the night air, and to the air of foggy or cloudy days, and also to the winds, particularly to the north wind, which even drove the rain into it.

"From this notice it is easy to understand the mischief done to the colours, which have lost all their vivacity, and above all to the half tints, which have, for the most part, disappeared, and universally to all the grounds which had become so black, that one could hardly tell that they had been painted with good azure, which, however, still shewed itself in some parts, that were either less exposed, or better painted. But, as this is an evil too difficult to repair, without offending the superstition of some persons, who would rather consent to the entire destruction of an excellent painting, than allow it to be touched by the hand of another person, however skilful and excellent he may be; it is certainly a popular error, to believe that nothing can be done, but to try to preserve, as well as possible, the relics of antiquity, and the venerable remains of such wonderful labours.

"It is also true that posterity will not be of the same opinion as our scrupulous moderns; for if the mere embrions of those productions, which they know were so perfect in our time, or a little previous are preserved with difficulty to their times, they will reproach us with want of love for the art, and perhaps even with injustice, for having denied to painting that assistance, which is extended to sculpture, in which art we frequently see statues restored by the renewal of the legs, or the arms, and sometimes of the head, to set off the trunk and the rest of the figure.

"Upon this consideration, *Sig. Carlo Maratti*, with the approbation of Sig. Felini, and of prudent persons, has repainted all the backgrounds, restoring them to that tone of colour which was still visible in those few parts of the ancient picture which has remained uninjured, as has been before mentioned; and moreover, as many figures had lost all their former force and spirit, either by the destruction of the middle tints, or by the greater darkening of the shaded parts, or by the entire fading away of the light parts of the eyes, we think proper to record here separately, all the repairs made by Sig. Maratti, in order that our contemporaries as well as posterity may know the obligation which they are under, to the preserving genius of this great man. The figures repaired by him are the following, namely; the *Bacchus* and the *Hercules* in the *Cena de' Dei.* In the *Concilio de' Dei*, the *Mercury* handing the cup to *Psyche*, and *Cupid* embracing *Psyche*, and the head of *Psyche* herself. Almost all the northern side, where the imposts and the spaces between the arches are situated, and particularly the *Psyche*, carried by the little Loves to Heaven, and the children holding the exploits of the Gods. Within the opposite imposts, he restored from a most deplorable state to its present perfection, the *Jove* and the *suppliant Venus*. This has been executed with such judgment, and with such skill, that certainly none of our professors would be able to point out which were the additions of modern art, unless he had learned it, either from this historical narration, or from others who had known it by ocular inspection, such has been the union of the modern with ancient art! and such the industry of this great man, in endeavouring to discover the exact positions in which the primitive tints were placed! And I know that where he was not sufficiently certain of the accuracy of his knowledge, owing to the total absence of any vestiges, he used to make drawings from ancient statues, as he did in particular, from the *Antinous*, and from the *Torso* of the *Ercole di Belvedere*, from which Raffaelle took the two above-mentioned figures.

"And really, whoever examines the effects of these beautiful restorations will confess, that *Sig. Felini* had good reason for saying that the age would not always have the good fortune to possess a Carlo Maratti, and in that case we might only be able to desire to accomplish that which has now been in our power to execute.

"We must not conceal from the knowledge of posterity another which on that occasion was conferred on this *Loggia*; and we must first consider that Raffaelle, and the excellent disciples of his school, did not finish the above-mentioned painting; because the festoons of flowers and fruits, painted by *Gio. da Udine* did not reach to the cornice, as the design of the painting required, but there remained a breadth of two or three palms to be painted, in order to make the festoon rest upon the cornice. The *Lunettes* also of the interior wall, opposite to the arches of the Loggia, were not painted, and were covered with the white priming only, and this white, added to that of the whole of the wall, below the cornice, produced a very great discordance with the roof, which was so beautifully painted, and made those beautiful figures appear crude and almost unpleasant to the eye. Now, however, these festoons are complete, and are continued to the top of the cornice; the before mentioned *lunettes* are also painted, imitating the spaces between the arches on the other side, (so beautifully painted by *Gio. da Udine*,) and the perspective appearance of the windows, and the cornices which close the above-mentioned arches. Besides, all that part, which extends from the cornice to the ground, has been painted over to imitate simple architectural designs, without figures, in order to preserve the effect of the roof above it. This work, which was always superintended by the great genius of *Sig. Carlo Maratti* has been wonderfully executed by *Sig. Domenico Paradisi*, and *Sig. Giuseppe Belletti*. And in order that this Loggia might become a perfect gallery, the two other doors of the four, which are seen at the top and bottom, have been opened; the door-posts are made of *Africano*, and the doors themselves made anew with veined nut wood, so that the whole agrees wonderfully together, and pleases the eye exceedingly.

" Lastly, we must not omit to speak of the restorations which were also made, on this occasion, to the contiguous Loggia, which faces the garden, and which was painted by *Baldassar da Siena*, and *Sebastiano del Piombo;* because as the priming of that roof had begun to drop off in small pieces, so as to leave a large blank space in the middle of it, where the figure of night had been painted, it was strengthened by driving in seven hundred and thirty nails, and the proper restorations were made in this blank space; fifty nails were also driven into the same wall, on the part where the splendid *Galathea* of Raffaelle is painted, to keep the priming better attached to the wall, and to give greater duration also to this splendid offspring of his divine pencil."

INDEX.

N.B.—The Roman numerals refer to the preliminary inquiry on Colours.

A CATALOG OF SELECTED

DOVER BOOKS

IN ALL FIELDS OF INTEREST

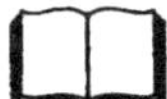

A CATALOG OF SELECTED DOVER BOOKS IN ALL FIELDS OF INTEREST

ALICE'S ADVENTURES IN WONDERLAND, Lewis Carroll. Beloved classic about a little girl lost in a topsy-turvy land and her encounters with the White Rabbit, March Hare, Mad Hatter, Cheshire Cat, and other delightfully improbable characters. 42 illustrations by Sir John Tenniel. 96pp. 5³⁄₁₆ x 8¼. 0-486-27543-4

AMERICA'S LIGHTHOUSES: An Illustrated History, Francis Ross Holland. Profusely illustrated fact-filled survey of American lighthouses since 1716. Over 200 stations — East, Gulf, and West coasts, Great Lakes, Hawaii, Alaska, Puerto Rico, the Virgin Islands, and the Mississippi and St. Lawrence Rivers. 240pp. 8 x 10¾. 0-486-25576-X

AN ENCYCLOPEDIA OF THE VIOLIN, Alberto Bachmann. Translated by Frederick H. Martens. Introduction by Eugene Ysaye. First published in 1925, this renowned reference remains unsurpassed as a source of essential information, from construction and evolution to repertoire and technique. Includes a glossary and 73 illustrations. 496pp. 6⅛ x 9¼. 0-486-46618-3

ANIMALS: 1,419 Copyright-Free Illustrations of Mammals, Birds, Fish, Insects, etc., Selected by Jim Harter. Selected for its visual impact and ease of use, this outstanding collection of wood engravings presents over 1,000 species of animals in extremely lifelike poses. Includes mammals, birds, reptiles, amphibians, fish, insects, and other invertebrates. 284pp. 9 x 12. 0-486-23766-4

THE ANNALS, Tacitus. Translated by Alfred John Church and William Jackson Brodribb. This vital chronicle of Imperial Rome, written by the era's great historian, spans A.D. 14-68 and paints incisive psychological portraits of major figures, from Tiberius to Nero. 416pp. 5³⁄₁₆ x 8¼. 0-486-45236-0

ANTIGONE, Sophocles. Filled with passionate speeches and sensitive probing of moral and philosophical issues, this powerful and often-performed Greek drama reveals the grim fate that befalls the children of Oedipus. Footnotes. 64pp. 5³⁄₁₆ x 8 ¼. 0-486-27804-2

ART DECO DECORATIVE PATTERNS IN FULL COLOR, Christian Stoll. Reprinted from a rare 1910 portfolio, 160 sensuous and exotic images depict a breathtaking array of florals, geometrics, and abstracts — all elegant in their stark simplicity. 64pp. 8⅜ x 11. 0-486-44862-2

THE ARTHUR RACKHAM TREASURY: 86 Full-Color Illustrations, Arthur Rackham. Selected and Edited by Jeff A. Menges. A stunning treasury of 86 full-page plates span the famed English artist's career, from *Rip Van Winkle* (1905) to masterworks such as *Undine, A Midsummer Night's Dream,* and *Wind in the Willows* (1939). 96pp. 8⅜ x 11. 0-486-44685-9

THE AUTHENTIC GILBERT & SULLIVAN SONGBOOK, W. S. Gilbert and A. S. Sullivan. The most comprehensive collection available, this songbook includes selections from every one of Gilbert and Sullivan's light operas. Ninety-two numbers are presented uncut and unedited, and in their original keys. 410pp. 9 x 12. 0-486-23482-7

THE AWAKENING, Kate Chopin. First published in 1899, this controversial novel of a New Orleans wife's search for love outside a stifling marriage shocked readers. Today, it remains a first-rate narrative with superb characterization. New introductory Note. 128pp. 5³⁄₁₆ x 8¼. 0-486-27786-0

BASIC DRAWING, Louis Priscilla. Beginning with perspective, this commonsense manual progresses to the figure in movement, light and shade, anatomy, drapery, composition, trees and landscape, and outdoor sketching. Black-and-white illustrations throughout. 128pp. 8⅜ x 11. 0-486-45815-6

THE BATTLES THAT CHANGED HISTORY, Fletcher Pratt. Historian profiles 16 crucial conflicts, ancient to modern, that changed the course of Western civilization. Gripping accounts of battles led by Alexander the Great, Joan of Arc, Ulysses S. Grant, other commanders. 27 maps. 352pp. 5⅜ x 8½. 0-486-41129-X

BEETHOVEN'S LETTERS, Ludwig van Beethoven. Edited by Dr. A. C. Kalischer. Features 457 letters to fellow musicians, friends, greats, patrons, and literary men. Reveals musical thoughts, quirks of personality, insights, and daily events. Includes 15 plates. 410pp. 5⅜ x 8½. 0-486-22769-3

BERNICE BOBS HER HAIR AND OTHER STORIES, F. Scott Fitzgerald. This brilliant anthology includes 6 of Fitzgerald's most popular stories: "The Diamond as Big as the Ritz," the title tale, "The Offshore Pirate," "The Ice Palace," "The Jelly Bean," and "May Day." 176pp. 5⅜ x 8½. 0-486-47049-0

BESLER'S BOOK OF FLOWERS AND PLANTS: 73 Full-Color Plates from Hortus Eystettensis, 1613, Basilius Besler. Here is a selection of magnificent plates from the *Hortus Eystettensis,* which vividly illustrated and identified the plants, flowers, and trees that thrived in the legendary German garden at Eichstätt. 80pp. 8⅜ x 11. 0-486-46005-3

THE BOOK OF KELLS, Edited by Blanche Cirker. Painstakingly reproduced from a rare facsimile edition, this volume contains full-page decorations, portraits, illustrations, plus a sampling of textual leaves with exquisite calligraphy and ornamentation. 32 full-color illustrations. 32pp. 9⅜ x 12¼. 0-486-24345-1

THE BOOK OF THE CROSSBOW: With an Additional Section on Catapults and Other Siege Engines, Ralph Payne-Gallwey. Fascinating study traces history and use of crossbow as military and sporting weapon, from Middle Ages to modern times. Also covers related weapons: balistas, catapults, Turkish bows, more. Over 240 illustrations. 400pp. 7¼ x 10⅞. 0-486-28720-3

THE BUNGALOW BOOK: Floor Plans and Photos of 112 Houses, 1910, Henry L. Wilson. Here are 112 of the most popular and economic blueprints of the early 20th century — plus an illustration or photograph of each completed house. A wonderful time capsule that still offers a wealth of valuable insights. 160pp. 8⅜ x 11. 0-486-45104-6

THE CALL OF THE WILD, Jack London. A classic novel of adventure, drawn from London's own experiences as a Klondike adventurer, relating the story of a heroic dog caught in the brutal life of the Alaska Gold Rush. Note. 64pp. 5³⁄₁₆ x 8¼. 0-486-26472-6

CANDIDE, Voltaire. Edited by Francois-Marie Arouet. One of the world's great satires since its first publication in 1759. Witty, caustic skewering of romance, science, philosophy, religion, government — nearly all human ideals and institutions. 112pp. 5³⁄₁₆ x 8¼. 0-486-26689-3

CELEBRATED IN THEIR TIME: Photographic Portraits from the George Grantham Bain Collection, Edited by Amy Pastan. With an Introduction by Michael Carlebach. Remarkable portrait gallery features 112 rare images of Albert Einstein, Charlie Chaplin, the Wright Brothers, Henry Ford, and other luminaries from the worlds of politics, art, entertainment, and industry. 128pp. 8⅜ x 11. 0-486-46754-6

CHARIOTS FOR APOLLO: The NASA History of Manned Lunar Spacecraft to 1969, Courtney G. Brooks, James M. Grimwood, and Loyd S. Swenson, Jr. This illustrated history by a trio of experts is the definitive reference on the Apollo spacecraft and lunar modules. It traces the vehicles' design, development, and operation in space. More than 100 photographs and illustrations. 576pp. 6¾ x 9¼. 0-486-46756-2

DOOMED SHIPS: Great Ocean Liner Disasters, William H. Miller, Jr. Nearly 200 photographs, many from private collections, highlight tales of some of the vessels whose pleasure cruises ended in catastrophe: the *Morro Castle, Normandie, Andrea Doria, Europa,* and many others. 128pp. 8⅞ x 11¾. 0-486-45366-9

THE DORÉ BIBLE ILLUSTRATIONS, Gustave Doré. Detailed plates from the Bible: the Creation scenes, Adam and Eve, horrifying visions of the Flood, the battle sequences with their monumental crowds, depictions of the life of Jesus, 241 plates in all. 241pp. 9 x 12. 0-486-23004-X

DRAWING DRAPERY FROM HEAD TO TOE, Cliff Young. Expert guidance on how to draw shirts, pants, skirts, gloves, hats, and coats on the human figure, including folds in relation to the body, pull and crush, action folds, creases, more. Over 200 drawings. 48pp. 8¼ x 11. 0-486-45591-2

DUBLINERS, James Joyce. A fine and accessible introduction to the work of one of the 20th century's most influential writers, this collection features 15 tales, including a masterpiece of the short-story genre, "The Dead." 160pp. 5³⁄₁₆ x 8¼. 0-486-26870-5

EASY-TO-MAKE POP-UPS, Joan Irvine. Illustrated by Barbara Reid. Dozens of wonderful ideas for three-dimensional paper fun — from holiday greeting cards with moving parts to a pop-up menagerie. Easy-to-follow, illustrated instructions for more than 30 projects. 299 black-and-white illustrations. 96pp. 8⅜ x 11. 0-486-44622-0

EASY-TO-MAKE STORYBOOK DOLLS: A "Novel" Approach to Cloth Dollmaking, Sherralyn St. Clair. Favorite fictional characters come alive in this unique beginner's dollmaking guide. Includes patterns for Pollyanna, Dorothy from *The Wonderful Wizard of Oz,* Mary of *The Secret Garden,* plus easy-to-follow instructions, 263 black-and-white illustrations, and an 8-page color insert. 112pp. 8¼ x 11. 0-486-47360-0

EINSTEIN'S ESSAYS IN SCIENCE, Albert Einstein. Speeches and essays in accessible, everyday language profile influential physicists such as Niels Bohr and Isaac Newton. They also explore areas of physics to which the author made major contributions. 128pp. 5 x 8. 0-486-47011-3

EL DORADO: Further Adventures of the Scarlet Pimpernel, Baroness Orczy. A popular sequel to *The Scarlet Pimpernel,* this suspenseful story recounts the Pimpernel's attempts to rescue the Dauphin from imprisonment during the French Revolution. An irresistible blend of intrigue, period detail, and vibrant characterizations. 352pp. 5³⁄₁₆ x 8¼. 0-486-44026-5

ELEGANT SMALL HOMES OF THE TWENTIES: 99 Designs from a Competition, Chicago Tribune. Nearly 100 designs for five- and six-room houses feature New England and Southern colonials, Normandy cottages, stately Italianate dwellings, and other fascinating snapshots of American domestic architecture of the 1920s. 112pp. 9 x 12. 0-486-46910-7

THE ELEMENTS OF STYLE: The Original Edition, William Strunk, Jr. This is the book that generations of writers have relied upon for timeless advice on grammar, diction, syntax, and other essentials. In concise terms, it identifies the principal requirements of proper style and common errors. 64pp. 5⅜ x 8½. 0-486-44798-7

THE ELUSIVE PIMPERNEL, Baroness Orczy. Robespierre's revolutionaries find their wicked schemes thwarted by the heroic Pimpernel — Sir Percival Blakeney. In this thrilling sequel, Chauvelin devises a plot to eliminate the Pimpernel and his wife. 272pp. 5³⁄₁₆ x 8¼. 0-486-45464-9

AN ENCYCLOPEDIA OF BATTLES: Accounts of Over 1,560 Battles from 1479 B.C. to the Present, David Eggenberger. Essential details of every major battle in recorded history from the first battle of Megiddo in 1479 B.C. to Grenada in 1984. List of battle maps. 99 illustrations. 544pp. 6½ x 9¼. 0-486-24913-1

ENCYCLOPEDIA OF EMBROIDERY STITCHES, INCLUDING CREWEL, Marion Nichols. Precise explanations and instructions, clearly illustrated, on how to work chain, back, cross, knotted, woven stitches, and many more — 178 in all, including Cable Outline, Whipped Satin, and Eyelet Buttonhole. Over 1400 illustrations. 219pp. 8⅜ x 11¼. 0-486-22929-7

ENTER JEEVES: 15 Early Stories, P. G. Wodehouse. Splendid collection contains first 8 stories featuring Bertie Wooster, the deliciously dim aristocrat and Jeeves, his brainy, imperturbable manservant. Also, the complete Reggie Pepper (Bertie's prototype) series. 288pp. 5⅜ x 8½. 0-486-29717-9

ERIC SLOANE'S AMERICA: Paintings in Oil, Michael Wigley. With a Foreword by Mimi Sloane. Eric Sloane's evocative oils of America's landscape and material culture shimmer with immense historical and nostalgic appeal. This original hardcover collection gathers nearly a hundred of his finest paintings, with subjects ranging from New England to the American Southwest. 128pp. 10⅝ x 9. 0-486-46525-X

ETHAN FROME, Edith Wharton. Classic story of wasted lives, set against a bleak New England background. Superbly delineated characters in a hauntingly grim tale of thwarted love. Considered by many to be Wharton's masterpiece. 96pp. 5³⁄₁₆ x 8 ¼. 0-486-26690-7

THE EVERLASTING MAN, G. K. Chesterton. Chesterton's view of Christianity — as a blend of philosophy and mythology, satisfying intellect and spirit — applies to his brilliant book, which appeals to readers' heads as well as their hearts. 288pp. 5⅜ x 8½. 0-486-46036-3

THE FIELD AND FOREST HANDY BOOK, Daniel Beard. Written by a co-founder of the Boy Scouts, this appealing guide offers illustrated instructions for building kites, birdhouses, boats, igloos, and other fun projects, plus numerous helpful tips for campers. 448pp. 5³⁄₁₆ x 8¼. 0-486-46191-2

FINDING YOUR WAY WITHOUT MAP OR COMPASS, Harold Gatty. Useful, instructive manual shows would-be explorers, hikers, bikers, scouts, sailors, and survivalists how to find their way outdoors by observing animals, weather patterns, shifting sands, and other elements of nature. 288pp. 5⅜ x 8½. 0-486-40613-X

FIRST FRENCH READER: A Beginner's Dual-Language Book, Edited and Translated by Stanley Appelbaum. This anthology introduces 50 legendary writers — Voltaire, Balzac, Baudelaire, Proust, more — through passages from *The Red and the Black, Les Misérables, Madame Bovary,* and other classics. Original French text plus English translation on facing pages. 240pp. 5⅜ x 8½. 0-486-46178-5

FIRST GERMAN READER: A Beginner's Dual-Language Book, Edited by Harry Steinhauer. Specially chosen for their power to evoke German life and culture, these short, simple readings include poems, stories, essays, and anecdotes by Goethe, Hesse, Heine, Schiller, and others. 224pp. 5⅜ x 8½. 0-486-46179-3

FIRST SPANISH READER: A Beginner's Dual-Language Book, Angel Flores. Delightful stories, other material based on works of Don Juan Manuel, Luis Taboada, Ricardo Palma, other noted writers. Complete faithful English translations on facing pages. Exercises. 176pp. 5⅜ x 8½. 0-486-25810-6

FIVE ACRES AND INDEPENDENCE, Maurice G. Kains. Great back-to-the-land classic explains basics of self-sufficient farming. The one book to get. 95 illustrations. 397pp. 5⅜ x 8½. 0-486-20974-1

FLAGG'S SMALL HOUSES: Their Economic Design and Construction, 1922, Ernest Flagg. Although most famous for his skyscrapers, Flagg was also a proponent of the well-designed single-family dwelling. His classic treatise features innovations that save space, materials, and cost. 526 illustrations. 160pp. 9⅜ x 12¼. 0-486-45197-6

FLATLAND: A Romance of Many Dimensions, Edwin A. Abbott. Classic of science (and mathematical) fiction — charmingly illustrated by the author — describes the adventures of A. Square, a resident of Flatland, in Spaceland (three dimensions), Lineland (one dimension), and Pointland (no dimensions). 96pp. 5³⁄₁₆ x 8¼. 0-486-27263-X

FRANKENSTEIN, Mary Shelley. The story of Victor Frankenstein's monstrous creation and the havoc it caused has enthralled generations of readers and inspired countless writers of horror and suspense. With the author's own 1831 introduction. 176pp. 5³⁄₁₆ x 8¼. 0-486-28211-2

THE GARGOYLE BOOK: 572 Examples from Gothic Architecture, Lester Burbank Bridaham. Dispelling the conventional wisdom that French Gothic architectural flourishes were born of despair or gloom, Bridaham reveals the whimsical nature of these creations and the ingenious artisans who made them. 572 illustrations. 224pp. 8⅜ x 11. 0-486-44754-5

THE GIFT OF THE MAGI AND OTHER SHORT STORIES, O. Henry. Sixteen captivating stories by one of America's most popular storytellers. Included are such classics as "The Gift of the Magi," "The Last Leaf," and "The Ransom of Red Chief." Publisher's Note. 96pp. 5³⁄₁₆ x 8¼. 0-486-27061-0

THE GOETHE TREASURY: Selected Prose and Poetry, Johann Wolfgang von Goethe. Edited, Selected, and with an Introduction by Thomas Mann. In addition to his lyric poetry, Goethe wrote travel sketches, autobiographical studies, essays, letters, and proverbs in rhyme and prose. This collection presents outstanding examples from each genre. 368pp. 5⅜ x 8½. 0-486-44780-4

GREAT EXPECTATIONS, Charles Dickens. Orphaned Pip is apprenticed to the dirty work of the forge but dreams of becoming a gentleman — and one day finds himself in possession of "great expectations." Dickens' finest novel. 400pp. 5³⁄₁₆ x 8¼. 0-486-41586-4

GREAT WRITERS ON THE ART OF FICTION: From Mark Twain to Joyce Carol Oates, Edited by James Daley. An indispensable source of advice and inspiration, this anthology features essays by Henry James, Kate Chopin, Willa Cather, Sinclair Lewis, Jack London, Raymond Chandler, Raymond Carver, Eudora Welty, and Kurt Vonnegut, Jr. 192pp. 5⅜ x 8½. 0-486-45128-3

HAMLET, William Shakespeare. The quintessential Shakespearean tragedy, whose highly charged confrontations and anguished soliloquies probe depths of human feeling rarely sounded in any art. Reprinted from an authoritative British edition complete with illuminating footnotes. 128pp. 5³⁄₁₆ x 8¼. 0-486-27278-8

THE HAUNTED HOUSE, Charles Dickens. A Yuletide gathering in an eerie country retreat provides the backdrop for Dickens and his friends — including Elizabeth Gaskell and Wilkie Collins — who take turns spinning supernatural yarns. 144pp. 5⅜ x 8½. 0-486-46309-5

HEART OF DARKNESS, Joseph Conrad. Dark allegory of a journey up the Congo River and the narrator's encounter with the mysterious Mr. Kurtz. Masterly blend of adventure, character study, psychological penetration. For many, Conrad's finest, most enigmatic story. 80pp. 5³⁄₁₆ x 8¼. 0-486-26464-5

HENSON AT THE NORTH POLE, Matthew A. Henson. This thrilling memoir by the heroic African-American who was Peary's companion through two decades of Arctic exploration recounts a tale of danger, courage, and determination. "Fascinating and exciting." — *Commonweal*. 128pp. 5⅜ x 8½. 0-486-45472-X

HISTORIC COSTUMES AND HOW TO MAKE THEM, Mary Fernald and E. Shenton. Practical, informative guidebook shows how to create everything from short tunics worn by Saxon men in the fifth century to a lady's bustle dress of the late 1800s. 81 illustrations. 176pp. 5⅜ x 8½. 0-486-44906-8

THE HOUND OF THE BASKERVILLES, Arthur Conan Doyle. A deadly curse in the form of a legendary ferocious beast continues to claim its victims from the Baskerville family until Holmes and Watson intervene. Often called the best detective story ever written. 128pp. 5³⁄₁₆ x 8¼. 0-486-28214-7

THE HOUSE BEHIND THE CEDARS, Charles W. Chesnutt. Originally published in 1900, this groundbreaking novel by a distinguished African-American author recounts the drama of a brother and sister who "pass for white" during the dangerous days of Reconstruction. 208pp. 5⅜ x 8½. 0-486-46144-0

THE HUMAN FIGURE IN MOTION, Eadweard Muybridge. The 4,789 photographs in this definitive selection show the human figure — models almost all undraped — engaged in over 160 different types of action: running, climbing stairs, etc. 390pp. 7⅞ x 10⅝. 0-486-20204-6

THE IMPORTANCE OF BEING EARNEST, Oscar Wilde. Wilde's witty and buoyant comedy of manners, filled with some of literature's most famous epigrams, reprinted from an authoritative British edition. Considered Wilde's most perfect work. 64pp. 5³⁄₁₆ x 8¼. 0-486-26478-5

THE INFERNO, Dante Alighieri. Translated and with notes by Henry Wadsworth Longfellow. The first stop on Dante's famous journey from Hell to Purgatory to Paradise, this 14th-century allegorical poem blends vivid and shocking imagery with graceful lyricism. Translated by the beloved 19th-century poet, Henry Wadsworth Longfellow. 256pp. 5³⁄₁₆ x 8¼. 0-486-44288-8

JANE EYRE, Charlotte Brontë. Written in 1847, *Jane Eyre* tells the tale of an orphan girl's progress from the custody of cruel relatives to an oppressive boarding school and its culmination in a troubled career as a governess. 448pp. 5³⁄₁₆ x 8¼. 0-486-42449-9

JAPANESE WOODBLOCK FLOWER PRINTS, Tanigami Kônan. Extraordinary collection of Japanese woodblock prints by a well-known artist features 120 plates in brilliant color. Realistic images from a rare edition include daffodils, tulips, and other familiar and unusual flowers. 128pp. 11 x 8¼. 0-486-46442-3

JEWELRY MAKING AND DESIGN, Augustus F. Rose and Antonio Cirino. Professional secrets of jewelry making are revealed in a thorough, practical guide. Over 200 illustrations. 306pp. 5⅜ x 8½. 0-486-21750-7

JULIUS CAESAR, William Shakespeare. Great tragedy based on Plutarch's account of the lives of Brutus, Julius Caesar and Mark Antony. Evil plotting, ringing oratory, high tragedy with Shakespeare's incomparable insight, dramatic power. Explanatory footnotes. 96pp. 5³⁄₁₆ x 8¼. 0-486-26876-4

THE JUNGLE, Upton Sinclair. 1906 bestseller shockingly reveals intolerable labor practices and working conditions in the Chicago stockyards as it tells the grim story of a Slavic family that emigrates to America full of optimism but soon faces despair. 320pp. 5³⁄₁₆ x 8¼. 0-486-41923-1

THE KINGDOM OF GOD IS WITHIN YOU, Leo Tolstoy. The soul-searching book that inspired Gandhi to embrace the concept of passive resistance, Tolstoy's 1894 polemic clearly outlines a radical, well-reasoned revision of traditional Christian thinking. 352pp. 5³⁄₁₆ x 8¼. 0-486-45138-0

THE LADY OR THE TIGER?: and Other Logic Puzzles, Raymond M. Smullyan. Created by a renowned puzzle master, these whimsically themed challenges involve paradoxes about probability, time, and change; metapuzzles; and self-referentiality. Nineteen chapters advance in difficulty from relatively simple to highly complex. 1982 edition. 240pp. 5⅜ x 8½. 0-486-47027-X

LEAVES OF GRASS: The Original 1855 Edition, Walt Whitman. Whitman's immortal collection includes some of the greatest poems of modern times, including his masterpiece, "Song of Myself." Shattering standard conventions, it stands as an unabashed celebration of body and nature. 128pp. 5³⁄₁₆ x 8¼. 0-486-45676-5

LES MISÉRABLES, Victor Hugo. Translated by Charles E. Wilbour. Abridged by James K. Robinson. A convict's heroic struggle for justice and redemption plays out against a fiery backdrop of the Napoleonic wars. This edition features the excellent original translation and a sensitive abridgment. 304pp. 6⅛ x 9¼. 0-486-45789-3

LILITH: A Romance, George MacDonald. In this novel by the father of fantasy literature, a man travels through time to meet Adam and Eve and to explore humanity's fall from grace and ultimate redemption. 240pp. 5⅜ x 8½. 0-486-46818-6

THE LOST LANGUAGE OF SYMBOLISM, Harold Bayley. This remarkable book reveals the hidden meaning behind familiar images and words, from the origins of Santa Claus to the fleur-de-lys, drawing from mythology, folklore, religious texts, and fairy tales. 1,418 illustrations. 784pp. 5⅜ x 8½. 0-486-44787-1

MACBETH, William Shakespeare. A Scottish nobleman murders the king in order to succeed to the throne. Tortured by his conscience and fearful of discovery, he becomes tangled in a web of treachery and deceit that ultimately spells his doom. 96pp. 5³⁄₁₆ x 8¼. 0-486-27802-6

MAKING AUTHENTIC CRAFTSMAN FURNITURE: Instructions and Plans for 62 Projects, Gustav Stickley. Make authentic reproductions of handsome, functional, durable furniture: tables, chairs, wall cabinets, desks, a hall tree, and more. Construction plans with drawings, schematics, dimensions, and lumber specs reprinted from 1900s *The Craftsman* magazine. 128pp. 8⅛ x 11. 0-486-25000-8

MATHEMATICS FOR THE NONMATHEMATICIAN, Morris Kline. Erudite and entertaining overview follows development of mathematics from ancient Greeks to present. Topics include logic and mathematics, the fundamental concept, differential calculus, probability theory, much more. Exercises and problems. 641pp. 5⅜ x 8½. 0-486-24823-2

MEMOIRS OF AN ARABIAN PRINCESS FROM ZANZIBAR, Emily Ruete. This 19th-century autobiography offers a rare inside look at the society surrounding a sultan's palace. A real-life princess in exile recalls her vanished world of harems, slave trading, and court intrigues. 288pp. 5⅜ x 8½. 0-486-47121-7

THE METAMORPHOSIS AND OTHER STORIES, Franz Kafka. Excellent new English translations of title story (considered by many critics Kafka's most perfect work), plus "The Judgment," "In the Penal Colony," "A Country Doctor," and "A Report to an Academy." Note. 96pp. 5$\frac{3}{16}$ x 8$\frac{1}{4}$. 0-486-29030-1

MICROSCOPIC ART FORMS FROM THE PLANT WORLD, R. Anheisser. From undulating curves to complex geometrics, a world of fascinating images abound in this classic, illustrated survey of microscopic plants. Features 400 detailed illustrations of nature's minute but magnificent handiwork. The accompanying CD-ROM includes all of the images in the book. 128pp. 9 x 9. 0-486-46013-4

A MIDSUMMER NIGHT'S DREAM, William Shakespeare. Among the most popular of Shakespeare's comedies, this enchanting play humorously celebrates the vagaries of love as it focuses upon the intertwined romances of several pairs of lovers. Explanatory footnotes. 80pp. 5$\frac{3}{16}$ x 8$\frac{1}{4}$. 0-486-27067-X

THE MONEY CHANGERS, Upton Sinclair. Originally published in 1908, this cautionary novel from the author of *The Jungle* explores corruption within the American system as a group of power brokers joins forces for personal gain, triggering a crash on Wall Street. 192pp. 5$\frac{3}{8}$ x 8$\frac{1}{2}$. 0-486-46917-4

THE MOST POPULAR HOMES OF THE TWENTIES, William A. Radford. With a New Introduction by Daniel D. Reiff. Based on a rare 1925 catalog, this architectural showcase features floor plans, construction details, and photos of 26 homes, plus articles on entrances, porches, garages, and more. 250 illustrations, 21 color plates. 176pp. 8$\frac{3}{8}$ x 11. 0-486-47028-8

MY 66 YEARS IN THE BIG LEAGUES, Connie Mack. With a New Introduction by Rich Westcott. A Founding Father of modern baseball, Mack holds the record for most wins — and losses — by a major league manager. Enhanced by 70 photographs, his warmhearted autobiography is populated by many legends of the game. 288pp. 5$\frac{3}{8}$ x 8$\frac{1}{2}$. 0-486-47184-5

NARRATIVE OF THE LIFE OF FREDERICK DOUGLASS, Frederick Douglass. Douglass's graphic depictions of slavery, harrowing escape to freedom, and life as a newspaper editor, eloquent orator, and impassioned abolitionist. 96pp. 5$\frac{3}{16}$ x 8$\frac{1}{4}$. 0-486-28499-9

THE NIGHTLESS CITY: Geisha and Courtesan Life in Old Tokyo, J. E. de Becker. This unsurpassed study from 100 years ago ventured into Tokyo's red-light district to survey geisha and courtesan life and offer meticulous descriptions of training, dress, social hierarchy, and erotic practices. 49 black-and-white illustrations; 2 maps. 496pp. 5$\frac{3}{8}$ x 8$\frac{1}{2}$. 0-486-45563-7

THE ODYSSEY, Homer. Excellent prose translation of ancient epic recounts adventures of the homeward-bound Odysseus. Fantastic cast of gods, giants, cannibals, sirens, other supernatural creatures — true classic of Western literature. 256pp. 5$\frac{3}{16}$ x 8$\frac{1}{4}$. 0-486-40654-7

OEDIPUS REX, Sophocles. Landmark of Western drama concerns the catastrophe that ensues when King Oedipus discovers he has inadvertently killed his father and married his mother. Masterly construction, dramatic irony. Explanatory footnotes. 64pp. 5$\frac{3}{16}$ x 8$\frac{1}{4}$. 0-486-26877-2

ONCE UPON A TIME: The Way America Was, Eric Sloane. Nostalgic text and drawings brim with gentle philosophies and descriptions of how we used to live — self-sufficiently — on the land, in homes, and among the things built by hand. 44 line illustrations. 64pp. 8$\frac{3}{8}$ x 11. 0-486-44411-2

ONE OF OURS, Willa Cather. The Pulitzer Prize–winning novel about a young Nebraskan looking for something to believe in. Alienated from his parents, rejected by his wife, he finds his destiny on the bloody battlefields of World War I. 352pp. 5³⁄₁₆ x 8¼. 0-486-45599-8

ORIGAMI YOU CAN USE: 27 Practical Projects, Rick Beech. Origami models can be more than decorative, and this unique volume shows how! The 27 practical projects include a CD case, frame, napkin ring, and dish. Easy instructions feature 400 two-color illustrations. 96pp. 8¼ x 11. 0-486-47057-1

OTHELLO, William Shakespeare. Towering tragedy tells the story of a Moorish general who earns the enmity of his ensign Iago when he passes him over for a promotion. Masterly portrait of an archvillain. Explanatory footnotes. 112pp. 5³⁄₁₆ x 8¼. 0-486-29097-2

PARADISE LOST, John Milton. Notes by John A. Himes. First published in 1667, *Paradise Lost* ranks among the greatest of English literature's epic poems. It's a sublime retelling of Adam and Eve's fall from grace and expulsion from Eden. Notes by John A. Himes. 480pp. 5³⁄₁₆ x 8¼. 0-486-44287-X

PASSING, Nella Larsen. Married to a successful physician and prominently ensconced in society, Irene Redfield leads a charmed existence — until a chance encounter with a childhood friend who has been "passing for white." 112pp. 5⅜ x 8½. 0-486-43713-2

PERSPECTIVE DRAWING FOR BEGINNERS, Len A. Doust. Doust carefully explains the roles of lines, boxes, and circles, and shows how visualizing shapes and forms can be used in accurate depictions of perspective. One of the most concise introductions available. 33 illustrations. 64pp. 5⅜ x 8½. 0-486-45149-6

PERSPECTIVE MADE EASY, Ernest R. Norling. Perspective is easy; yet, surprisingly few artists know the simple rules that make it so. Remedy that situation with this simple, step-by-step book, the first devoted entirely to the topic. 256 illustrations. 224pp. 5⅜ x 8½. 0-486-40473-0

THE PICTURE OF DORIAN GRAY, Oscar Wilde. Celebrated novel involves a handsome young Londoner who sinks into a life of depravity. His body retains perfect youth and vigor while his recent portrait reflects the ravages of his crime and sensuality. 176pp. 5³⁄₁₆ x 8¼. 0-486-27807-7

PRIDE AND PREJUDICE, Jane Austen. One of the most universally loved and admired English novels, an effervescent tale of rural romance transformed by Jane Austen's art into a witty, shrewdly observed satire of English country life. 272pp. 5³⁄₁₆ x 8¼. 0-486-28473-5

THE PRINCE, Niccolò Machiavelli. Classic, Renaissance-era guide to acquiring and maintaining political power. Today, nearly 500 years after it was written, this calculating prescription for autocratic rule continues to be much read and studied. 80pp. 5³⁄₁₆ x 8¼. 0-486-27274-5

QUICK SKETCHING, Carl Cheek. A perfect introduction to the technique of "quick sketching." Drawing upon an artist's immediate emotional responses, this is an extremely effective means of capturing the essential form and features of a subject. More than 100 black-and-white illustrations throughout. 48pp. 11 x 8¼. 0-486-46608-6

RANCH LIFE AND THE HUNTING TRAIL, Theodore Roosevelt. Illustrated by Frederic Remington. Beautifully illustrated by Remington, Roosevelt's celebration of the Old West recounts his adventures in the Dakota Badlands of the 1880s, from roundups to Indian encounters to hunting bighorn sheep. 208pp. 6¼ x 9¼. 0-486-47340-6

THE RED BADGE OF COURAGE, Stephen Crane. Amid the nightmarish chaos of a Civil War battle, a young soldier discovers courage, humility, and, perhaps, wisdom. Uncanny re-creation of actual combat. Enduring landmark of American fiction. 112pp. 5$\frac{3}{16}$ x 8¼. 0-486-26465-3

RELATIVITY SIMPLY EXPLAINED, Martin Gardner. One of the subject's clearest, most entertaining introductions offers lucid explanations of special and general theories of relativity, gravity, and spacetime, models of the universe, and more. 100 illustrations. 224pp. 5⅜ x 8½. 0-486-29315-7

REMBRANDT DRAWINGS: 116 Masterpieces in Original Color, Rembrandt van Rijn. This deluxe hardcover edition features drawings from throughout the Dutch master's prolific career. Informative captions accompany these beautifully reproduced landscapes, biblical vignettes, figure studies, animal sketches, and portraits. 128pp. 8⅜ x 11. 0-486-46149-1

THE ROAD NOT TAKEN AND OTHER POEMS, Robert Frost. A treasury of Frost's most expressive verse. In addition to the title poem: "An Old Man's Winter Night," "In the Home Stretch," "Meeting and Passing," "Putting in the Seed," many more. All complete and unabridged. 64pp. 5$\frac{3}{16}$ x 8¼. 0-486-27550-7

ROMEO AND JULIET, William Shakespeare. Tragic tale of star-crossed lovers, feuding families and timeless passion contains some of Shakespeare's most beautiful and lyrical love poetry. Complete, unabridged text with explanatory footnotes. 96pp. 5$\frac{3}{16}$ x 8¼. 0-486-27557-4

SANDITON AND THE WATSONS: Austen's Unfinished Novels, Jane Austen. Two tantalizing incomplete stories revisit Austen's customary milieu of courtship and venture into new territory, amid guests at a seaside resort. Both are worth reading for pleasure and study. 112pp. 5⅜ x 8½. 0-486-45793-1

THE SCARLET LETTER, Nathaniel Hawthorne. With stark power and emotional depth, Hawthorne's masterpiece explores sin, guilt, and redemption in a story of adultery in the early days of the Massachusetts Colony. 192pp. 5$\frac{3}{16}$ x 8¼. 0-486-28048-9

THE SEASONS OF AMERICA PAST, Eric Sloane. Seventy-five illustrations depict cider mills and presses, sleds, pumps, stump-pulling equipment, plows, and other elements of America's rural heritage. A section of old recipes and household hints adds additional color. 160pp. 8⅜ x 11. 0-486-44220-9

SELECTED CANTERBURY TALES, Geoffrey Chaucer. Delightful collection includes the General Prologue plus three of the most popular tales: "The Knight's Tale," "The Miller's Prologue and Tale," and "The Wife of Bath's Prologue and Tale." In modern English. 144pp. 5$\frac{3}{16}$ x 8¼. 0-486-28241-4

SELECTED POEMS, Emily Dickinson. Over 100 best-known, best-loved poems by one of America's foremost poets, reprinted from authoritative early editions. No comparable edition at this price. Index of first lines. 64pp. 5$\frac{3}{16}$ x 8¼. 0-486-26466-1

SIDDHARTHA, Hermann Hesse. Classic novel that has inspired generations of seekers. Blending Eastern mysticism and psychoanalysis, Hesse presents a strikingly original view of man and culture and the arduous process of self-discovery, reconciliation, harmony, and peace. 112pp. 5$\frac{3}{16}$ x 8¼. 0-486-40653-9

SKETCHING OUTDOORS, Leonard Richmond. This guide offers beginners step-by-step demonstrations of how to depict clouds, trees, buildings, and other outdoor sights. Explanations of a variety of techniques include shading and constructional drawing. 48pp. 11 x 8¼. 0-486-46922-0

SMALL HOUSES OF THE FORTIES: With Illustrations and Floor Plans, Harold E. Group. 56 floor plans and elevations of houses that originally cost less than $15,000 to build. Recommended by financial institutions of the era, they range from Colonials to Cape Cods. 144pp. 8⅜ x 11. 0-486-45598-X

SOME CHINESE GHOSTS, Lafcadio Hearn. Rooted in ancient Chinese legends, these richly atmospheric supernatural tales are recounted by an expert in Oriental lore. Their originality, power, and literary charm will captivate readers of all ages. 96pp. 5⅜ x 8½. 0-486-46306-0

SONGS FOR THE OPEN ROAD: Poems of Travel and Adventure, Edited by The American Poetry & Literacy Project. More than 80 poems by 50 American and British masters celebrate real and metaphorical journeys. Poems by Whitman, Byron, Millay, Sandburg, Langston Hughes, Emily Dickinson, Robert Frost, Shelley, Tennyson, Yeats, many others. Note. 80pp. 5³⁄₁₆ x 8¼. 0-486-40646-6

SPOON RIVER ANTHOLOGY, Edgar Lee Masters. An American poetry classic, in which former citizens of a mythical midwestern town speak touchingly from the grave of the thwarted hopes and dreams of their lives. 144pp. 5³⁄₁₆ x 8¼. 0-486-27275-3

STAR LORE: Myths, Legends, and Facts, William Tyler Olcott. Captivating retellings of the origins and histories of ancient star groups include Pegasus, Ursa Major, Pleiades, signs of the zodiac, and other constellations. "Classic." — *Sky & Telescope*. 58 illustrations. 544pp. 5⅜ x 8½. 0-486-43581-4

THE STRANGE CASE OF DR. JEKYLL AND MR. HYDE, Robert Louis Stevenson. This intriguing novel, both fantasy thriller and moral allegory, depicts the struggle of two opposing personalities — one essentially good, the other evil — for the soul of one man. 64pp. 5³⁄₁₆ x 8¼. 0-486-26688-5

SURVIVAL HANDBOOK: The Official U.S. Army Guide, Department of the Army. This special edition of the Army field manual is geared toward civilians. An essential companion for campers and all lovers of the outdoors, it constitutes the most authoritative wilderness guide. 288pp. 5³⁄₁₆ x 8¼. 0-486-46184-X

A TALE OF TWO CITIES, Charles Dickens. Against the backdrop of the French Revolution, Dickens unfolds his masterpiece of drama, adventure, and romance about a man falsely accused of treason. Excitement and derring-do in the shadow of the guillotine. 304pp. 5³⁄₁₆ x 8¼. 0-486-40651-2

TEN PLAYS, Anton Chekhov. *The Sea Gull, Uncle Vanya, The Three Sisters, The Cherry Orchard,* and *Ivanov,* plus 5 one-act comedies: *The Anniversary, An Unwilling Martyr, The Wedding, The Bear,* and *The Proposal.* 336pp. 5³⁄₁₆ x 8¼. 0-486-46560-8

THE FLYING INN, G. K. Chesterton. Hilarious romp in which pub owner Humphrey Hump and friend take to the road in a donkey cart filled with rum and cheese, inveighing against Prohibition and other "oppressive forms of modernity." 320pp. 5⅜ x 8½. 0-486-41910-X

THIRTY YEARS THAT SHOOK PHYSICS: The Story of Quantum Theory, George Gamow. Lucid, accessible introduction to the influential theory of energy and matter features careful explanations of Dirac's anti-particles, Bohr's model of the atom, and much more. Numerous drawings. 1966 edition. 240pp. 5⅜ x 8½. 0-486-24895-X

TREASURE ISLAND, Robert Louis Stevenson. Classic adventure story of a perilous sea journey, a mutiny led by the infamous Long John Silver, and a lethal scramble for buried treasure — seen through the eyes of cabin boy Jim Hawkins. 160pp. 5³⁄₁₆ x 8¼. 0-486-27559-0

THE TRIAL, Franz Kafka. Translated by David Wyllie. From its gripping first sentence onward, this novel exemplifies the term "Kafkaesque." Its darkly humorous narrative recounts a bank clerk's entrapment in a bureaucratic maze, based on an undisclosed charge. 176pp. 5³⁄₁₆ x 8¼. 0-486-47061-X

THE TURN OF THE SCREW, Henry James. Gripping ghost story by great novelist depicts the sinister transformation of 2 innocent children into flagrant liars and hypocrites. An elegantly told tale of unspoken horror and psychological terror. 96pp. 5³⁄₁₆ x 8¼. 0-486-26684-2

UP FROM SLAVERY, Booker T. Washington. Washington (1856-1915) rose to become the most influential spokesman for African-Americans of his day. In this eloquently written book, he describes events in a remarkable life that began in bondage and culminated in worldwide recognition. 160pp. 5³⁄₁₆ x 8¼. 0-486-28738-6

VICTORIAN HOUSE DESIGNS IN AUTHENTIC FULL COLOR: 75 Plates from the "Scientific American – Architects and Builders Edition," 1885-1894, Edited by Blanche Cirker. Exquisitely detailed, exceptionally handsome designs for an enormous variety of attractive city dwellings, spacious suburban and country homes, charming "cottages" and other structures — all accompanied by perspective views and floor plans. 80pp. 9¼ x 12¼. 0-486-29438-2

VILLETTE, Charlotte Brontë. Acclaimed by Virginia Woolf as "Brontë's finest novel," this moving psychological study features a remarkably modern heroine who abandons her native England for a new life as a schoolteacher in Belgium. 480pp. 5³⁄₁₆ x 8¼. 0-486-45557-2

THE VOYAGE OUT, Virginia Woolf. A moving depiction of the thrills and confusion of youth, Woolf's acclaimed first novel traces a shipboard journey to South America for a captivating exploration of a woman's growing self-awareness. 288pp. 5³⁄₁₆ x 8¼. 0-486-45005-8

WALDEN; OR, LIFE IN THE WOODS, Henry David Thoreau. Accounts of Thoreau's daily life on the shores of Walden Pond outside Concord, Massachusetts, are interwoven with musings on the virtues of self-reliance and individual freedom, on society, government, and other topics. 224pp. 5³⁄₁₆ x 8¼. 0-486-28495-6

WILD PILGRIMAGE: A Novel in Woodcuts, Lynd Ward. Through startling engravings shaded in black and red, Ward wordlessly tells the story of a man trapped in an industrial world, struggling between the grim reality around him and the fantasies his imagination creates. 112pp. 6⅛ x 9¼. 0-486-46583-7

WILLY POGÁNY REDISCOVERED, Willy Pogány. Selected and Edited by Jeff A. Menges. More than 100 color and black-and-white Art Nouveau–style illustrations from fairy tales and adventure stories include scenes from Wagner's "Ring" cycle, *The Rime of the Ancient Mariner, Gulliver's Travels,* and *Faust.* 144pp. 8⅜ x 11. 0-486-47046-6

WOOLLY THOUGHTS: Unlock Your Creative Genius with Modular Knitting, Pat Ashforth and Steve Plummer. Here's the revolutionary way to knit — easy, fun, and foolproof! Beginners and experienced knitters need only master a single stitch to create their own designs with patchwork squares. More than 100 illustrations. 128pp. 6½ x 9¼. 0-486-46084-3

WUTHERING HEIGHTS, Emily Brontë. Somber tale of consuming passions and vengeance — played out amid the lonely English moors — recounts the turbulent and tempestuous love story of Cathy and Heathcliff. Poignant and compelling. 256pp. 5³⁄₁₆ x 8¼. 0-486-29256-8

www.ingramcontent.com/pod-product-compliance
Lightning Source LLC
Chambersburg PA
CBHW071423180526
45170CB00001B/200

* 9 7 8 0 4 8 6 4 3 2 9 3 9 *